HANDY REFERENCE (1)

Tips For Good Document Design

- Use the Master pages as fully as possible to set up a consistent design which is carried throughout your document.
- Use columns and guidelines to create a layout grid. If you keep text and graphic elements aligned to this grid then your document will assume a clear structure.
- Try not to use too many fonts or text effects. Often good results can be gained from restricting yourself to two basic fonts, one for headings and one for body text.
- Allow yourself the use of white space. It is usually not necessary to completely fill each page.
- Make sure that text is always readable. Too many characters to a line, or too little space between lines (leading) can create a solid mass of text which is very tiring to read.
- Use style sheets as much as possible. This way you have the flexibility to make design alterations to, for example, all of your headings in one simple manoeuvre at any time.
- Feel free to experiment with dummy text and graphics on the page in the early stages of your design. Try to form a clear idea of your document margins, text columns and page structure right from the beginning.
- Keep your design as simple and consistent as possible.

HANDY REFERENCE (2)

Keyboard Shortcuts

^ represents Control key

File menu

New	^N
Open	^O
Save	^S
Place	^D
Links	^ Shift D
Print	^P
Exit	^Q
Save all publications	Shift "Save"
Close all publications	Shift "Close"
Revert to last mini-save	Shift "Revert"

Edit menu

Undo	^Z or Alt Backspace
Cut	^X or Shift Delete
Copy	^C or ^ Insert
Paste	^V or Shift Insert
Clear	Delete
Select all	^A
Story/Layout view	^E
Power paste	^ Shift P
Multiple paste bypassing dialog box	Shift "Multiple Paste"

Utilities menu

Find	^F
Find next	^G
Spelling	^L
Index entry	^;
Show index for current publication only	^ "Show Index"
Make index entry bypassing dialog box	^ Shift ;
Add proper name to index	^ Shift Z
Copy book list to all publications	^ "Book"

Story menu (in Story Editor)

Close all stories in current publication	Shift "Close story"

Layout menu

Fit in window	^0
50% view	^5
Actual size	^1
200% view	^2
Show Pasteboard	^ Shift W
Actual size/Fit in window toggle	Right button
Actual size/200% toggle	Shift Right button
Set view for all pages	^ Alt Page view
Set page to Fit in Window	Shift Click on page icon
Show rulers	^R
Snap to rulers	^ Shift Y
Show guides	^J
Snap to guides	^ Shift 5
Go to page	^/

Type menu

Type specs	^T
Paragraph	^M
Indents/tabs	^I
Define styles	^3
Increase font size 1 point	^ Shift >
Decrease font size 1 point	^ Shift <
Increase font to next standard size	^ >
Decrease font to next standard size	^ <
Left align	^ Shift L
Right align	^ Shift R
Centre	^ Shift C
Justify	^ Shift J
Force Justify	^ Shift F
All caps on/off	^ Shift K
Subscript	^\
Superscript	^ Shift \
Autoleading	^ Shift A
Normal width	^ Shift X
No tracking	^ Shift Q
Bold	^ Shift B
Italic	^ Shift I
Underline	^ Shift U
Strikethrough	^ Shift S
Normal	^ Shift Space
Reverse	^ Shift V

Arrange menu

Bring to front	^F
Send to back	^B
Bring Forward	^8
Send Backward	^9

Window menu

Style palette	^Y
Colour palette	^K
Control palette	^#
Cascade all open stories	Shift "Cascade"
Tile all open stories	Shift "Tile"

Help menu

Contents	F1
Help within dialog box	Shift Right button
Context sensitive help	Shift F1
List installation options	^ "About PageMaker"

HANDY REFERENCE (3)

Keyboard Shortcuts

^ represents Control key

Toolbox

Text tool	Shift F2
Ellipse tool	Shift F3
Rectangle tool	Shift F4
Line tool	Shift F5
Perpendicular line tool	Shift F6
Polygon tool	Shift F7
Zoom tool	Shift F8
Rotation tool	Shift F9
Cropping tool	Shift F11
Toggle between current tool and pointer	F9

Control palette

Focus on Control palette	^#
Character/paragraph mode toggle	^ Shift '
Next option	Tab
Previous option	Shift Tab
Revert to last valid value	Esc
Apply	Enter
Apply retaining focus on Control palette	Shift Enter
Activate/deactivate current button	Spacebar
Change unit of measurement	Shift F12
Nudge	Arrow keys
Nudge by 10 times the normal amount	^ Arrow keys
Select tracking, style or font name	Type first few characters

Style palette

Edit style	^ Click on name
New style	^ Click on "No style"

Colour palette

Edit colour	^ Click on name
New colour	^ Click on "Registration"
Toggle between spot and process colour	^ Alt Shift Click on name

Graphics

Draw regular shape	Shift
Select multiple objects	Shift Click
Select object behind	^ Click
Horizontal or vertical move	Shift Drag
Group	^G
Ungroup	^U
Align	^4
Lock	^L
Restore proportions	Shift Click on corner handle
Proportional stretch	Shift Stretch
Resize bitmap to printer resolution	^ Stretch

Text

Select word	Double-click
Select paragraph	Triple-click
Move up/down screen	Pg Up/Pg Dn
Move to beginning/end of line	Home/End
Move to beginning/end of sentence	^ Home/^ End
Move to beginning/end of story	^ Pg Up/^ Pg Dn
Move left/right one word	^ left/right arrow
Move up/down one paragraph	^ Up/Down arrow
Kern 0.01 em space	^ Shift Keypad + or -
Kern 0.04 em space	^ Keypad + or -
Remove manual kerning	^ Shift 0 (zero)

Print dialog box

Set options without printing	Shift Click on "Print"

Place dialog box

Moderate TIFF compression	^ Alt "OK"
(Wait a few seconds before releasing these keys)	
Maximum TIFF compression	^ Alt Shift "OK"
Decompress TIFF	^ "OK"

General

Exit from nested dialog boxes	Shift "OK" or "Cancel"
Auto/Manual text flow	^
Semi-auto text flow	Shift
Edit OLE object	Double-click
Edit non-OLE object	Alt Double-click
Choose Editor for object	Shift Alt Double-click
Redraw page at high resolution	^ Shift F12
Previous/Next page	F11/F12
Grabber hand	Alt Drag

ABOUT THE SERIES

In easy steps series is developed for time-sensitive people who want results fast. It is designed for quick, easy and effortless learning.

By using the best authors in the field, and with our experience in writing computer training materials, this series is ideal for today's computer users. It explains the essentials simply, concisely and clearly - without the unnecessary verbal blurb. We strive to ensure that each book is technically superior, effective for easy learning and offers the best value.

Learn the essentials **in easy steps** - accept no substitutes!

Titles in the series include:

Title	Author	ISBN
Windows 95	Harshad Kotecha	1-874029-28-8
Microsoft Office	Stephen Copestake	1-874029-37-7
Internet UK	Andy Holyer	1-874029-31-8
CompuServe UK	John Clare	1-874029-33-4
CorelDRAW	Stephen Copestake	1-874029-32-6
PageMaker	Scott Basham	1-874029-35-0
Quicken UK	John Sumner	1-874029-30-X
Microsoft Works	Stephen Copestake	1-874029-41-5
Word	Scott Basham	1-874029-39-3
Excel	Pamela Roach	1-874029-40-7
Sage Sterling for Windows	Ralf Kirchmayr	1-874029-43-1
Sage Instant Accounting	Ralf Kirchmayr	1-874029-44-X
SmartSuite	Stephen Copestake	1-874029-42-3
HTML	Andy Holyer	1-874029-46-6
Netscape Navigator	Mary Lojkine	1-874029-47-4
PagePlus	Richard Hunt	1-874029-49-0
Publisher	Brian Austin	1-874029-56-3
Access	Stephen Copestake	1-874029-57-1
Internet Explorer	Mary Lojkine	1-874029-58-X
WordPerfect	Stephen Copestake	1-874029-59-8

PAGEMAKER
in easy steps

Scott Basham

COMPUTER STEP

In easy steps is an imprint of Computer Step
5c Southfield Road, Southam
Warwickshire CV33 OJH England
☎01926 817999

This edition 1996
Earlier editions 1993, 1994

Notice of Liability
Every effort has been made to ensure that this book contains accurate and current information. However, Computer Step and the author shall not be liable for any loss or damage suffered by readers as a result of any information contained herein.

Trademarks
Adobe, PageMaker and PostScript are registered trademarks of Adobe Systems Incorporated. Windows is a registered trademark of Microsoft Corporation. All other trademarks are acknowledged as belonging to their respective companies.

For all sales and volume discounts please contact Computer Step on Tel: 01926 817999.

For export orders and reprint/translation rights write to the address above or Fax: (+44) 1926 817005.

Comments to the publisher can be e-mailed to:
harshad@compstep.demon.co.uk

Printed and bound in the United Kingdom

ISBN 1-874029-35-0

Contents

1. The Basics 7

Introduction 8
Starting PageMaker 9
The PageMaker Screen 10
Floating Palettes 11
The Rulers 12
Repositioning the Zero Point 13
Viewing the Page 14
Other Page Views 15
The Zoom Tool 16

2. Working with a Publication 17

New Publication 18
Opening a Publication From Disk 20
The Page Icons 21
Inserting/Removing Pages 22
Saving a Document 23
Closing a Document 24

3. The Drawing Tools 25

Lines 26
Boxes 27
Ellipses 27
Polygons 27
Selecting Elements 28
Deleting Elements 28
Moving Elements 29
Resizing Elements 29
Selecting Multiple Elements 30
Grouping and Ungrouping 32
Manipulating Elements using the Control Palette 33
Moving Elements using the Control Palette 35
Resizing Elements using the Control Palette 36
Aligning Elements using the Control Palette 37

Aligning Objects using the Align Dialog 39
Using Fill and Line 40
Cut, Copy and Paste 43
Power Pasting 44
Multiple Paste 45
Magnetic Guidelines 47
Using Guidelines 49
Defaults 50
The Rotation Tool 53
Front and Back 54

4. Importing Graphics 55

The Place Command 56
Graphic File Formats 58
The Cropping Tool 61
Image Control 62

5. The Text Tool 63

Adding Text 64
Changing Text 65
Manipulating Text 66
Default Text Settings 68
Working with Blocks of Text 69
More Advanced Text Effects 71

6. Transformations 75

Skewing 76
Reflecting 76
Cropping and Resizing with the Control Palette 77
Combining Effects 78
Rotating with the Control Palette 79
Locking Elements 80

7. Importing Text 81

Placing Text 82
Threaded Text 84
Manipulating Threaded Text Blocks 86
Autoflow 88

8. Master Pages 89

Master Pages 90
Multiple Master Pages 92
Column Guides 93

9. Working with Large Amounts of Text 95

Type Specifications 96
Paragraph Specifications 97
Widows and Orphans 98
The Keep With Next Command 100
Column and Page Breaks 101
Paragraph Rules 102
Indents/Tabs 104
Hyphenation 107
Inline Graphics 108
Text Wrap 110
The Guide Manager 112

10. The Story Editor 113

Using the Story Editor 114
The Spelling Checker 115
Find and Change 116
Story and Layout Views 118

11. Style Sheets 119

Paragraph Styles 120
Using Styles 121
Changing a Style 122
Style by Example 123
Styles in the Story Editor 124
Copying Styles From Another Document 124

12. Long Document Features 125

The Book Command 126
Table of Contents 127
Rebuilding the Table of Contents 129
Making Index Entries 130

More Complex Entries 131
Creating the Index 134
Indexing with the Story Editor 136
The Colour Palette 137
Links 138
The Print Dialog 138

13. Utilities 139

The Table Editor 140
The Library Palette 142
Sorting Pages 143
HTML Author 143
Create PDF 143
Open Template 144
Compressing TIFF Files 144

14. Tips and Techniques 145

Template Documents 146
Using a Template 147
Creating Your Own Template 149
Copying From One Document to Another 150
Special Keyboard Characters 151
Using PageMaker on the Mac 152

Index 153

CHAPTER ONE

The Basics

This chapter gets you started with PageMaker. It shows you how to open the application, and make sense of its screen layout.

Covers

Introduction 8

Starting PageMaker 9

The PageMaker Screen 10

Floating Palettes 11

The Rulers 12

Repositioning the Zero Point 13

Viewing the Page 14

Other Page Views 15

The Zoom Tool 16

Introduction

Desktop Publishing can mean different things to different people. Back in 1984, the term DTP was first used to describe the newly released PageMaker version 1. In those days it meant the ability to combine text and graphics on the same page using a personal computer system.

Today many wordprocessors have this capability, while DTP has developed and expanded to cover a much greater range of features and accuracy of control. Systems based on PCs are now being used to create virtually any kind of document previously associated with traditional publishing: from novels and technical manuals to glossy magazines and marketing flyers.

PageMaker version 6 has a rich array of facilities to import text and artwork from other computer application packages, as well as allowing you to generate these directly from within PageMaker itself. It allows precision alignment, sizing and orientation of elements either using the mouse or by working numerically with dialog boxes and an on-screen Control palette. There is a high level of typographical control, as well as a host of features to help with the organisation and management of long documents.

In this guide you will be taken through all the essential features of the various versions of PageMaker for Windows. To get the most out of this book, it is recommended that you are first familiar with the Windows operating environment (i.e. using a mouse, icons, menus, dialog boxes etc.). The objective of this guide is to show you PageMaker using pictures and concise explanations rather than endless pages of technical detail. Remember that it is also important to experiment using your own examples; like many things you will find that practice is the key to competence.

Starting PageMaker

If You Are Using Windows 95

Use the Start button to access the Programs menu, and select the PageMaker icon (usually located within the Adobe submenu).

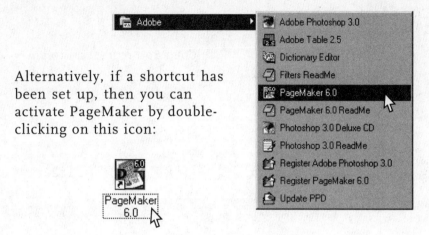

Alternatively, if a shortcut has been set up, then you can activate PageMaker by double-clicking on this icon:

If You Are Using Windows 3.1

From the Windows 3.1 Program Manager, you can start PageMaker by double-clicking directly on its icon.

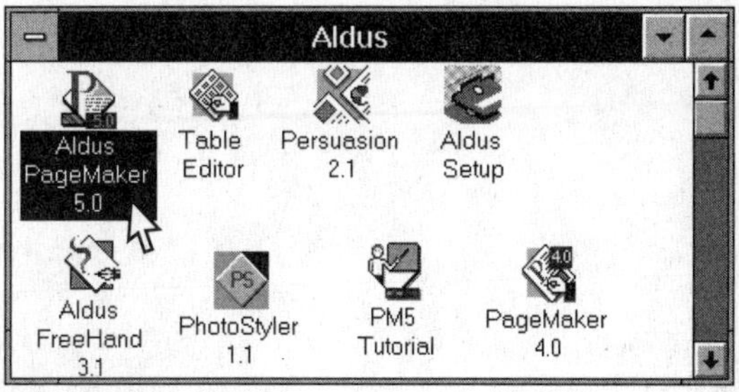

HANDY TIP **If you double-click on a PageMaker file, your machine will load PageMaker and then automatically open the file.**

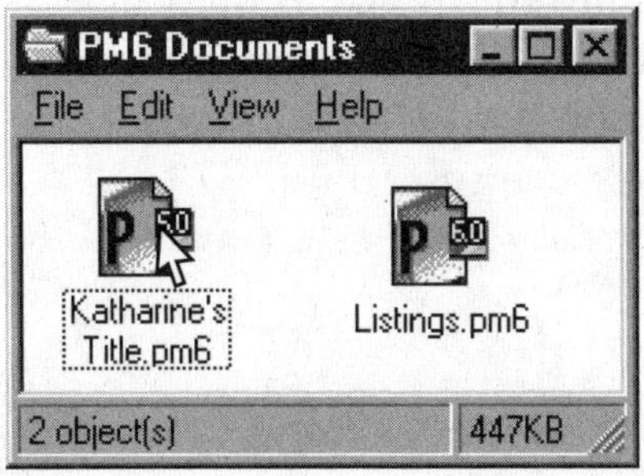

The PageMaker Screen

The PageMaker window

The document window

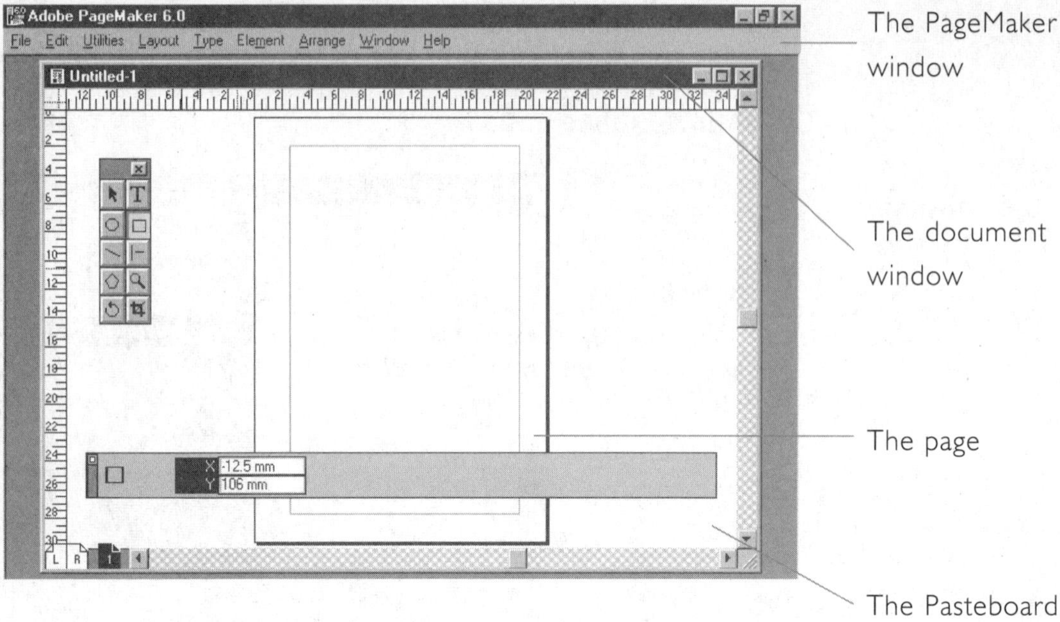

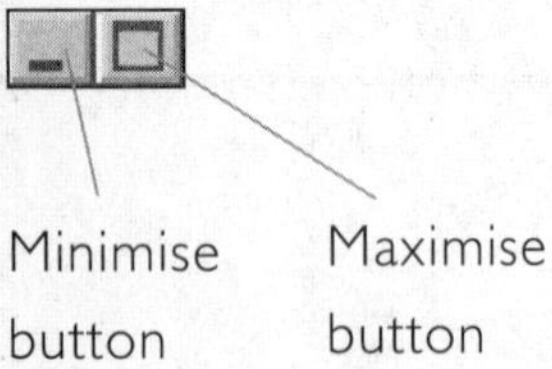

The page

The Pasteboard

1 Choose **New...** from the File menu.

2 Click **OK**.

The PageMaker screen is arranged as follows:

The PageMaker Window
Note: Clicking on the Close box ☒ will close PageMaker.

The Document Window
You can work on more than one document at a time using PageMaker, each with its own window. Note the Maximise and Minimise buttons will expand the window or shrink it to a single icon.

The Page and Pasteboard
All items positioned on the page will normally be printed. The surrounding Pasteboard is a working area.

Minimise button Maximise button

In Windows 3.1 these buttons look like this:

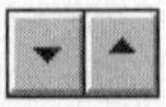

Floating Palettes

These give you immediate on-screen access to tools and commands. You can move palettes to the most convenient screen position, or close them down altogether if not required.

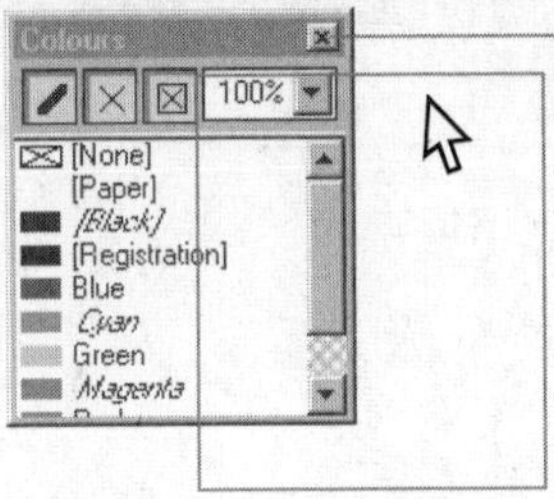

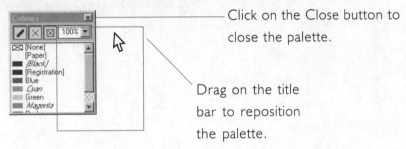

Click on the Close button to close the palette.

Drag on the title bar to reposition the palette.

Palettes can be turned on and off from the Window menu...

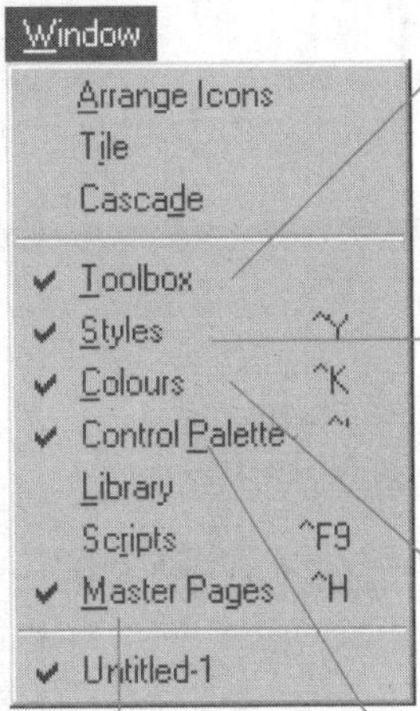

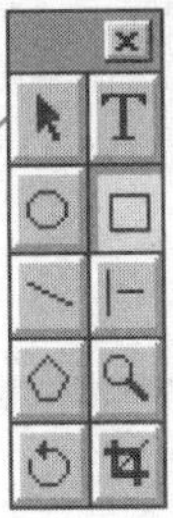

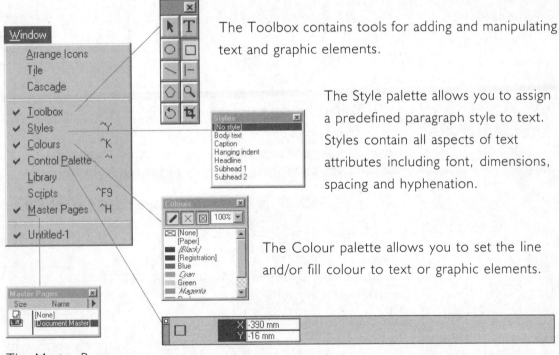

The Toolbox contains tools for adding and manipulating text and graphic elements.

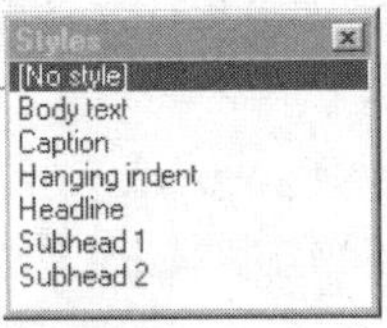

The Style palette allows you to assign a predefined paragraph style to text. Styles contain all aspects of text attributes including font, dimensions, spacing and hyphenation.

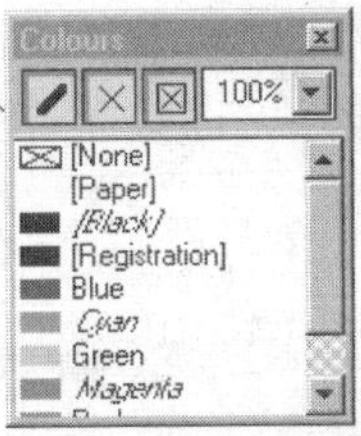

The Colour palette allows you to set the line and/or fill colour to text or graphic elements.

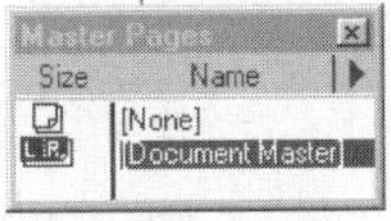

The Master Pages palette lets you create and apply consistent page designs.

The Control palette gives you full numeric control over elements as an alternative to making adjustments manually with the mouse or by dialog box. The controls which appear in the palette depend on the type of element(s) being edited.

The Rulers

The rulers help you make measurements on screen. Dotted line markers appear in each ruler to indicate your current position.

Horizontal ruler

Horizontal ruler position marker

Vertical ruler

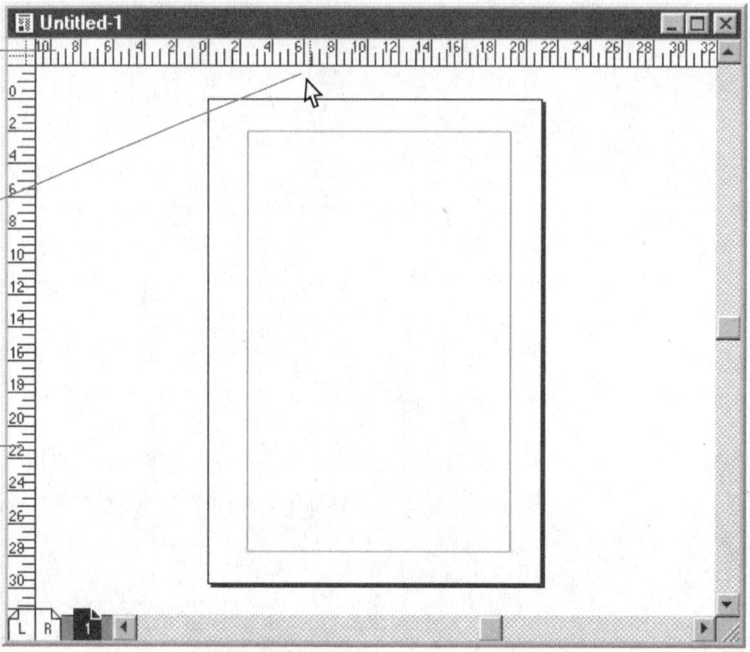

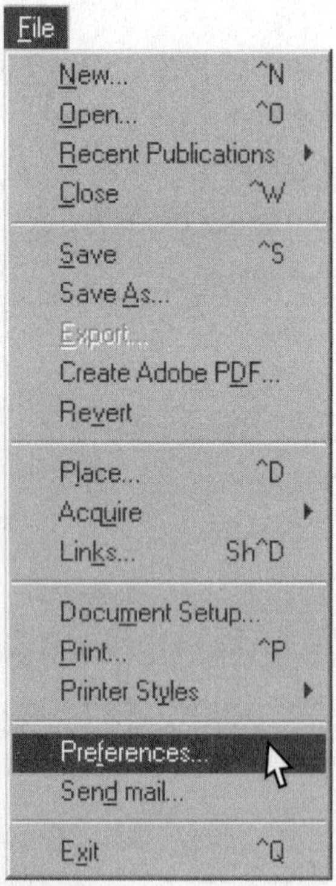

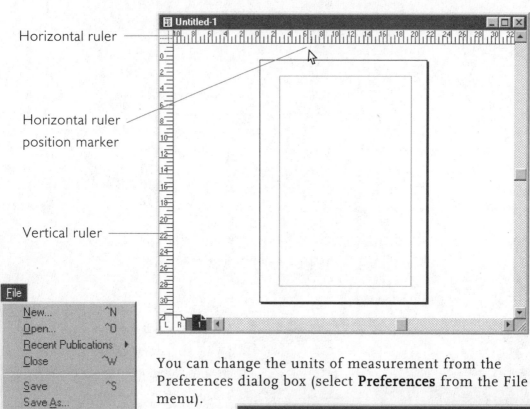

You can change the units of measurement from the Preferences dialog box (select **Preferences** from the File menu).

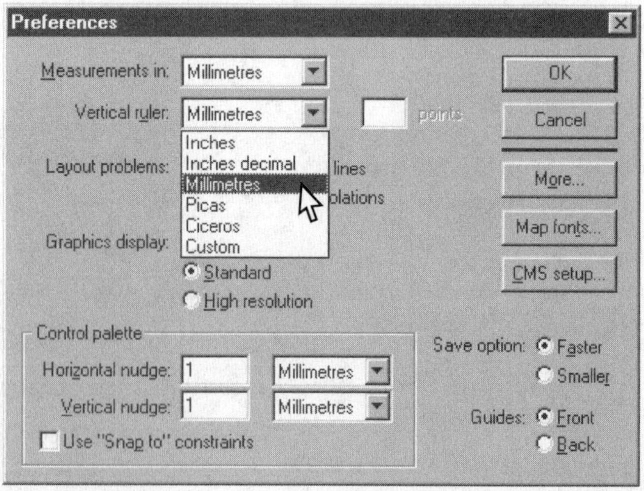

Repositioning the Zero Point

Initially all measurements are from the top left corner of the page. This can be changed by moving the Zero point.

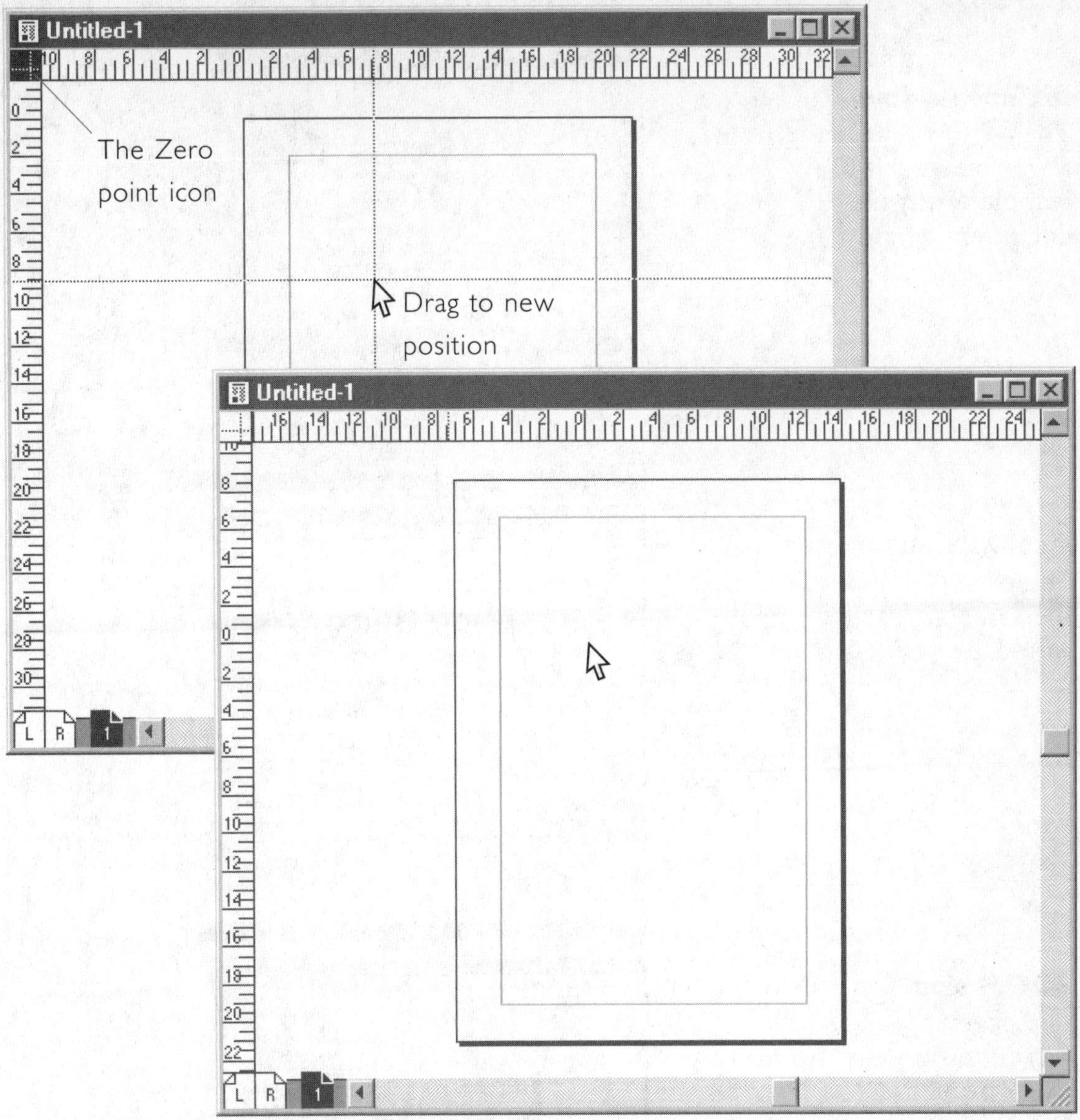

1. Move the mouse pointer directly over the Zero point icon.
2. Drag downwards and to the right until you reach the desired position for the new Zero point.

Viewing the Page

There are eight levels of page magnification. The three most often used can be accessed directly with the mouse.

Fit in Window
The page is reduced to a size where it will fit completely in the document window.

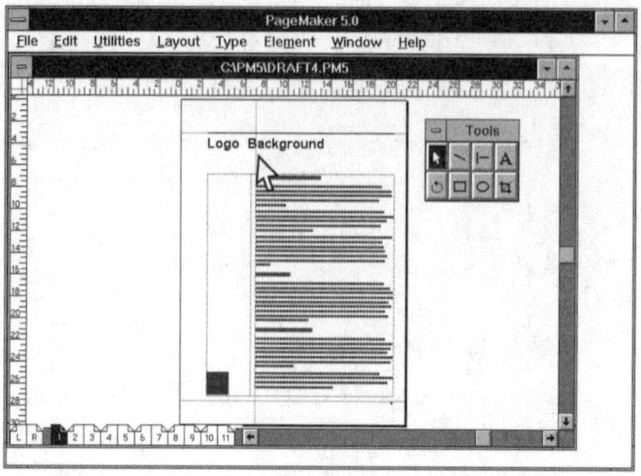

Point to area of interest and click right mouse button

Actual Size
The page is displayed the same size as it would be printed.

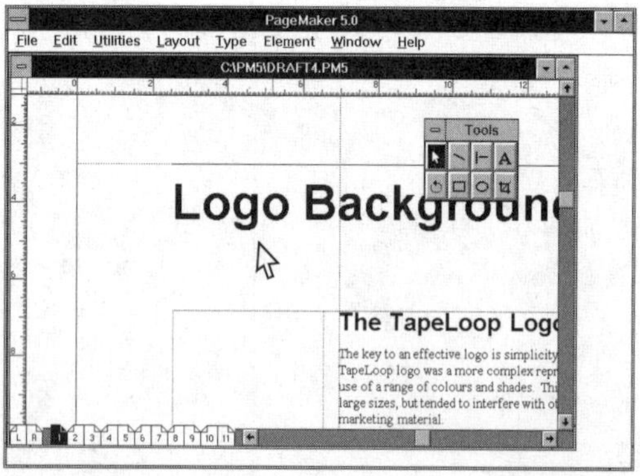

Click right mouse button while pressing Shift

200% size
The page appears twice the size as when printed.

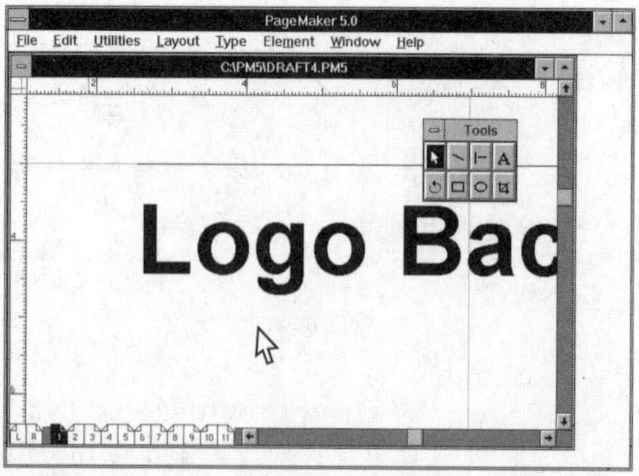

Other Page Views

1 Open the Layout menu.

2 Select the View submenu.

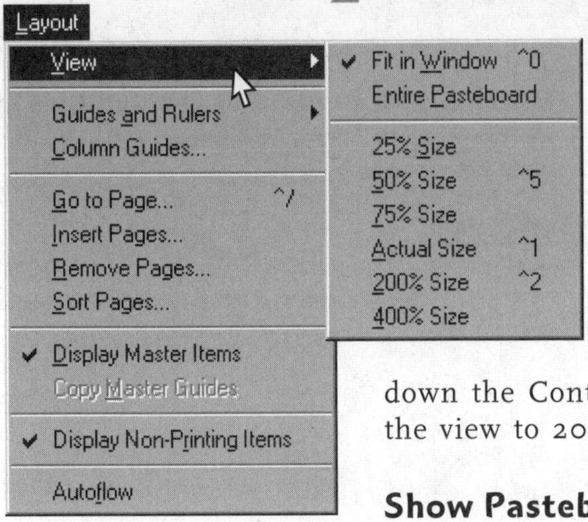

3 Choose one of the eight view options. Note that the rulers expand to reveal more detail as you zoom in.

The keyboard shortcuts are listed next to each menu option. The ^ symbol means "hold down the Control key". For example, holding down the Control key while pressing "2" will switch the view to 200% size.

Show Pasteboard

This zooms out to reveal the entire pasteboard area. The area beyond its perimeter is out of bounds.

Many keyboard shortcuts have changed with the advent of PageMaker version 6. Watch out for "Fit in Window" which has changed from ^W to ^O. ^W now closes your document down completely, a problem for PageMaker veterans who have developed a reflex action of frequently hitting ^W as they work.

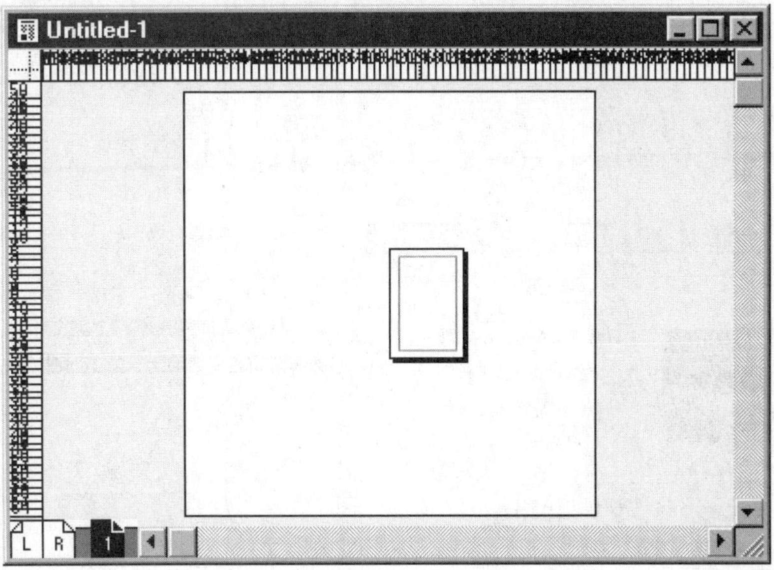

In all views you have access to all PageMaker's layout editing features.

The Zoom Tool

HANDY TIP **Double-clicking on the zoom tool returns you to 100% view.**

1. Select the zoom tool.
2. Position to the area where you want to zoom in and click.
3. Alternatively, use the tool to draw a rectangle area (drag with the mouse). When you release the mouse button PageMaker will zoom in to fill the screen with this area.

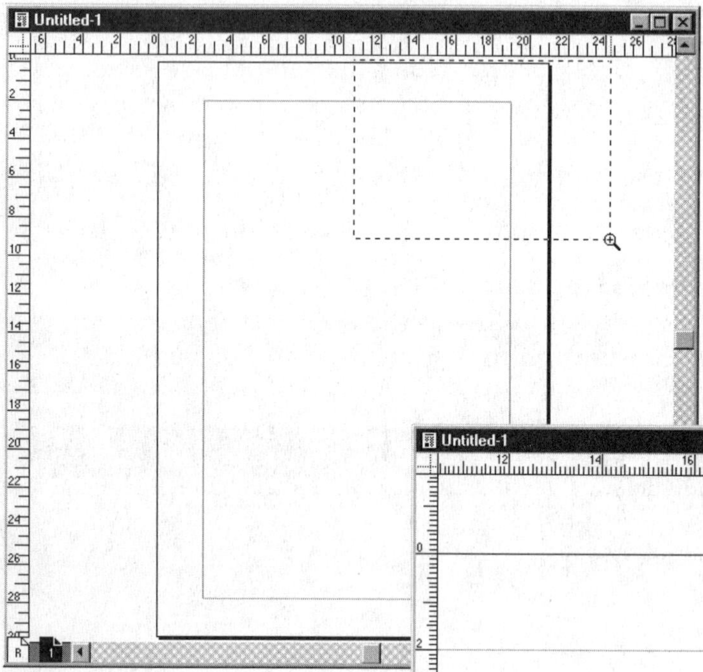

Using the zoom tool, you can magnify the page up to 800% actual size.

To zoom out, hold down the Control key as you click or drag.

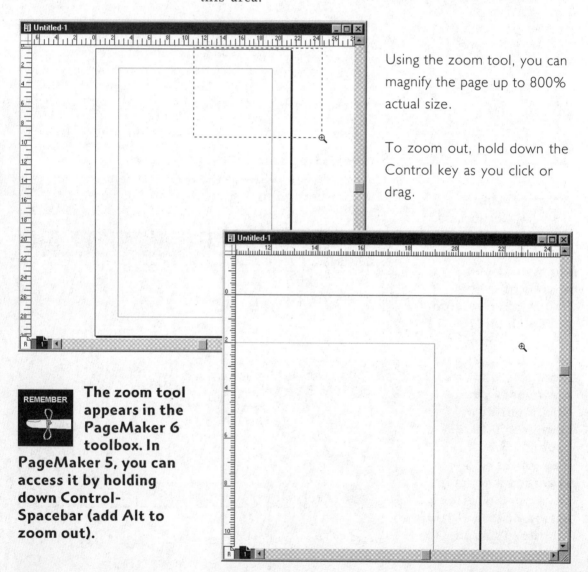

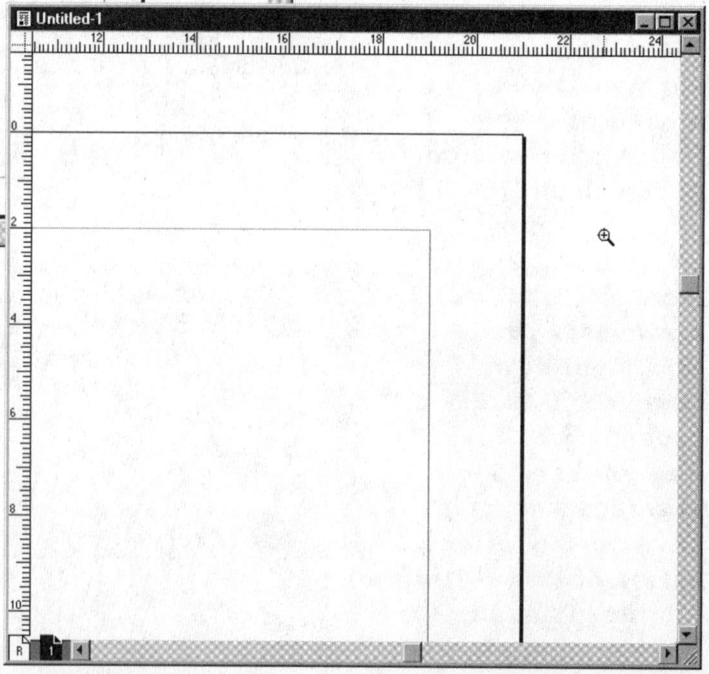

REMEMBER **The zoom tool appears in the PageMaker 6 toolbox. In PageMaker 5, you can access it by holding down Control-Spacebar (add Alt to zoom out).**

CHAPTER TWO

Working with a Publication

This chapter shows you how to store and retrieve your documents from disk. It also deals with navigation between pages within a publication.

Covers

New Publication 18

Opening a Publication From Disk 20

The Page Icons 21

Inserting/Removing Pages 22

Saving a Document 23

Closing a Document 24

New Publication

1 Choose **New...** from the File menu to display the initial Document Setup dialog box.

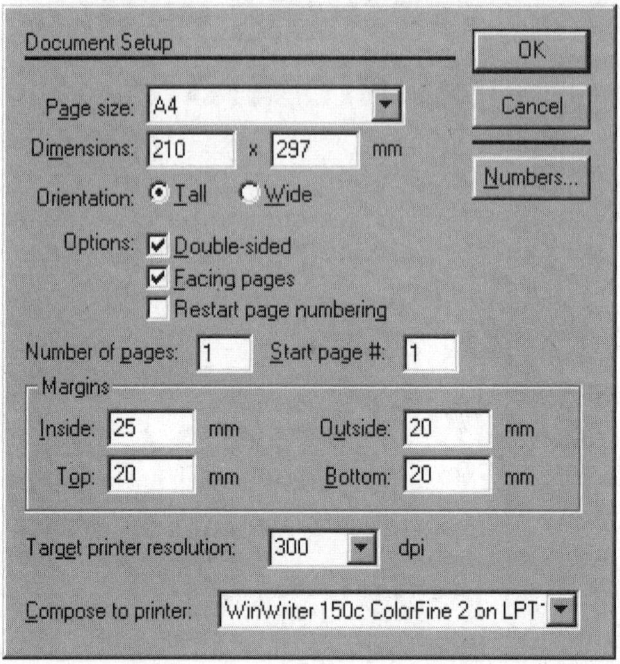

2 Choose from one of the preset page sizes in the **Page size** drop-down menu, or enter values directly into the **Dimensions** boxes (this allows you create a custom page size).

Tall orientation

3 Click on the **Tall** or **Wide** radio button to choose Page orientation (note this affects the entire document).

Wide orientation

4 The starting page number will normally be 1, but you may change this by entering a value in the **Start page #** box.

5 If you know how many pages you require, then enter this value in the **Number of pages** box. However, it is easy to add or remove pages later on.

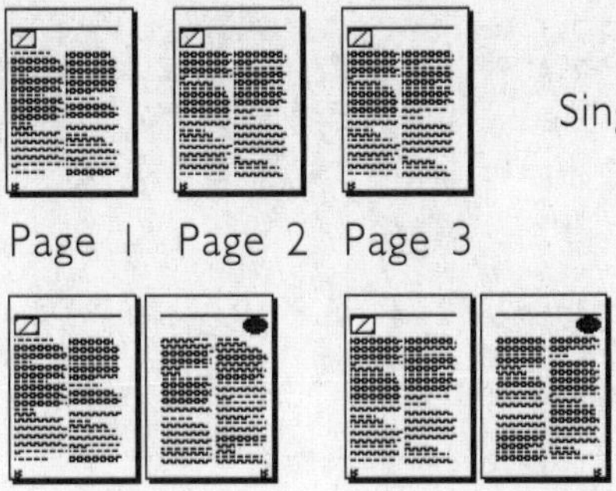

HANDY TIP

You can view your pages as thumbnail images using the Sort pages command from the Layout menu (PageMaker 6 or above), or the "Sort Pages" addition (PageMaker 5).

6 If your document is to be single-sided (printed on only one side of the paper) then remove the cross from the **Double-sided** checkbox. If the Double-sided option is active then you have a further choice to display **Facing pages**. This causes PageMaker to show you pages as "spreads" with left and right pages next to each other.

7 If your document is part of a larger Book list (see Chapter 12), then you have the option to **Restart page numbering** from this point.

8 Enter your page margins. Note that if your document is double-sided then you can set inner and outer margins (the inner margin is at the spine of a bound publication).

9 Choose your target printer from the **Compose to printer** drop-down menu. This will give you a list of printers installed in Windows. It is important to specify from the outset the printer used for your final, not draft, output if these are different. This gives PageMaker information about the text capabilities, graphics and printable page area which can be used.

10 The **Target printer resolution** will normally be set automatically according to your choice of printer, but you can alter this manually.

HANDY TIP

You can return to the Document Setup dialog box by choosing Document Setup from the File menu. In this way you can alter settings even once you have begun work on a document.

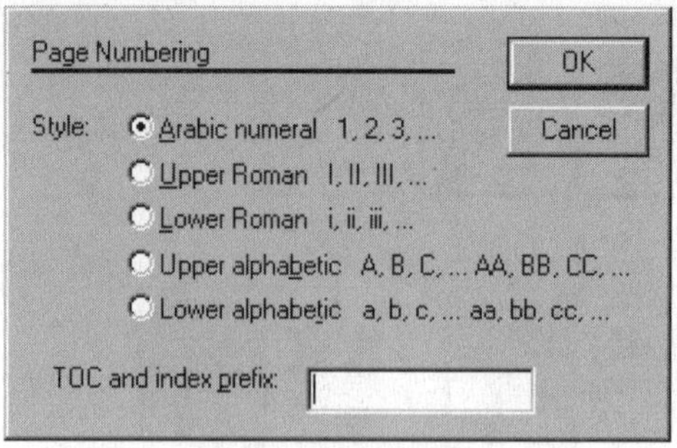

11 Click on the **Numbers...** button to alter the style of page numbering. Options include Roman numerals and alphabetic numbering.

Opening a Publication From Disk

1 Go to the File menu and choose **Open**.

HANDY TIP

From this pop-up list you can also select "Older PageMaker Files". This allows you to convert from previous version formats.

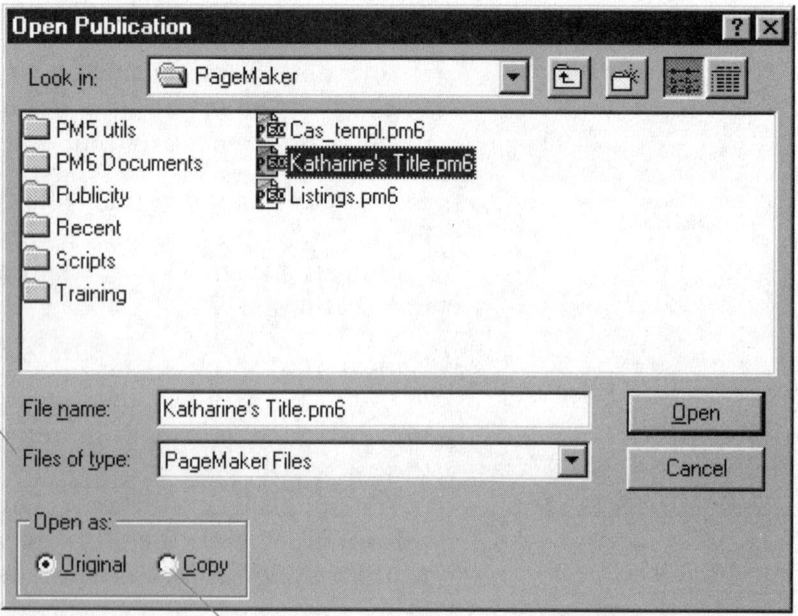

You can open an untitled copy of an existing document by clicking on the **Copy** radio button.

You can open as many publications as memory will allow. Each can be activated either by clicking on a visible part of its window or via the Window menu.

2 The dialog box displays all valid PageMaker files in the current directory. If necessary change directory by typing its path in the File name box or clicking on items in the Directories box.

3 Type or select the file name of the document you wish to open. Click **OK**.

The Page Icons

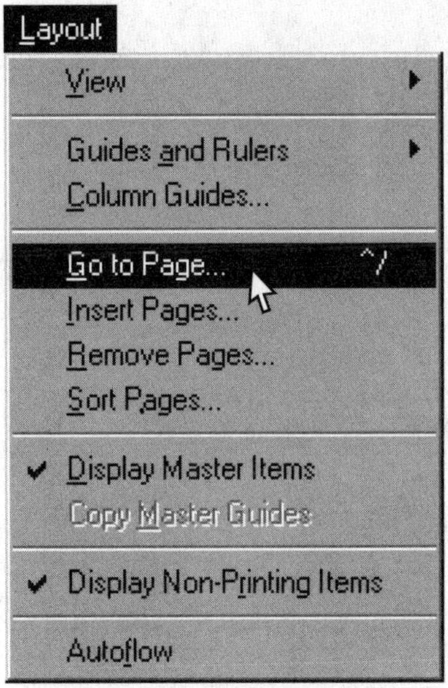

The page icons appear at the bottom left corner of the document window. The currently active page is highlighted.

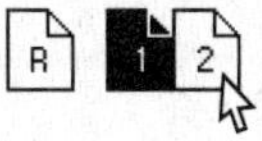

To move to another page simply click on its icon, or use the **Go to Page** option from the Layout menu.

Master Pages

These are labelled L and R (R only if the document is single-sided). These do not print but can act as a background for the "real" pages in your publication (see Chapter 8). In PageMaker 6 or above, you can use the Master Pages palette to switch between different Master Page designs.

Every time you move to a new page, PageMaker performs a mini-save as a security measure. If your machine crashed during use, you should be able to recover your document. If your document is currently untitled, the mini-saved version will be on disk as a .TMP file, within your Windows temporary directory.

If you rename this as a .PM6 file (or whichever extension is appropriate to your PageMaker version), you can open it within PageMaker. After this you should immediately save to another file name.

Inserting/Removing Pages

Inserting

1 Select the page either immediately before or after the place you want the new page(s) to go.

2 Choose **Insert Pages...** from the Layout menu.

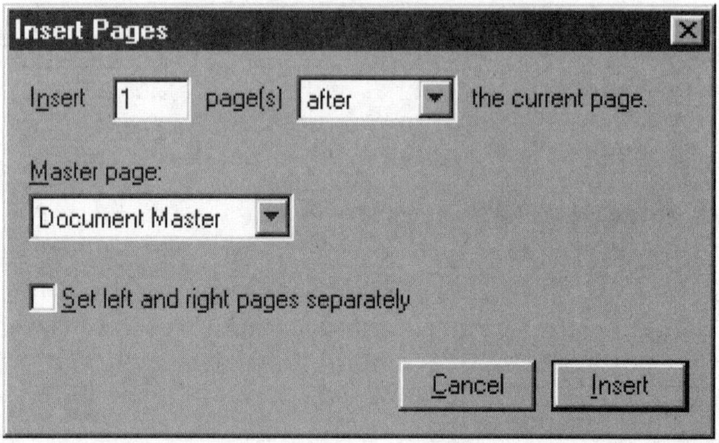

If you are using a double-sided document, there may be two current pages, and you will have a third option to add new pages between them.

3 Enter the number of pages to be inserted.

4 Select the position for the new pages, either before or after the current page.

Removing

The **Remove Pages...** option from the Layout menu works in the same way as Insert Pages...

There is an additional warning dialog box which asks you to verify the deletion:

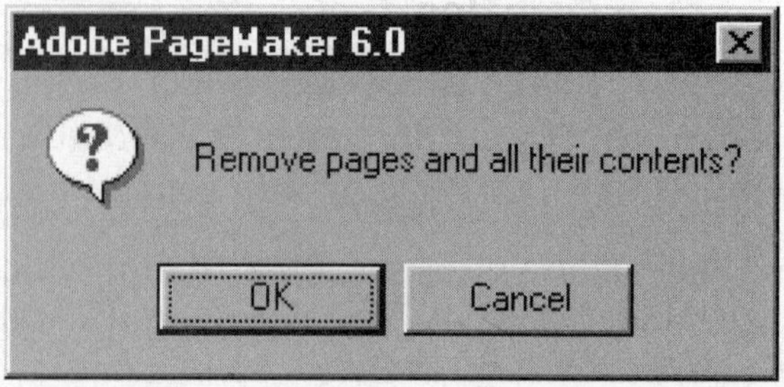

Saving a Document

REMEMBER

An untitled document window indicates that a file has not yet been saved.

REMEMBER

If you are using PageMaker 6 or above with Windows 95, then you can move, rename or delete files from within any of the File dialog boxes (e.g. Save, Open or Place) – just right-click on a file. With previous versions, use the Windows file-managing system(s).

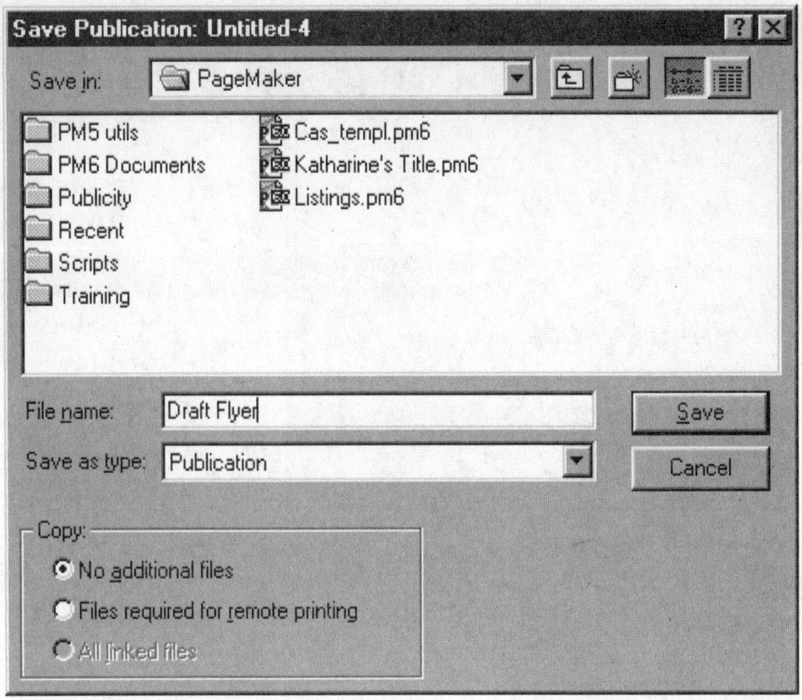

1. If you have more than one publication open, then make active the one you want to save by clicking in its window (or selecting from the Window menu).
2. Choose **Save** from the File menu. If your document already has a name then the save action will be automatic.
3. If you are saving the document for the first time the Save Publication dialog box will appear. Make sure the correct directory is active (if necessary type in the path or navigate using the drop-down menu).
4. Type in a valid document name (8 characters or less, no punctuation if you are using Windows 3.1).

If you wish to save to a file name different to the current document, choose **Save As...** from the File menu.

Closing a Document

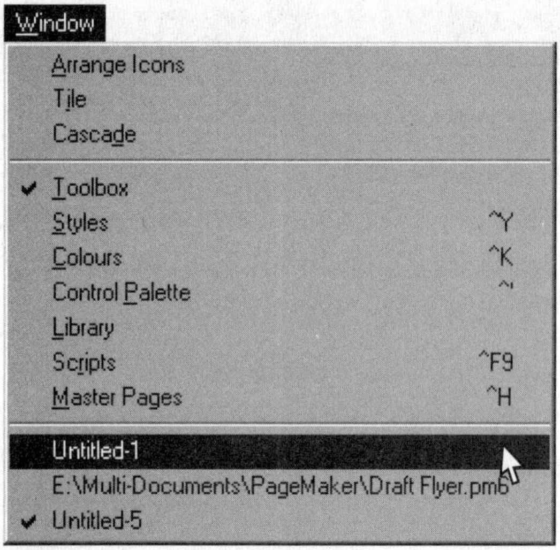

A document is closed when it is no longer required on screen.

1. If you have more than one document open, then make sure the one you want to close is active. This can be done by clicking on a visible part of the document window, or selecting the document name from the Window menu.

2. Either click on the document's Close box (Windows 95) or choose **Close** from the File menu.

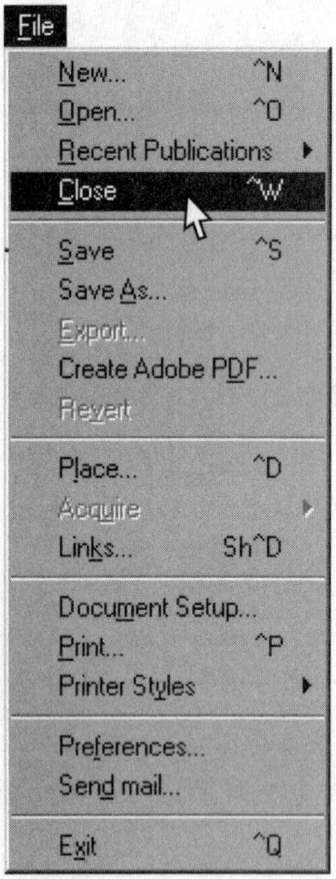

3. If the document has not been saved then the following dialog box will appear as a security measure:

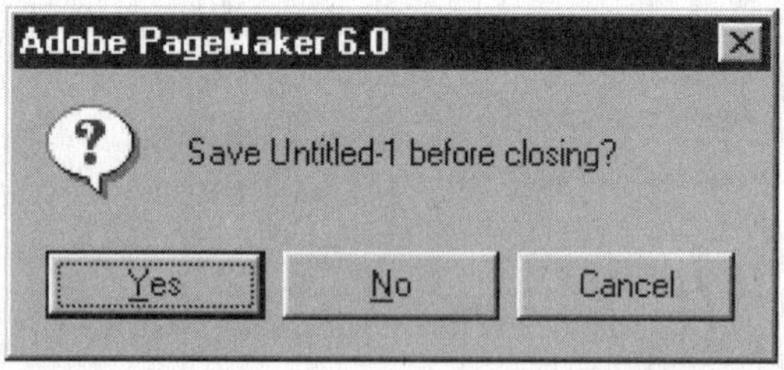

If you click **No** then the document will close without saving.

Clicking **Yes** will save your work (you may be asked for a file name if the document is currently untitled).

Cancel will abort the Close operation and return you to your document window.

CHAPTER THREE

The Drawing Tools

This chapter covers PageMaker's built-in drawing facilities. In later chapters you will see that many of the techniques you learn here will apply equally well to text and elements imported from other packages.

Covers

Lines, Boxes, Ellipses, Polygons 26

Selecting, Deleting, Moving, Resizing 28

Selecting Multiple Elements 30

Grouping and Ungrouping 32

The Control Palette 33

Aligning Objects using the Align dialog 39

Using Fill and Line 40

Cut, Copy and Paste 43

Power Pasting 44

Multiple Paste 45

Magnetic Guidelines 47

Using Guidelines 49

Defaults 50

The Rotation Tool 53

Front and Back 54

Lines

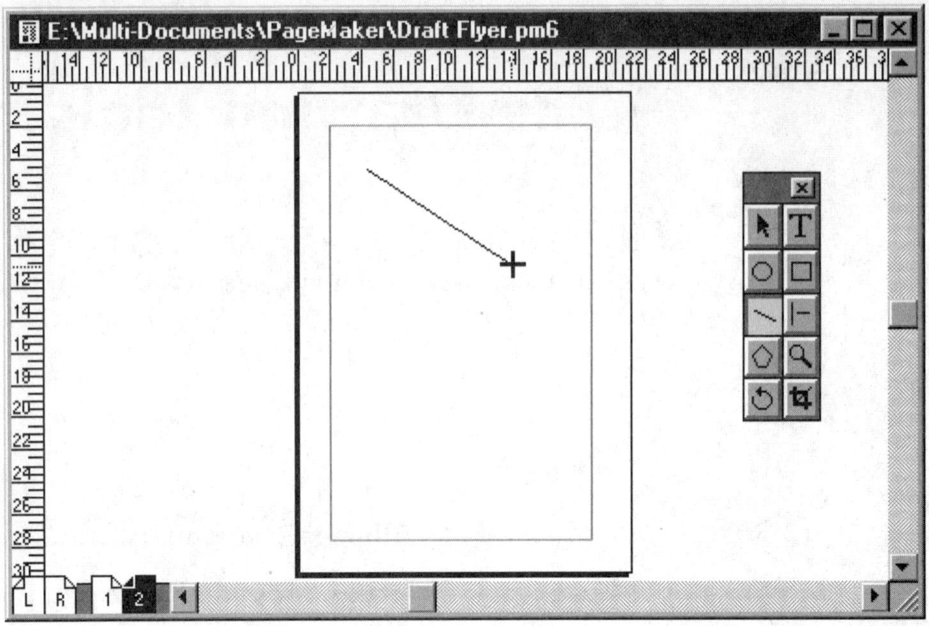

1. Select the line tool from the toolbox. The pointer will turn into a cross (to aid accurate drawing).

2. Drag from one end of the line to another.

The Constrained Line Tool

This will draw lines at 45 degree intervals, i.e. horizontally, vertically or diagonally.

You can achieve the same effect with the normal line tool if you hold down the Shift key while drawing.

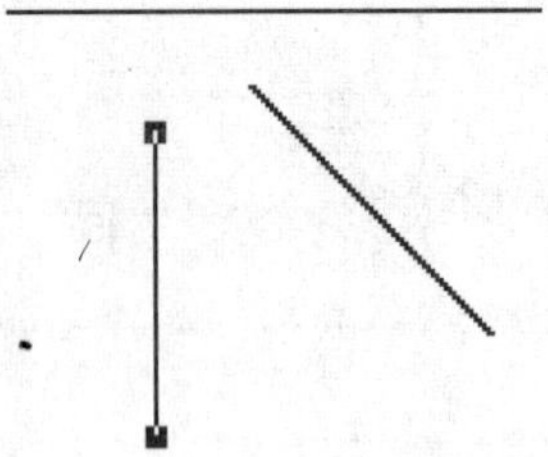

Boxes 

To draw a rectangle, select the box tool and drag from one corner to the other.

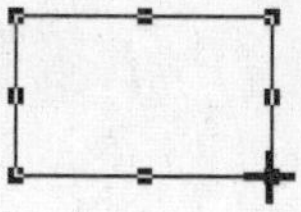

Ellipses 

To draw an oval shape, select the ellipse tool and drag diagonally.

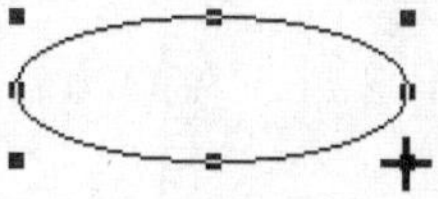

Polygons 

To draw a polygon, select the polygon tool and drag diagonally.

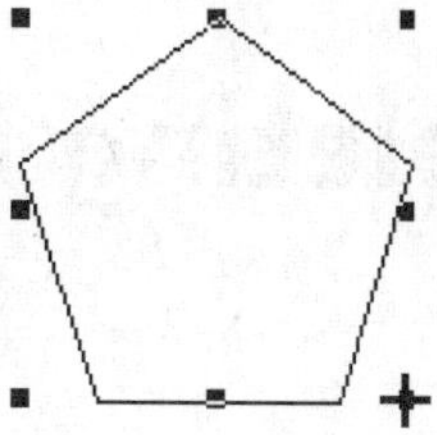

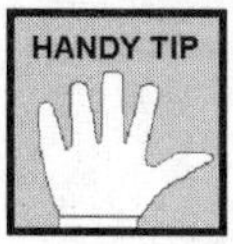

If you hold down Shift when drawing, all shapes will be made regular. Boxes will be kept square, and ellipses constrained as circles.

If you double-click on the polygon tool, the Polygon Settings dialog appears, allowing you to set the number of sides. You can also use the **Star inset** bar to change the shape gradually from a regular polygon to a wire-frame star.

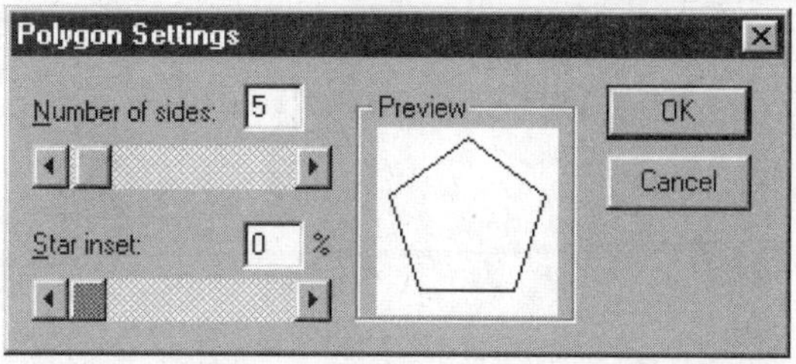

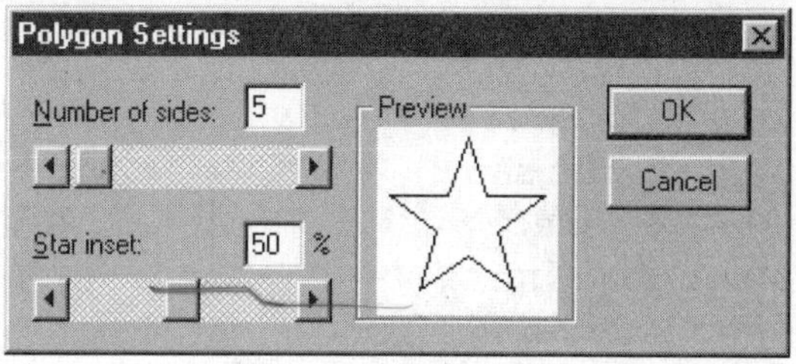

You can change settings to an existing polygon by selecting it, then choosing **Polygon Settings** from the Element menu.

Selecting Elements

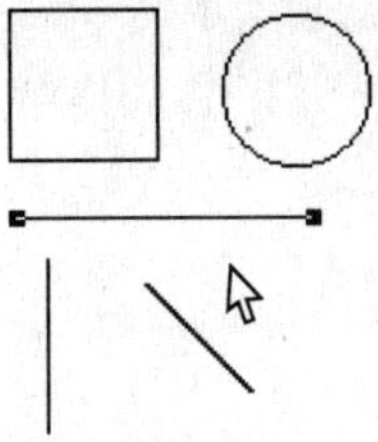

Normally, the element most recently drawn is selected.

You can tell that a shape is selected by the square handles (blocks) which appear at each corner.

To Select an Element

1. Choose the pointer tool. 
2. Click directly on the shape with the tip of the pointer.

Deleting Elements

1. Select the element to be deleted
2. Press the Delete or Backspace key.

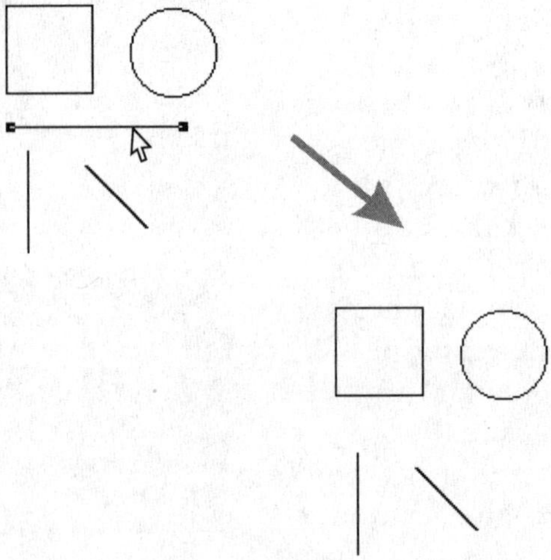

Moving Elements

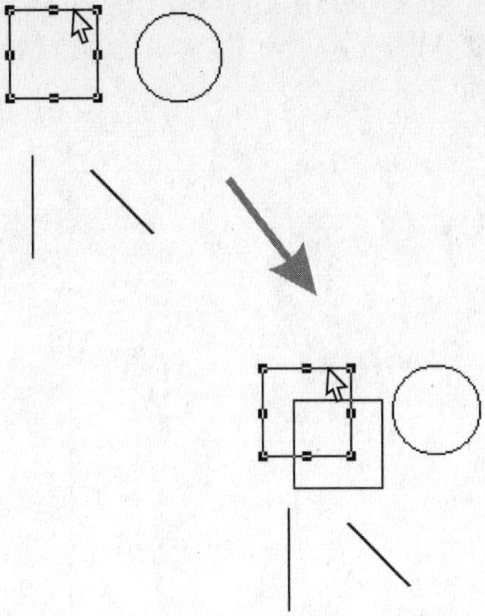

1 Select the element to be moved.

2 Drag to the new location.

Resizing Elements

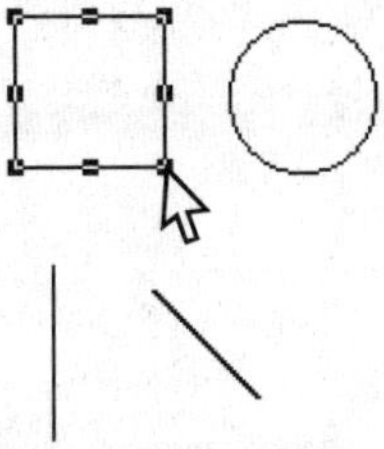

1 Select the element to be resized.

2 Drag directly on one of its handles.

Dragging on an edge handle will let you resize a shape horizontally or vertically, whilst dragging on a corner handle lets you stretch in both directions at once.

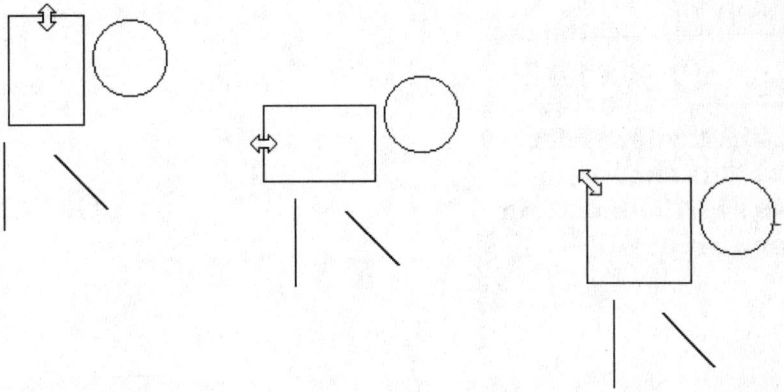

Selecting Multiple Elements

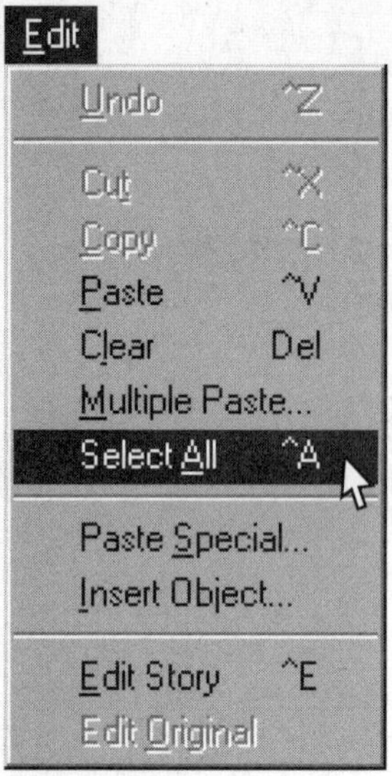

To select all elements on the page and pasteboard choose **Select All** from the Edit menu.

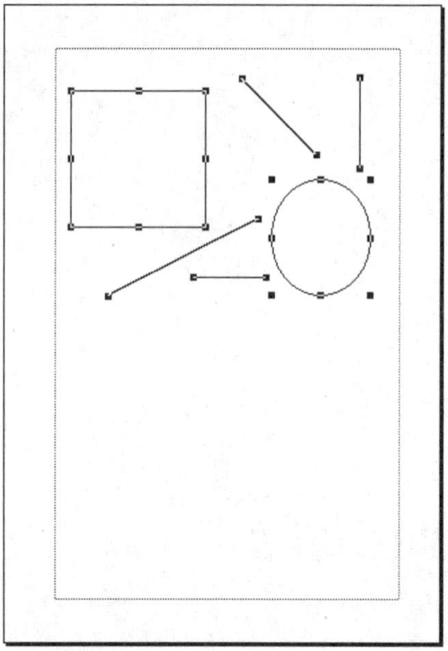

Shift-clicking

Normally when you click on an object any previously selected objects will be deselected.

If you hold down **Shift** while clicking successively on different objects, you can select as many as you wish.

HANDY TIP

Shift-clicking on an already-selected object will deselect it. This allows you to switch objects on and off at will.

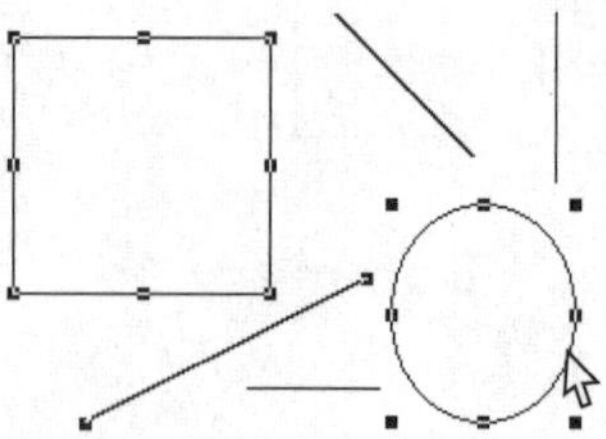

Creating a Selection Box

1. Select the pointer tool
2. Move to a blank area of the page or Pasteboard.
3. Drag diagonally. As you drag, a box bordered by a dotted line will appear.

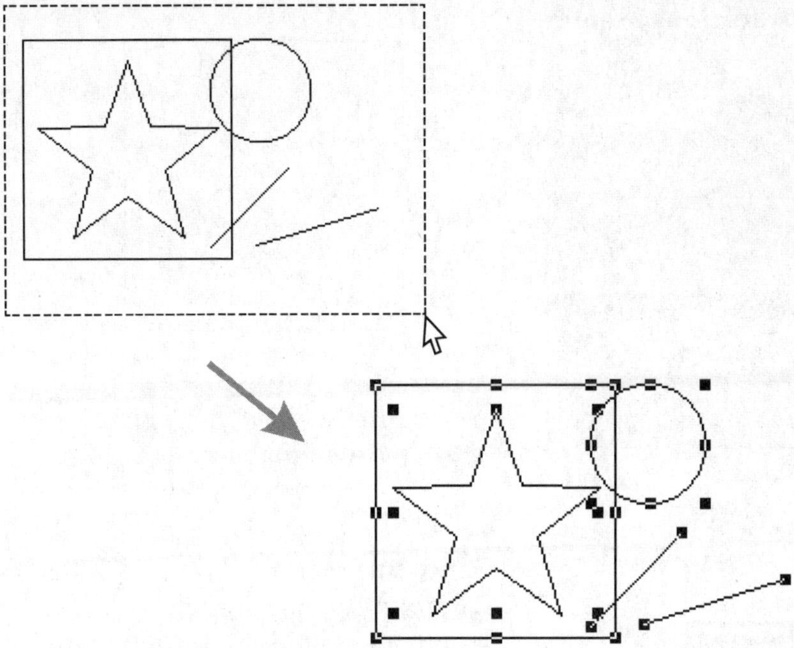

HANDY TIP **You can combine these techniques; e.g. Select All followed by Shift-clicking on one element (to deselect) will have the overall effect of selecting all elements but one.**

4. When you release the mouse button, all objects *completely* enclosed by this box will be selected.

Summary

There are three ways to make multiple selections:

- Select All
- Shift-clicking
- Selection box

Grouping and Ungrouping (PageMaker version 6 or above)

Grouping is a feature new to PageMaker 6, although PageMaker 5 has a PostScript Group function in its Additions menu.

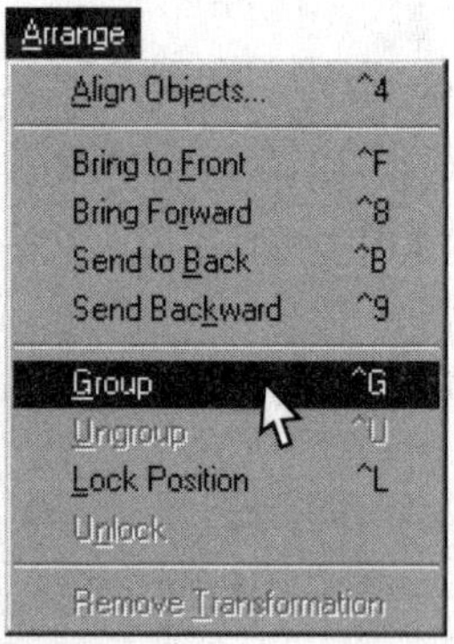

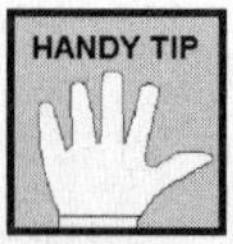

It is possible to edit individual group elements without ungrouping. Simply hold down the Control key and click on the element you wish to edit.

Grouping is useful because it allows you to create shapes using a combination of simpler shapes, thereafter treating them as a single object

To Group Elements

1. Select the elements to be grouped.
2. Choose **Group** from the Arrange menu (or ^G).

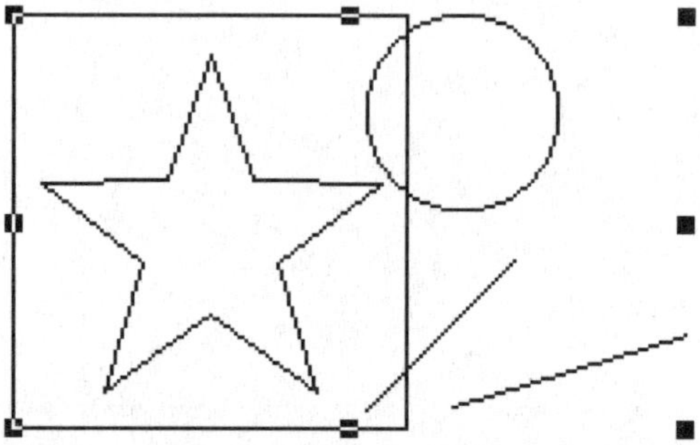

You can now move or resize the group as a single shape.

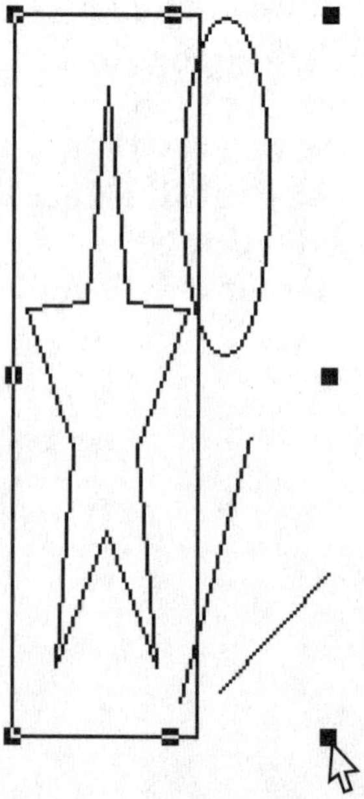

Ungrouping

To ungroup, simply select the group and choose **Ungroup** from the Arrange menu (or ^U).

Manipulating Elements using the Control Palette

If the Control palette is not active, choose the Control Palette option from the Window menu.

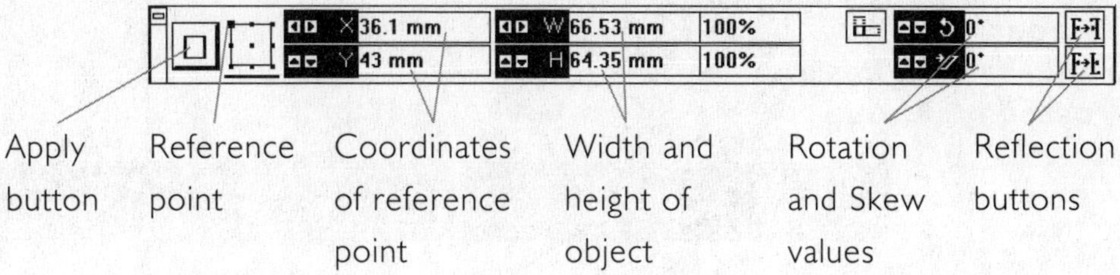

In PageMaker you have the choice to manipulate elements either visually using the mouse, or numerically with the Control palette.

The Control palette gives you the opportunity to specify the size, position or special effects applied to an object with complete precision.

Resizing an Element using the Control Palette

1. Select the element to be resized. The Control palette will display the object's attributes.
2. Edit the width and height values within the Control palette.

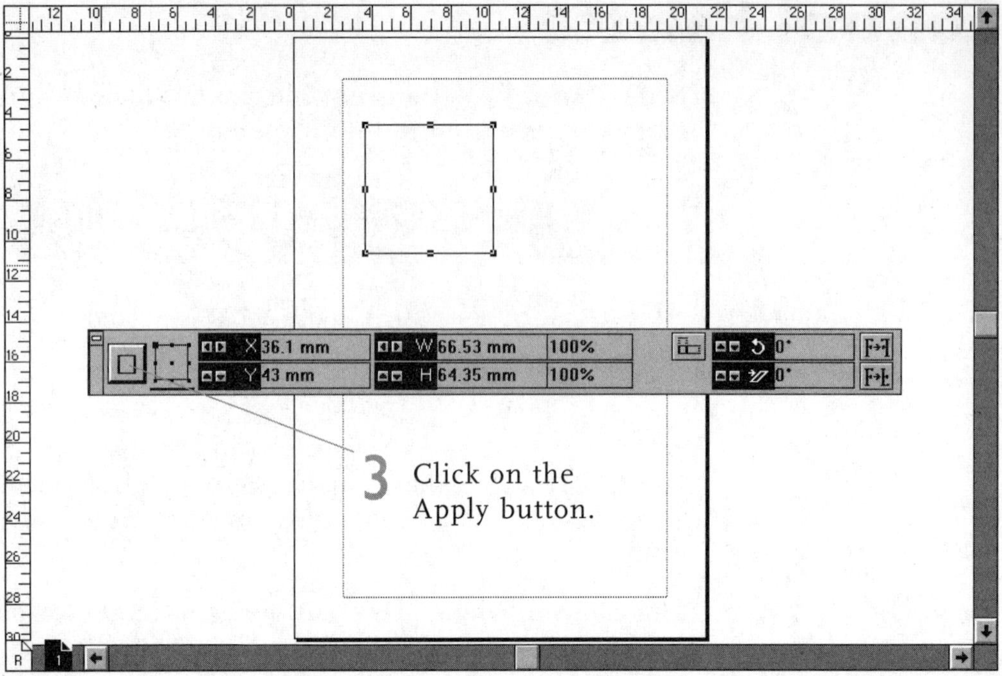

3 Click on the Apply button.

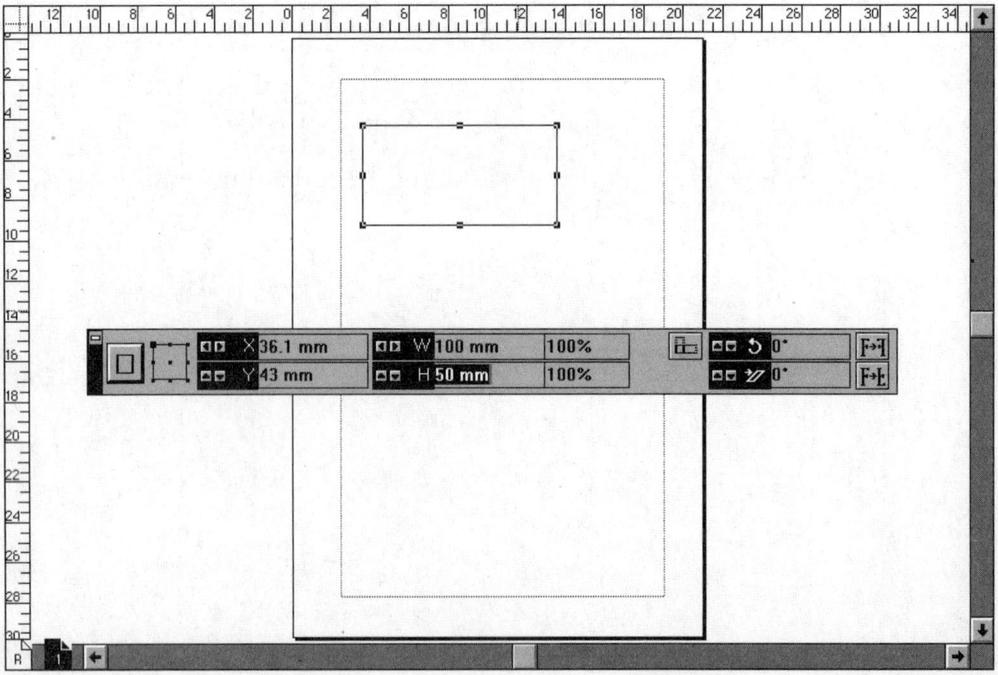

Moving Elements using the Control Palette

When moving a shape using the Control palette, you can set the reference point by clicking on the symbol to the right of the Apply button.

Changing the Coordinates of the Top-left Corner of a Shape

1. Select the shape with the pointer tool.

Click here to select the top-left reference point (repositioning mode).

2. Make sure the top-left reference point is active by clicking on its symbol in the Control palette. The point should be marked by a small square block (if it is marked by a double arrow then click once more on the point).
3. Type in the new coordinates for this point.
4. Click on the Apply button. The shape will be moved so that its top-left corner has the specified coordinates.

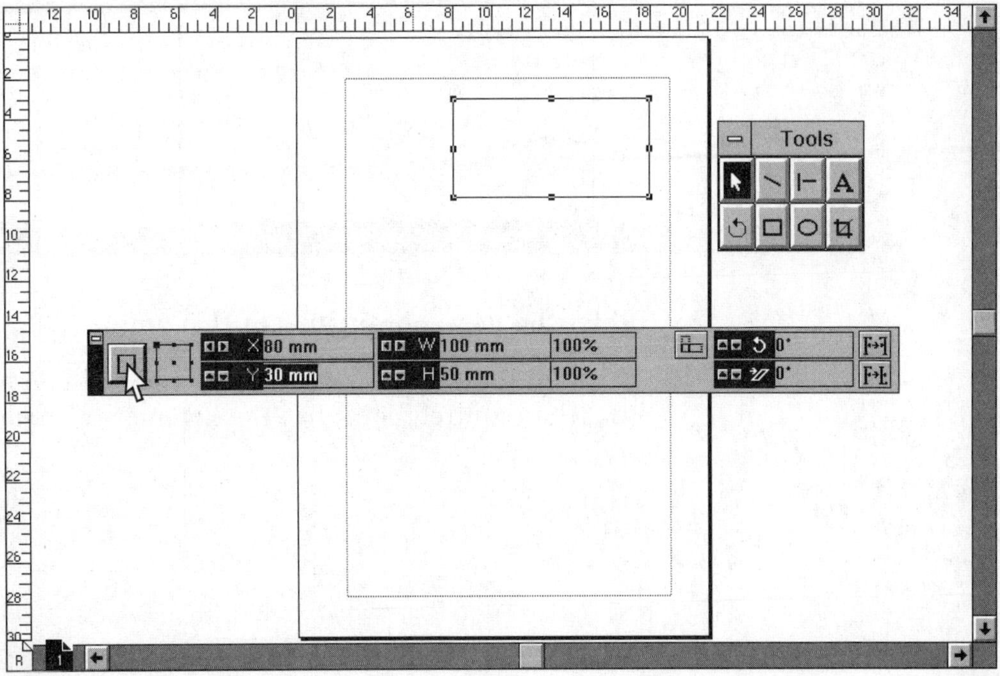

Resizing Elements using the Control Palette

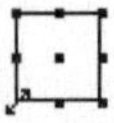

Lower-left reference point selected (resizing mode).

1. Select the shape to be resized.
2. Choose the reference point by clicking on the Control palette symbol. If necessary, click a second time to ensure that the point is marked by a double arrow. (This arrow indicates that resizing mode is active.)

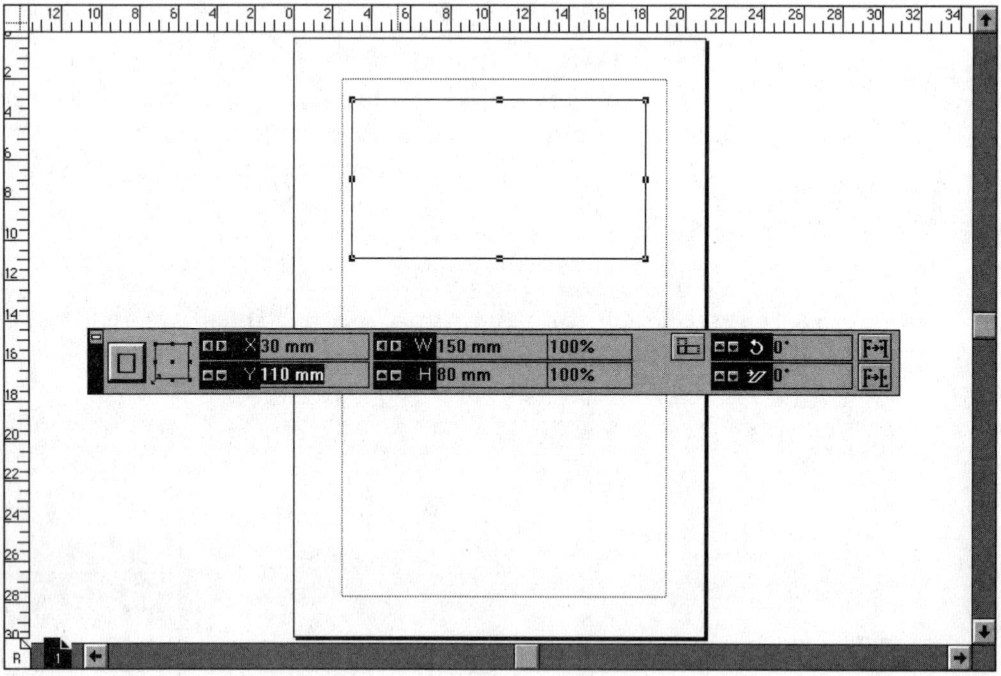

3. Enter the new coordinates for this point.
4. Click on the Apply button. The shape will be resized so that the required point has the given coordinates.

Aligning Elements using the Control Palette

In this example we have two shapes we wish to align.

We would like to move the circle so that its centre has the same coordinates as that of the rectangle...

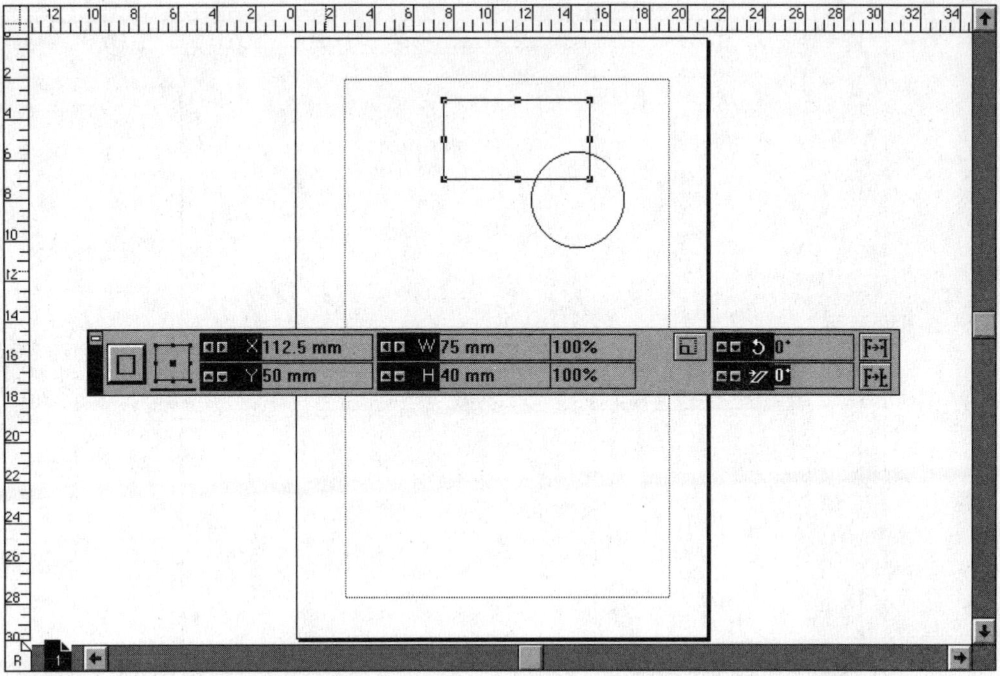

1 Click on the first shape (the rectangle) with the pointer tool and make the centre reference point active.

2 Note the X coordinate, in this case 112.5mm.

3. Click on the second shape (the circle).
4. Enter the same X value, 112.5mm.
5. Click on the Apply button. The circle's centre will now have the same X coordinate value as that of the rectangle.

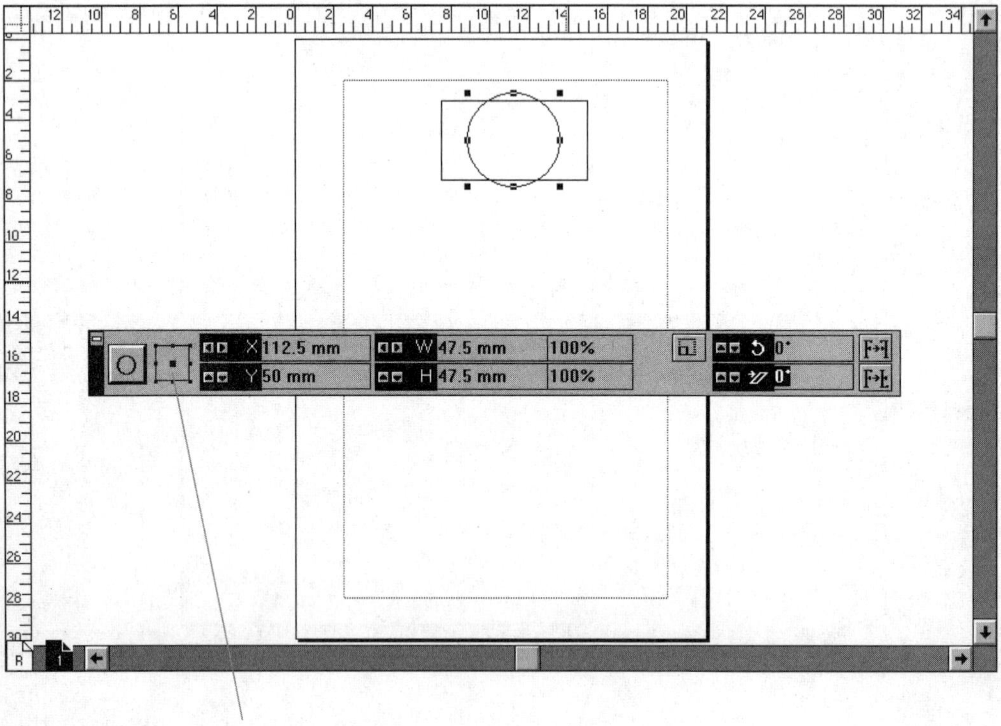

Centre point active. Note we are using repositioning (rather than resizing) mode.

Aligning Objects using the Align Dialog (PageMaker version 6 or above)

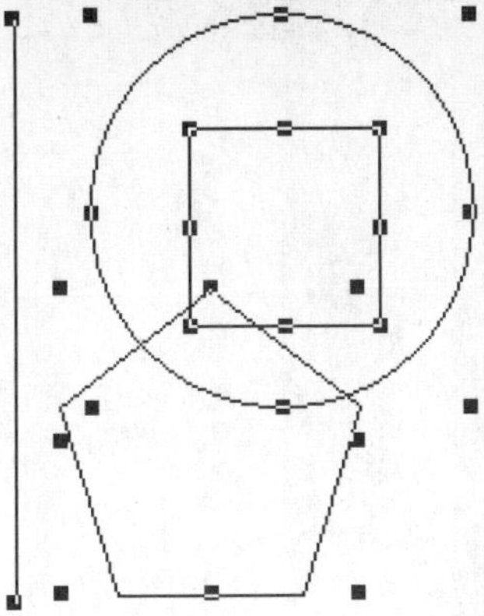

To align or distribute objects automatically in relation to each other, do the following:

1. Select the elements to be aligned.
2. Choose **Align Objects** from the Arrange menu.
3. Choose the appropriate Align or Distribute option for both the vertical and horizontal position of the elements.

Select this button if no change is required.

If you select this option then you can use the Revert command (File menu) to undo the alignment once you've seen its effect.

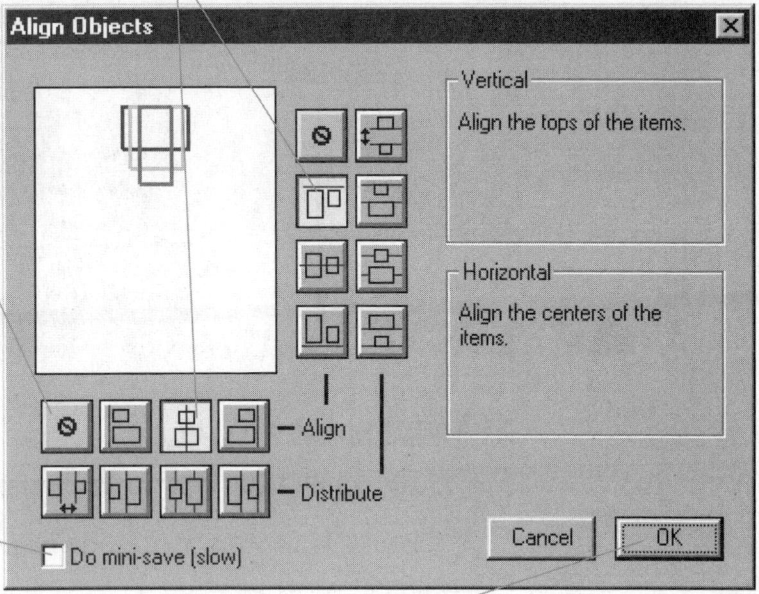

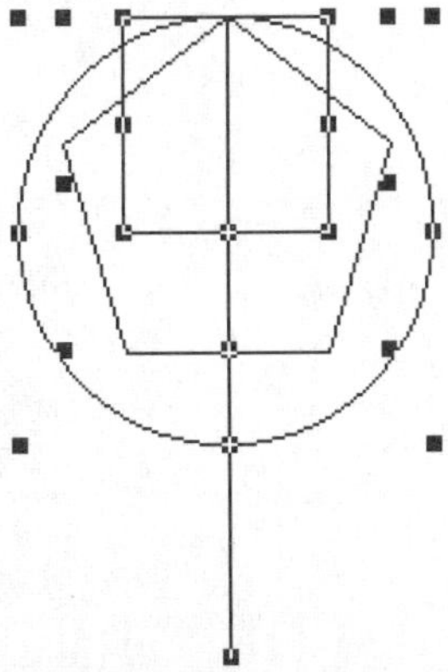

4. Click **OK**. The shapes will be aligned or distributed accordingly.

Using Fill and Line

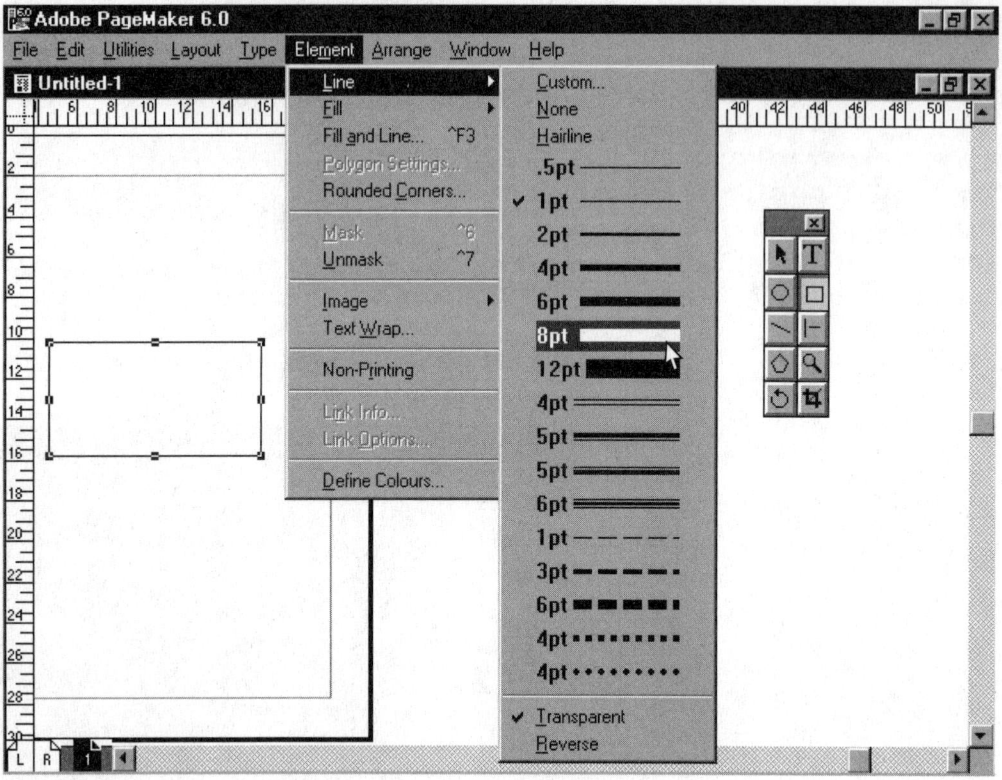

Changing Line Style

1. Select the element(s) to be changed.
2. Choose **Line** from the Element menu.
3. Select the desired line style.

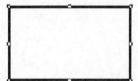

You can control the line style more accurately by using the Custom option from the Line submenu of the Element menu.

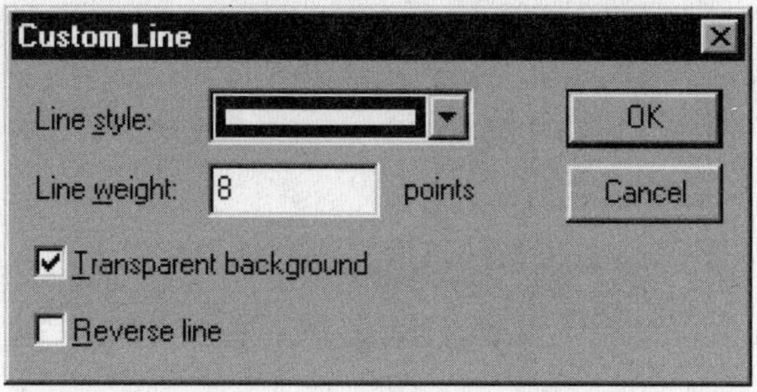

Here you can specify an exact line weight as well as style type.

Changing an Element's Fill

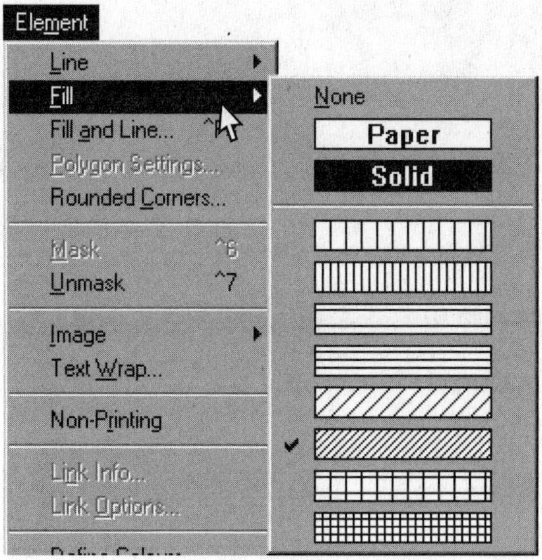

1 Select the element(s) to be changed.

2 Choose **Fill** from the Element menu.

3 Select the desired fill.

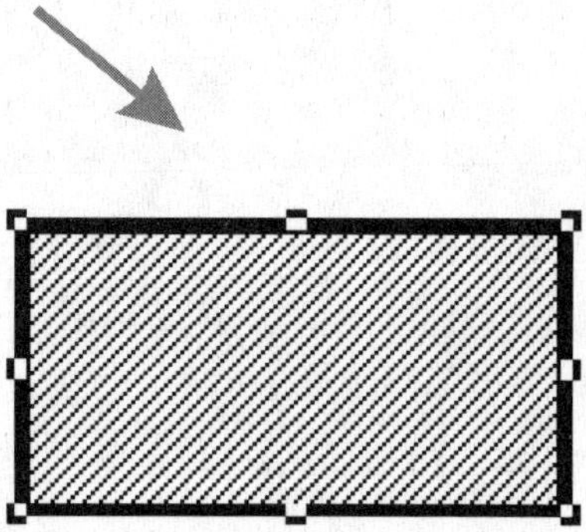

The Fill and Line dialog

The Fill and Line dialog box (Element menu) allows you to specify both colour and type of fill and line in one operation.

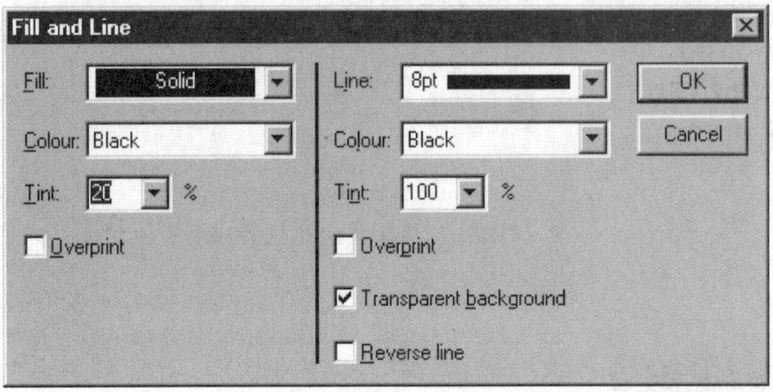

Note the subtle difference between a shape filled with "none", and another filled with "paper". The paper-filled shape is opaque – objects behind it cannot be seen.

The unfilled shape can only be selected from its perimeter, whereas a shape with any type of fill can be moved or selected from any point on its surface.

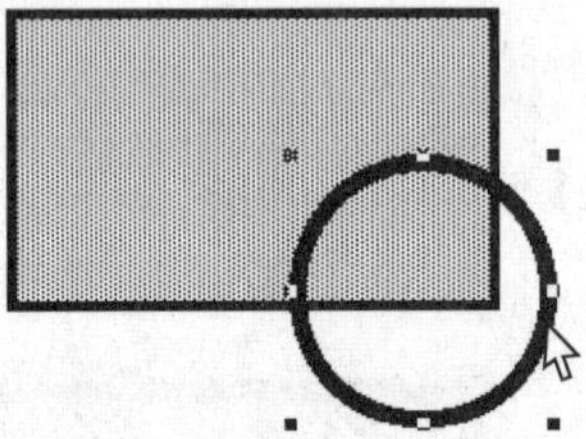

Select/move from edge only

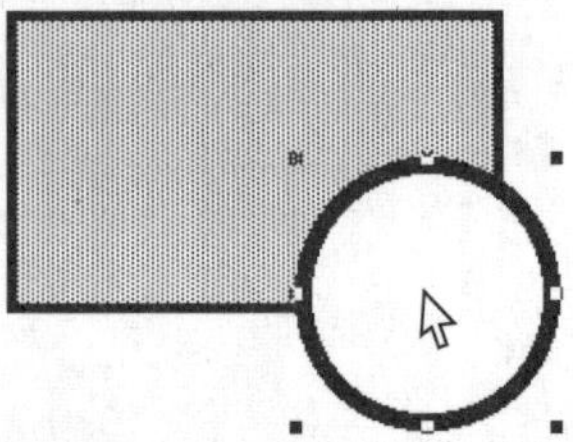

Select/move from any part of the object

Cut, Copy and Paste

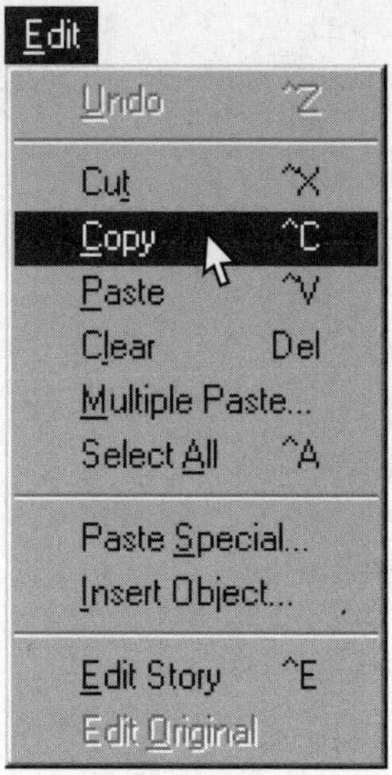

Copying

1. Select the Element(s) to copy.

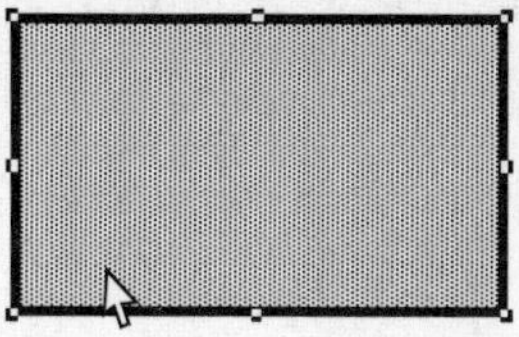

2. Choose **Copy** from the Edit menu. A copy of the element(s) will be made and stored in the Clipboard.
3. Choose **Paste** from the Edit menu. The Clipboard contents will be copied back to the page, slightly offset from the original.

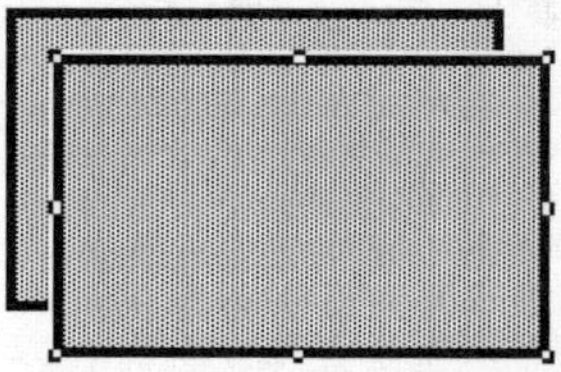

4. Position the new element(s) as desired.

Choosing Paste does not deplete the Clipboard contents, so pasting several times will give you additional copies.

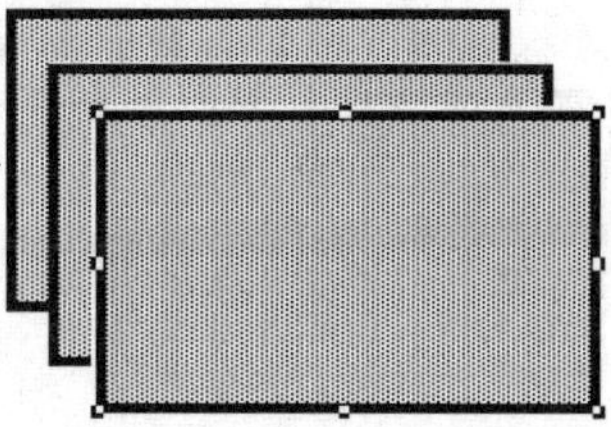

Cut

1. Select one or more elements.
2. Choose **Cut** from the Edit menu. The shapes will disappear from the page or pasteboard and are moved into the Clipboard.
3. To bring back the elements, choose **Paste**. This is useful when you want to move shapes from one page to another. For example, you may cut all elements from page 3, turn to page 7, and then paste them back.

Power Pasting

1. Select an element with the pointer tool.
2. Choose **Copy** from the Edit menu.

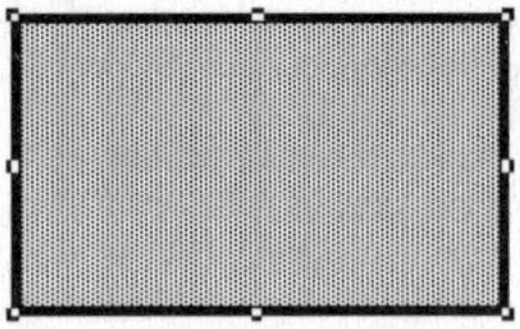

3. Instead of **Paste**, type **Control-Shift-P**. The copy will appear positioned directly over the original. (This is useful if you want to copy items from one page to another whilst maintaining their exact position.)
4. Move the new element by dragging with the pointer tool. Make sure that you move it only once, and do not deselect.

Instead of manually dragging the shape, you could adjust its position numerically with the Control palette.

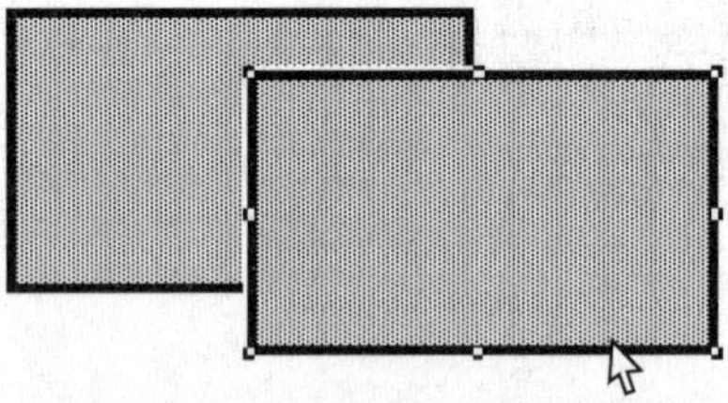

5. Type **Control-Shift-P** again. An additional copy will appear offset by the same distance as exists between the first two elements.

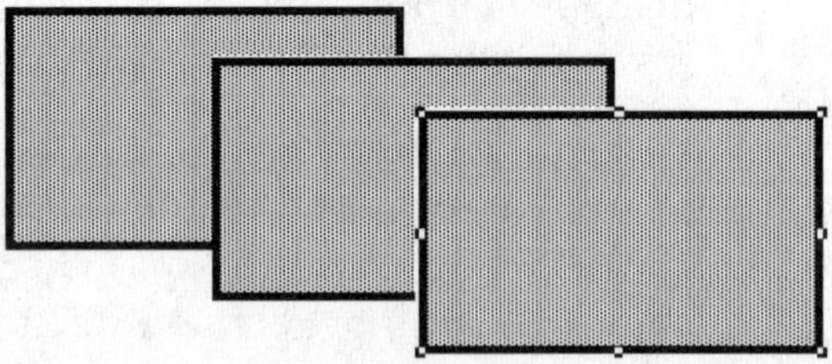

6. You can use **Control-Shift-P** to produce more copies at equal intervals. This technique is known as Power Pasting.

Multiple Paste

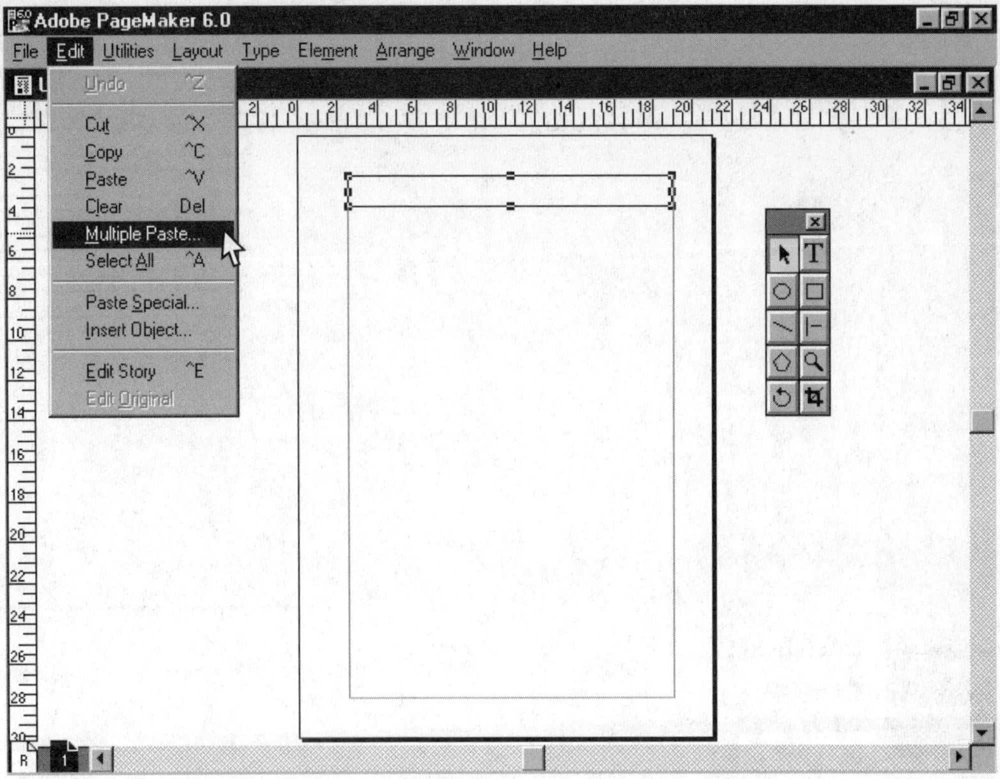

1. Select a shape with the pointer tool.
2. Choose **Copy** from the Edit menu.
3. Choose **Multiple Paste**, also from the Edit menu.
4. In the dialog box which appears, enter the number of copies required and the offsets (vertical and horizontal) for each successive copy, then click **OK**.

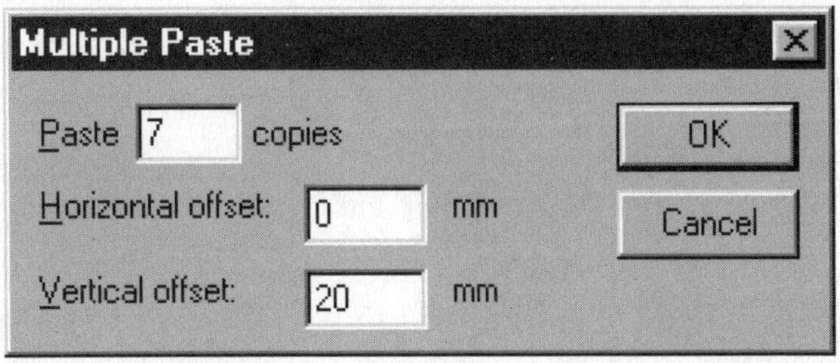

In this example seven copies are made, each 20mm directly below its neighbour.

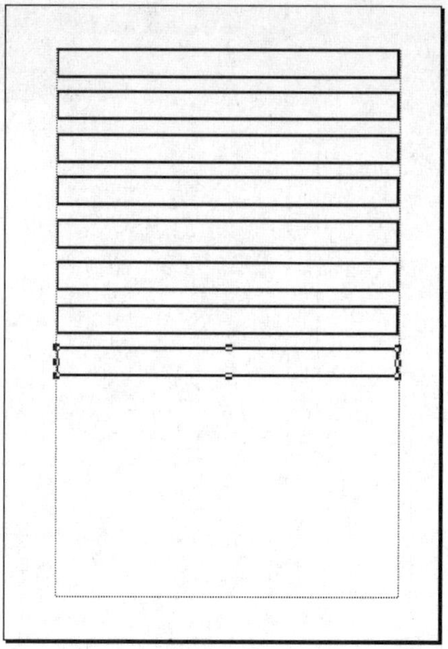

Multiple Pasting was introduced with PageMaker version 5. However, Power Pasting (see page 44) was present in earlier versions.

Magnetic Guidelines

Provided the **Snap to Guides** option is active (from the Layout menu, Guides and Rulers submenu), you will notice that the page margins are magnetic, i.e. elements tend to "snap to" the margin lines once within a certain distance. This makes it easy to align shapes.

Setting Your Own Vertical Guide Lines

1. With the pointer tool, move into the vertical ruler (the arrow should turn white).
2. Click the left mouse button and drag onto the page. A light blue vertical guideline will appear.
3. You can reposition this guide at any time, or delete by dragging it back onto the pasteboard.

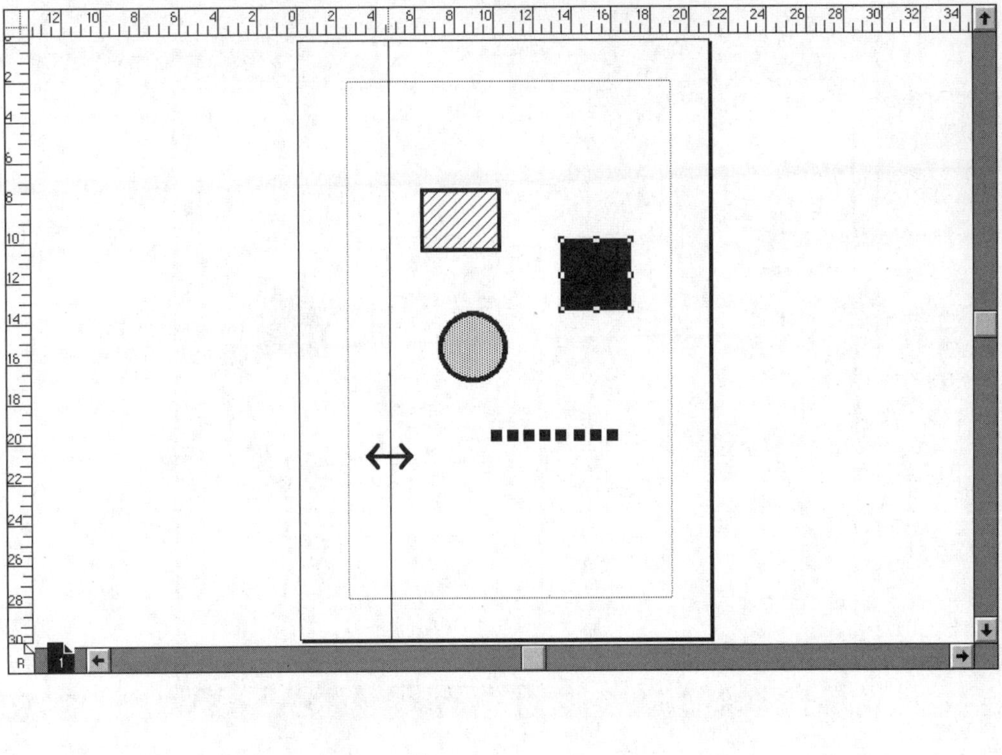

Creating Horizontal Guidelines

These are created in the same way:

1. Move into the horizontal ruler, and drag down onto the page.

2. You can repeat this process to create more guidelines, as long as the total count of horizontal plus vertical does not exceed 120 (in PageMaker 6) or 40 (in PageMaker 5).

Guides normally appear in front of PageMaker elements. Sometimes this may make it difficult to see thin objects such as hairlines. There is, however, an option to display guides "at the back" in the **Preferences** dialog box (File menu). In PageMaker 6 and above you can also set this from the Layout menu, Guides and Rulers submenu.

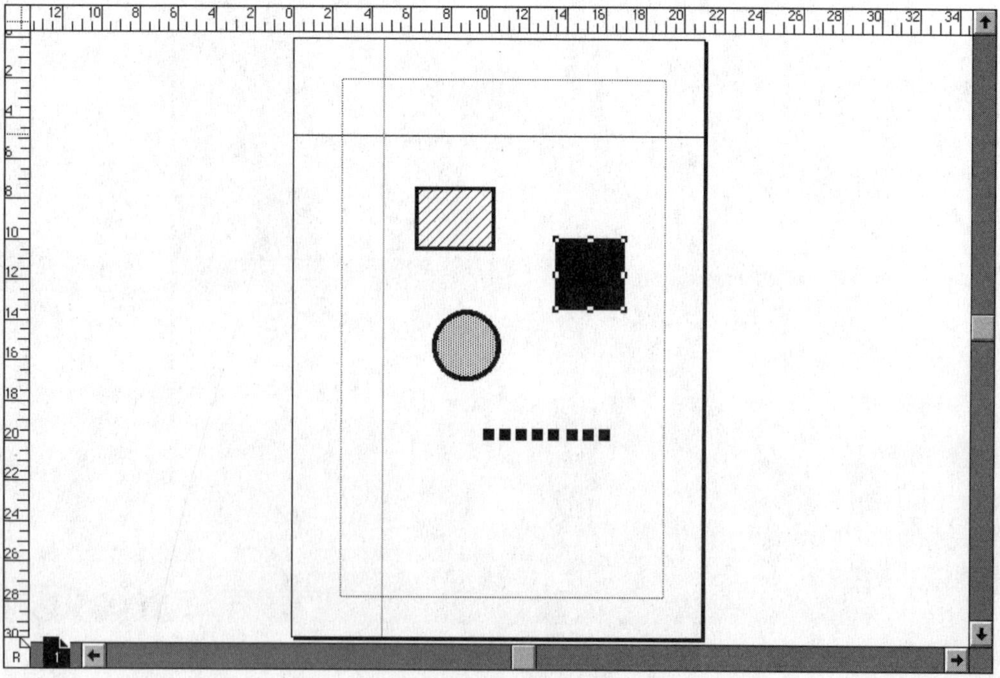

Using Guidelines

Provided the **Snap to Guides** feature is active (Layout menu, Guides and Rulers submenu), all guidelines will be magnetic. As you move or resize shapes using the mouse, they will snap into place when close to a guideline. This helps you to control the structure of your page design.

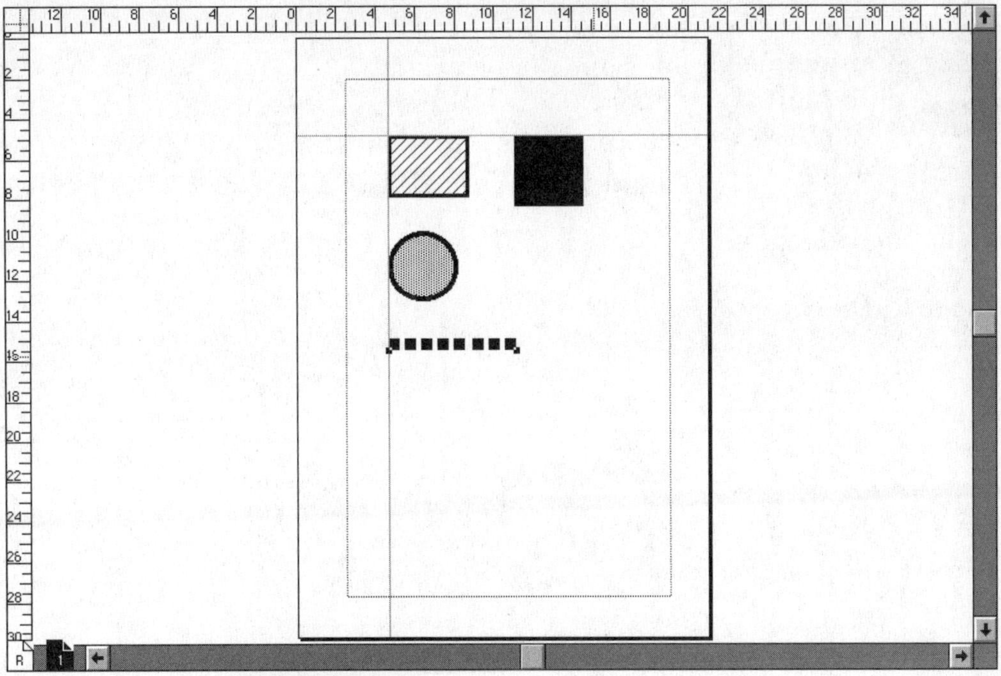

REMEMBER

You can lock your guides to prevent the possibility of accidentally moving them later on.

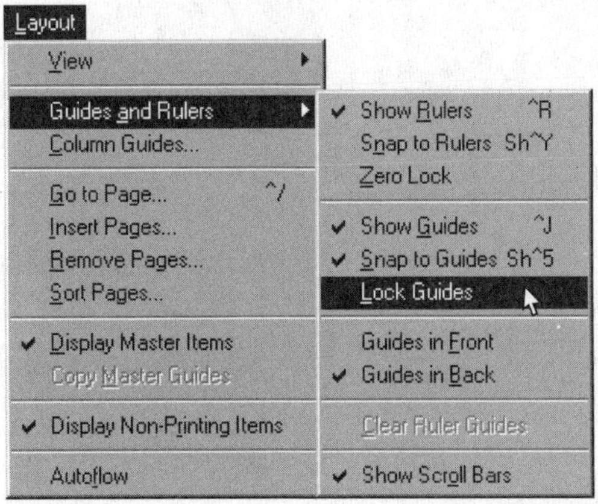

Defaults

Defaults determine the initial effects applied to newly created PageMaker elements.

For example, if the defaults have not been changed since PageMaker was installed, you will find that all new shapes have a default line style of one point, and a default fill of none.

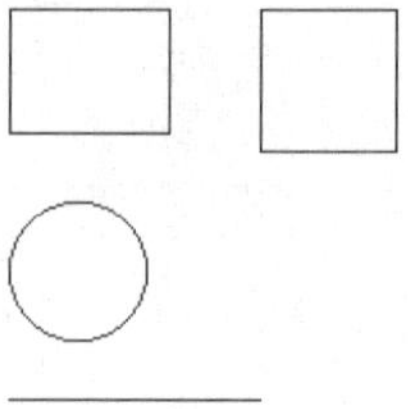

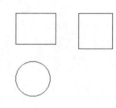

REMEMBER **The principle of defaults applies to all PageMaker attributes, including fill, colour and type specifications.**

Changing a Document's Default Line Style

1. Deselect any elements by clicking on the pointer tool.
2. Choose the required default line style from the Element menu. Because nothing was selected the default line style will change.

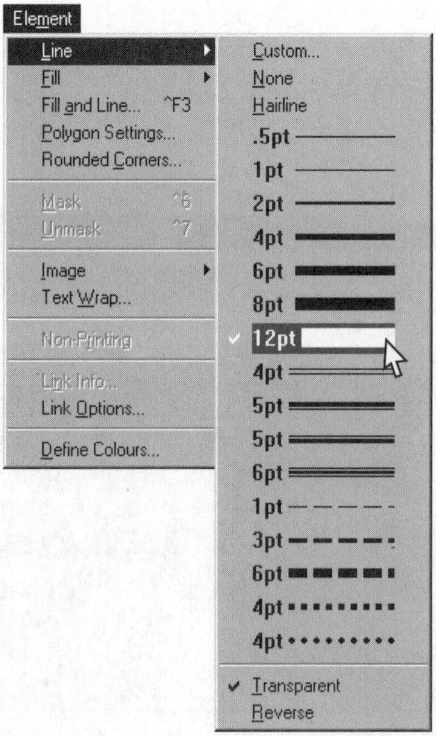

In this example all new shapes will now initially have a line style of 12 points.

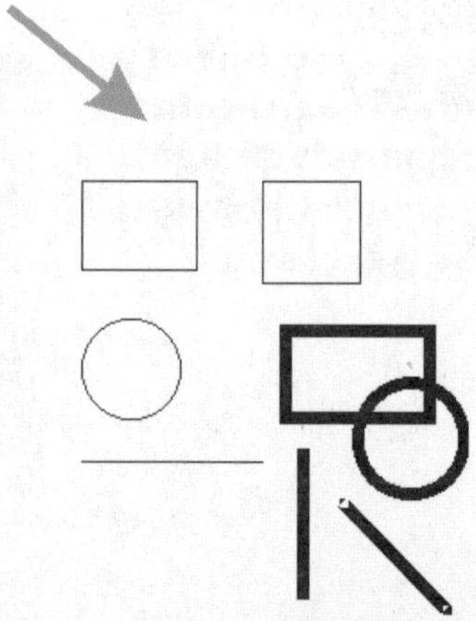

Changing PageMaker's Global Defaults

The previous example demonstrated altering defaults which apply to the working document only. This information is always saved as part of the document file.

It is also possible to change the global defaults, which will affect initial default values for all new PageMaker documents.

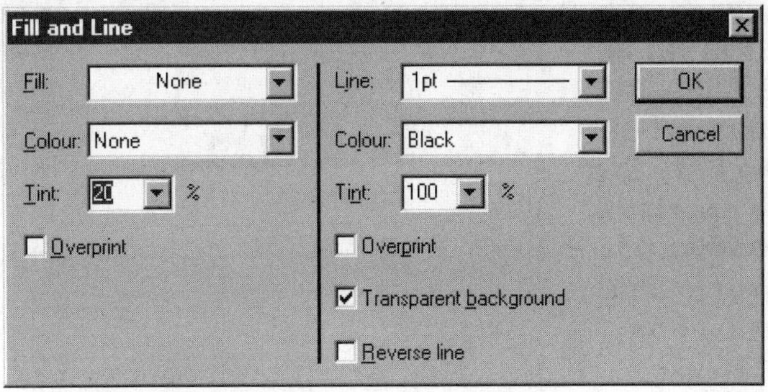

1. Close any open documents (File menu).
2. Any settings you make now will change PageMaker's general defaults. In this example, from now onwards all new PageMaker documents will use a 20% grey tint for boxes and circles.

HANDY TIP

Choosing Document Setup from the File menu at this time will let you specify default attributes for new documents.

The PMx.CNF File

This file contains PageMaker's global default information. You may wish to access this file for the following reasons:

The "x" here is used to denote the PageMaker version number, e.g. if you are using version 6 then the file should be called PM6.CNF.

This illustration shows the PMx.CNF file being accessed from Windows 95 My Computer. For Windows 3.1 you will need to use DOS or the File Manager.

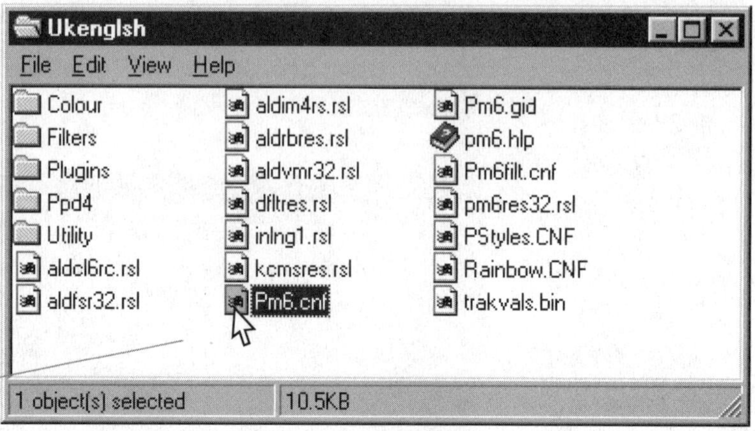

1. **Restoring Defaults to the Factory Settings**
   Simply delete the PMx.CNF file. A new one will be created the next time you launch PageMaker.

2. **Backing up Default Settings**
   If you back up PMx.CNF to floppy disk, you will be able to restore your default settings later on by copying the file back again. This is particularly useful if someone else has been using your machine and changing the settings from those which you prefer.

3. **Copying Defaults to Other Machines**
   Simply copy the PMx.CNF file to the same directory on other machines which have PageMaker installed. This allows you to develop company-wide standards for text and graphic defaults (including colour schemes and corporate fonts) on one PC which you may then copy across to others.

The Rotation Tool 

This allows you to freely rotate any PageMaker element directly on screen using the mouse.

1 Select the item to be rotated.

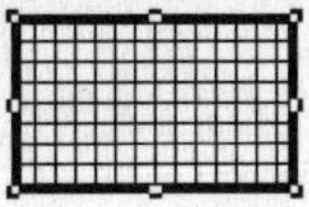

2 Choose the rotation tool.

3 Move to the point where you wish the *pivot* for rotation to be. Hold down the mouse button and drag several centimetres to the right. (Do not let go of the button yet.)

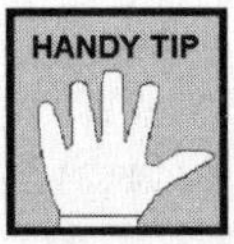

The further you initially drag from the pivot point, the better your control over the rotation angle.

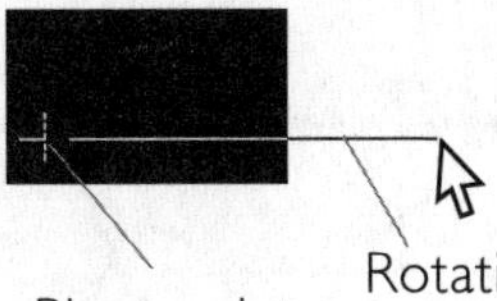
Rotation lever
Pivot point

4 A line will appear which can be used as a rotation lever. By dragging in a circular motion around the pivot point you can rotate the element in either a clockwise or anticlockwise direction.

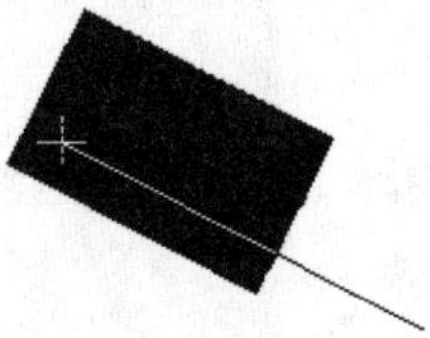
Dragging in a clockwise direction about the pivot point

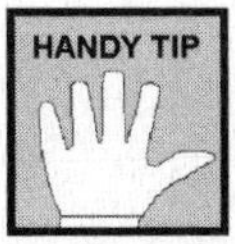

If the Control palette is active, then you will be able to read off the angle of rotation in degrees as you rotate.

5 When you have achieved the desired angle, release the mouse button. The element has been rotated.

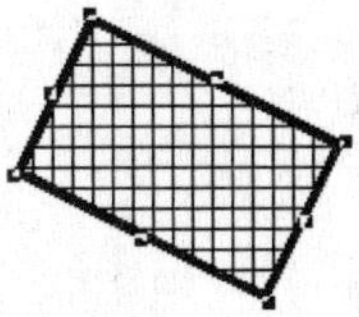

To rotate using the numeric Control palette, see Chapter 6, "Transformations".

Front and Back

Items created more recently tend to appear in front of those which are older. Before version 6 of PageMaker, moving an element had the side-effect of bringing it in front of all others. However, in version 6 and above the order of elements is preserved even when they are edited.

You can control the stacking order of elements using the Arrange menu.

To Bring Elements to the Front of Others

1. Select the element(s).

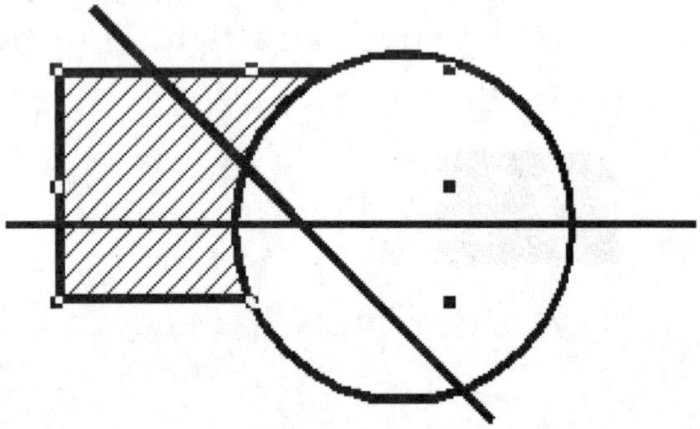

2. Choose **Bring to Front** from the Arrange menu.

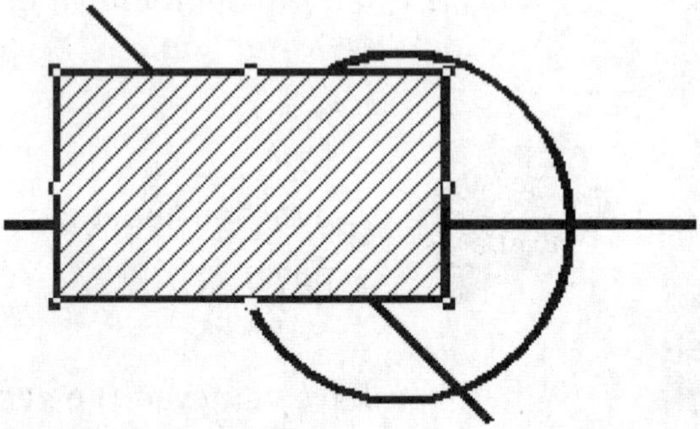

In PageMaker 6 (and above) you can also move elements one "layer" at a time using the Bring Forward and Send Backward commands from the Arrange menu.

To Send Elements to the Back of Others

1. Select the element(s).
2. Choose **Send to Back** from the Arrange menu.

CHAPTER FOUR

Importing Graphics

This chapter shows you how to import graphic elements from other application packages. Once inside your PageMaker document these can be treated in much the same way as internal elements. Additionally, they can be cropped, and TIFF files can be adjusted using Image Control.

Covers

The Place Command **56**

Graphic File Formats **58**

The Cropping Tool **61**

Image Control **62**

The Place Command

Graphics generated in other application packages can be brought into a PageMaker document by using the **Place** command.

1 Choose **Place** from the File menu. The Place dialog box will appear.

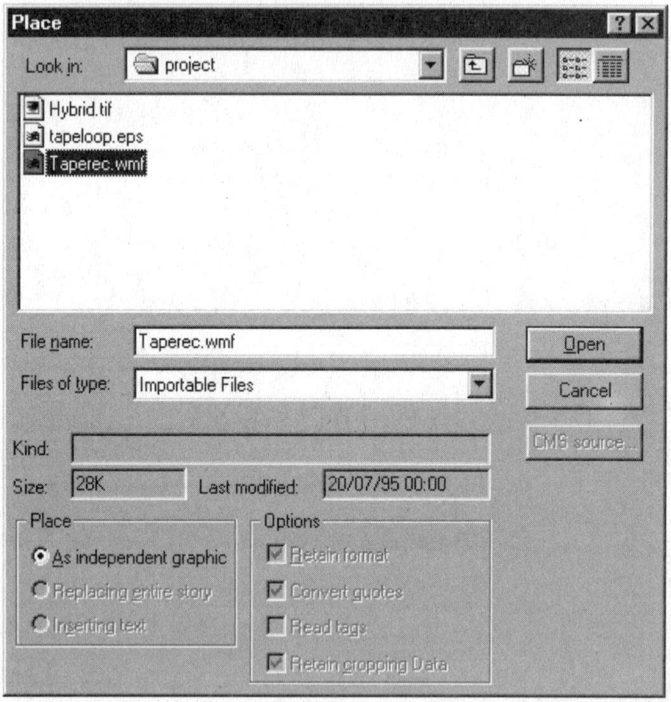

2 Use the directory list to find the location of the file to be imported, or type the path manually.

3 Either type the file name followed by **Return**, or double-click directly on a name displayed in the directory list.

4 Back on the page, your pointer will change into a loaded graphic icon. This gives you the opportunity to decide where the graphic will be positioned initially.

Loaded icons indicating type of graphic file about to be imported.

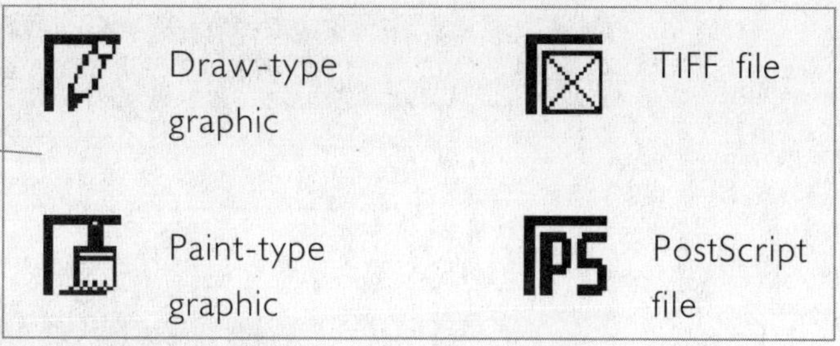

5 Position the loaded icon and click once.

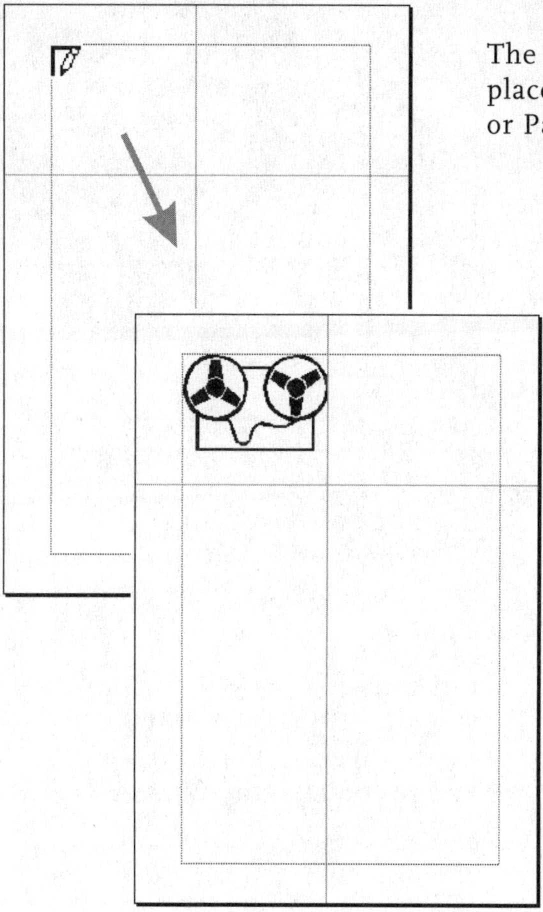

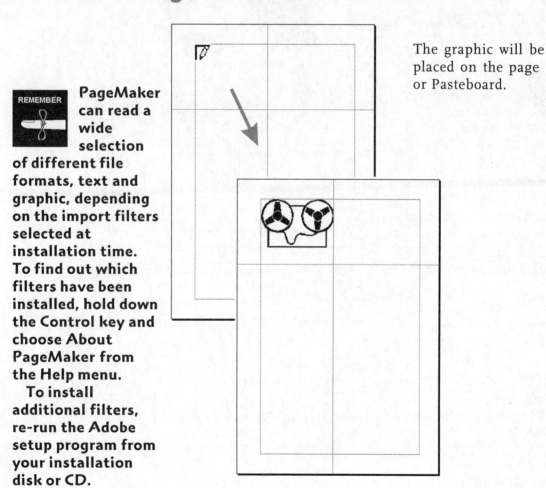

The graphic will be placed on the page or Pasteboard.

PageMaker can read a wide selection of different file formats, text and graphic, depending on the import filters selected at installation time. To find out which filters have been installed, hold down the Control key and choose About PageMaker from the Help menu.

To install additional filters, re-run the Adobe setup program from your installation disk or CD.

Graphic File Formats

This picture started life as two images digitised using a video still camera. They were then enhanced and combined using an image editing application to produce a grey-level TIFF file composite.

REMEMBER

High resolution images look clearer when printed out (provided the printer can match the resolution), but take up proportionately more storage space.

Bitmapped Graphics

TIFF files and Paint files are bitmapped. This means that they are represented as a series of dots (or blocks) which build up an image.

It is important to note the *resolution* of bitmapped graphics. If the resolution is high then the component dots will be small, which improves the quality of the image. Resolution is normally measured in dots per inch (dpi).

HANDY TIP

Holding down the Control key while resizing a bitmapped graphic will size it in "jumps", limiting you to sizes which work best with your selected printing device.

At 400% view size you can clearly see the blocks which make up the image...

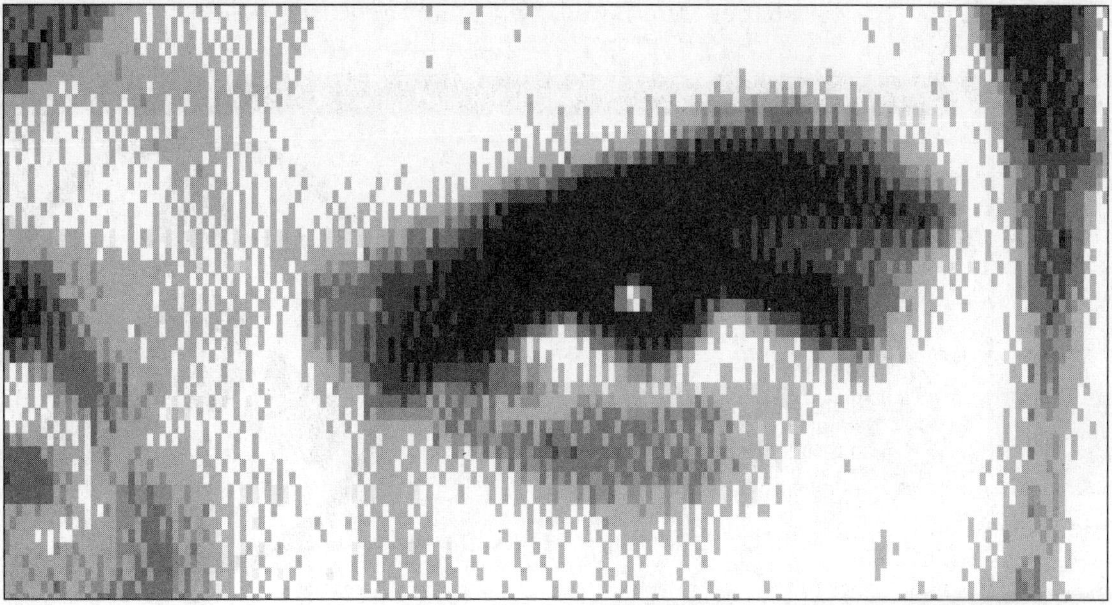

Resizing Imported Graphics

1. Click on the element with the pointer tool
2. Resize in the normal way (as for native PageMaker elements) by dragging on the object handles.
3. Hold down the **Shift** key if you want the graphic to remain in its original proportions.

Remember that you can also move or resize any element using the Control palette. This will give you precise numeric control (see Chapter 3).

Moving Imported Graphics

1. Again, make sure the element has been selected with the pointer tool.
2. Move by dragging anywhere within the shape.

The Draw-type loaded graphic icon

Draw-type Graphics

These are stored not as images, but as objects. The graphic is created as a series of (sometimes complex) mathematical shapes, and is redrawn to any required resolution.

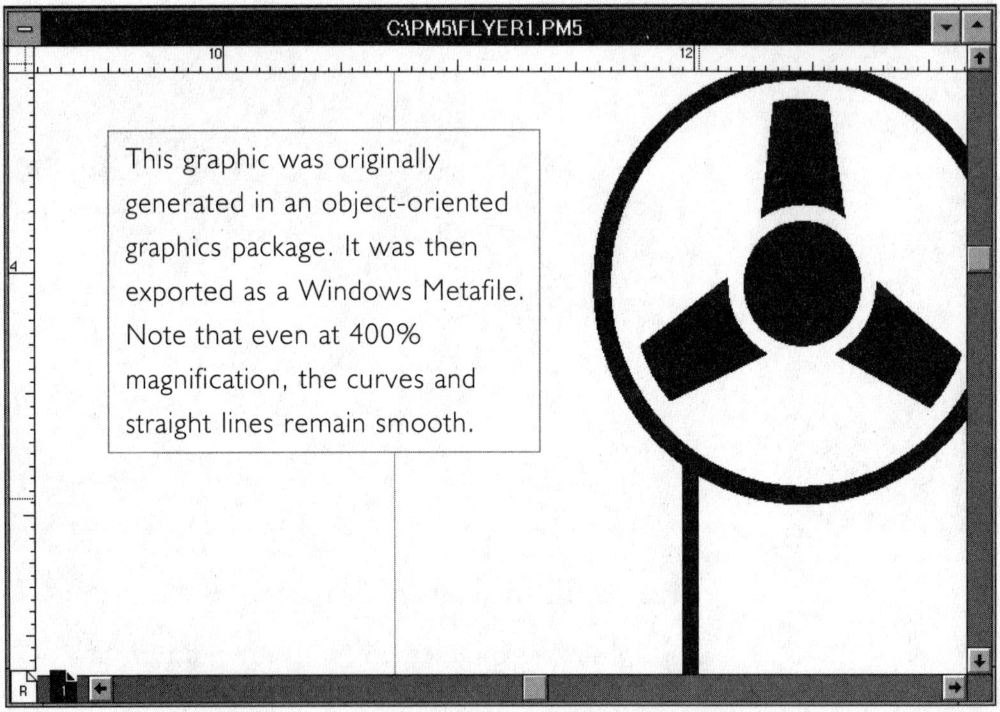

C:\PM5\FLYER1.PM5
This graphic was originally generated in an object-oriented graphics package. It was then exported as a Windows Metafile. Note that even at 400% magnification, the curves and straight lines remain smooth.

You can freely resize these graphics without losing definition. The final resolution is determined by the output device.

EPS Files

EPS files are represented by this icon.

EPS stands for Encapsulated PostScript. This is a page description language, a widely used standard in professional printing. EPS files may contain a combination of bitmapped and Draw-type graphics as well as text.

Since PostScript is a printer language, your EPS file may not display on the screen. Some EPS files get around this by incorporating a TIFF preview image, which may still look "grainier" than the final printed version.

The Cropping Tool

Cropping is used to "cut away" any unwanted parts of an imported graphic.

1 Select the cropping tool from the Toolbox.

2 Click once on the imported graphic to display its handles.

3 Line up the *centre* of the cropping tool with a handle.

4 Hold down the mouse button (you may have to wait a few seconds while the image is prepared for cropping).

5 Drag towards the centre of the object. Part of the image will disappear.

Dragging inwards with the cropping tool.

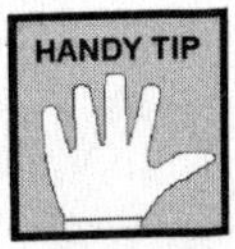

If you move within the shape and then hold down the mouse button, the cropping icon will change into a grabber hand. You will then be able to reposition the whole shape within its cropped "window".

6 Repeat this process with other handles if necessary.

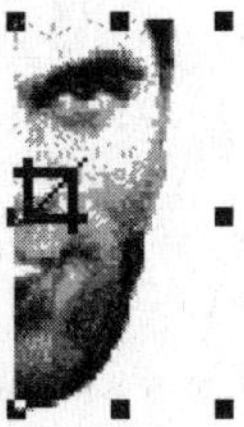

Dragging within the shape with the cropping tool.

Cropping is non-destructive. This means that you can always restore the shape by pulling the handles back out again.

Image Control

1 Select an imported TIFF file with the pointer tool.

2 Choose **Image Control** from the Image submenu of the Element menu.

The following dialog box will appear:

HANDY TIP **Image Control can be used to help "balance" several images on the page, so they appear to have the same lightness and contrast.**

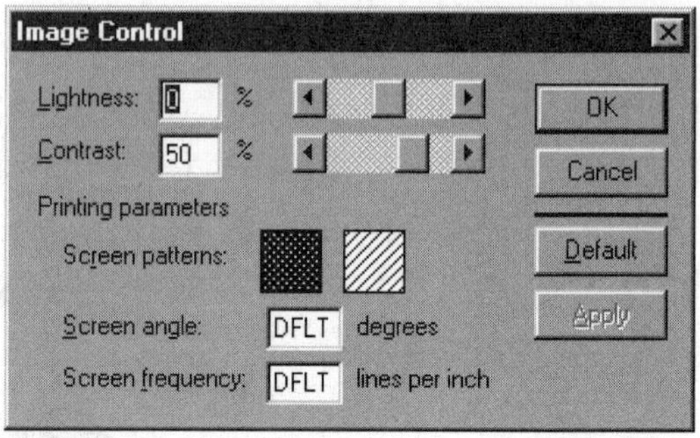

3 Make a change and click the **Apply** button to preview the effect on the image.

4 Click **OK** when satisfied, or **Cancel** to abort.

Lightness increased to 30%

Contrast increased to 100% (pure black and white)

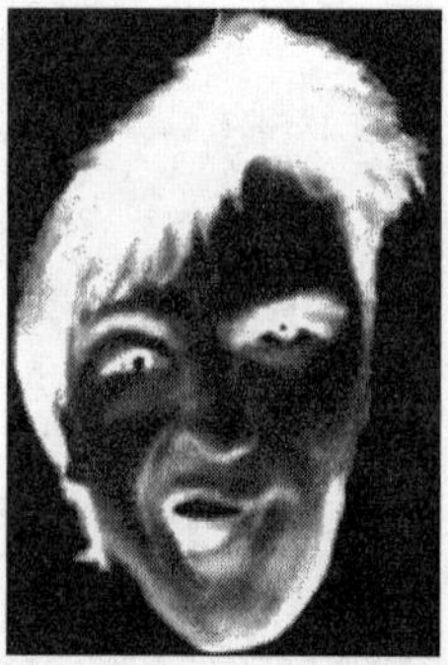

Contrast of minus 50% (inverted image)

Screening is the process where grey levels are simulated with solid black dots. This is done by printing a fine pattern of dots; the further apart the dots the lighter the overall grey effect.

This also applies to colour: for example, screened red dots will simulate a shade of pink.

CHAPTER FIVE

The Text Tool

PageMaker contains a wealth of text-editing features. In this chapter we'll look at how to enter and edit text, as well as the range of character and paragraph attributes which can be changed.

Covers

Adding Text 64

Changing Text 65

Manipulating Text 66

Default Text Settings 68

Working with Blocks of Text 69

More Advanced Text Effects 71

Adding Text

The text tool

1. Select the text tool.
2. Click anywhere on the page within the margin guides. An insertion point (text cursor) will appear at the left margin.
3. Type in the text.

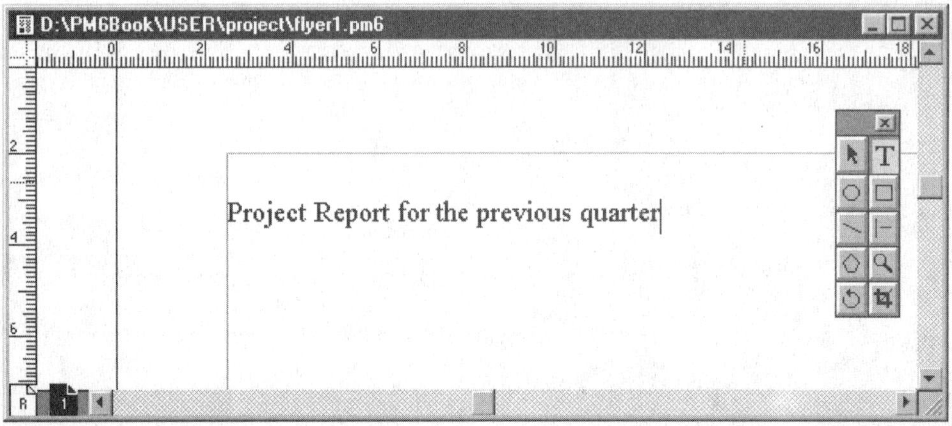
D:\PM6Book\USER\project\flyer1.pm6
Project Report for the previous quarter

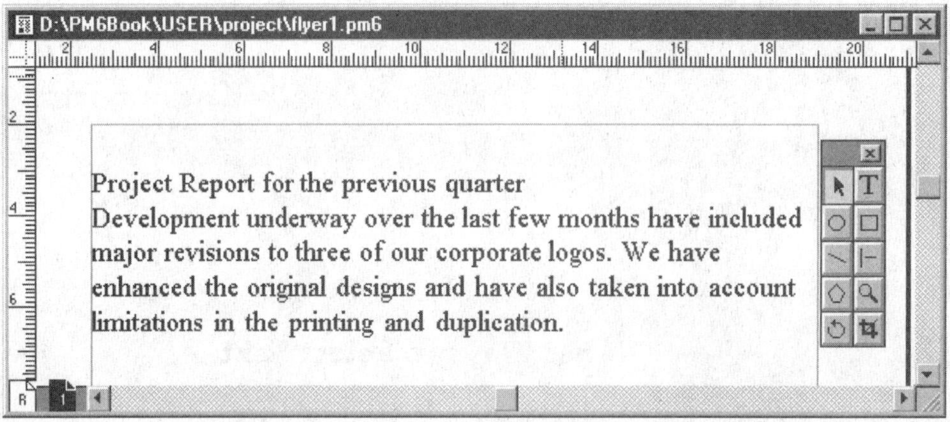
D:\PM6Book\USER\project\flyer1.pm6
Project Report for the previous quarter
Development underway over the last few months have included major revisions to three of our corporate logos. We have enhanced the original designs and have also taken into account limitations in the printing and duplication.

Changing Text

1 With the text tool, drag across the text you wish to select.

2 You now have the opportunity to make changes to this text.

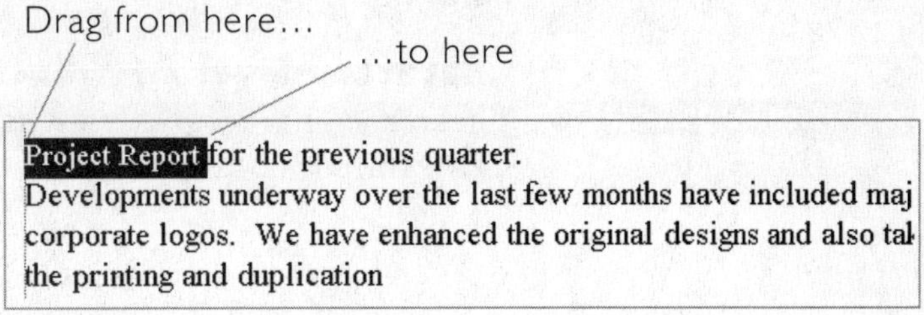
Drag from here...
...to here
Project Report for the previous quarter.
Developments underway over the last few months have included maj
corporate logos. We have enhanced the original designs and also tal
the printing and duplication

REMEMBER **You can activate or deactivate the Control palette from the Window menu.**

3 You can use the Control palette to alter any of the text attributes. Note that changes only affect the selected text.

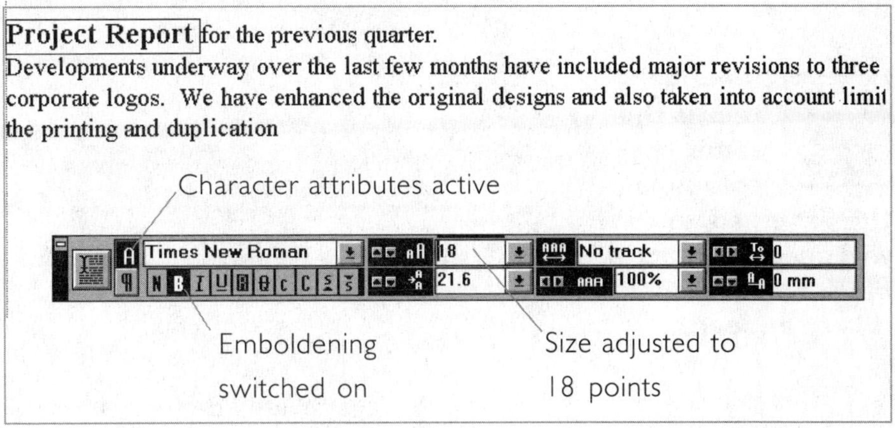
Project Report for the previous quarter.
Developments underway over the last few months have included major revisions to three
corporate logos. We have enhanced the original designs and also taken into account limit
the printing and duplication
Character attributes active
Times New Roman
18
No track
0
21.6
100%
0 mm
Emboldening switched on
Size adjusted to 18 points

Other Ways to Select Text

Double-click:	selects a word
Triple-click:	selects the surrounding paragraph
Select All:	(from the Edit menu) selects all text in a story
Shift-click:	selects from previous insertion point to mouse location

Manipulating Text

Selected text can be copied, cut and pasted (from the Edit menu) in the same manner as graphics (see Chapter 3).

Changing text attributes is achieved most easily with the Control palette. This operates in two modes, character and paragraph level.

Character-level Attributes

These are characteristics which can be applied to one or more individual characters.

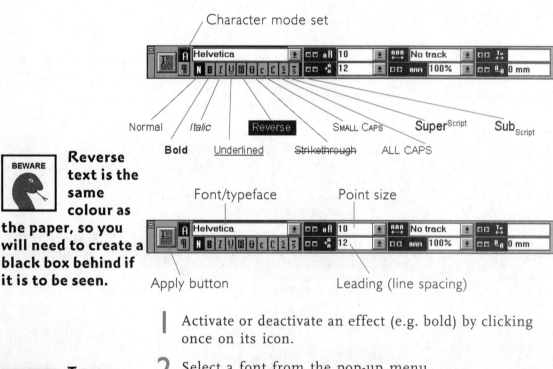

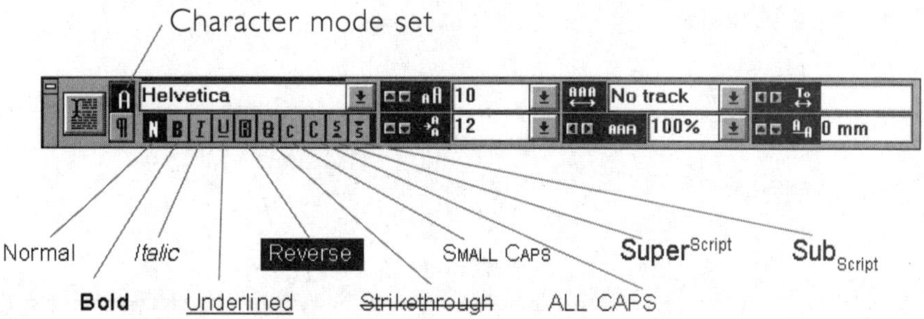

BEWARE **Reverse text is the same colour as the paper, so you will need to create a black box behind if it is to be seen.**

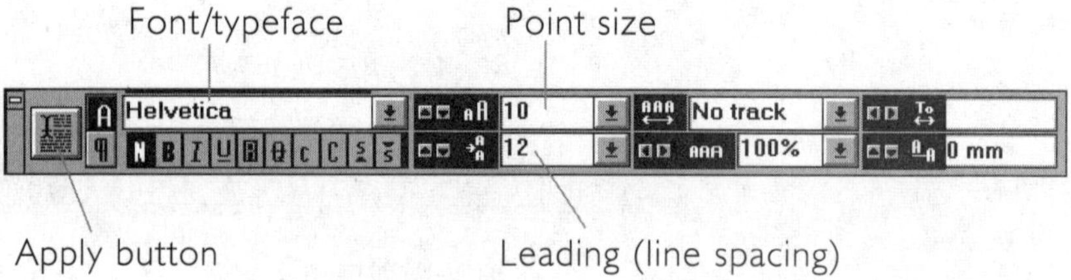

1. Activate or deactivate an effect (e.g. bold) by clicking once on its icon.
2. Select a font from the pop-up menu.
3. Enter a new point size or select from the pop-up menu.
4. Leading is the vertical space given to a line of text (usually measured in points). An automatic setting is available from the pop-up menu.

HANDY TIP **To see how the changes affect the text, click on the Apply button, or press Escape to abort the new setting.**

...contd

Paragraph-level Attributes

These are characteristics which affect entire paragraphs of text.

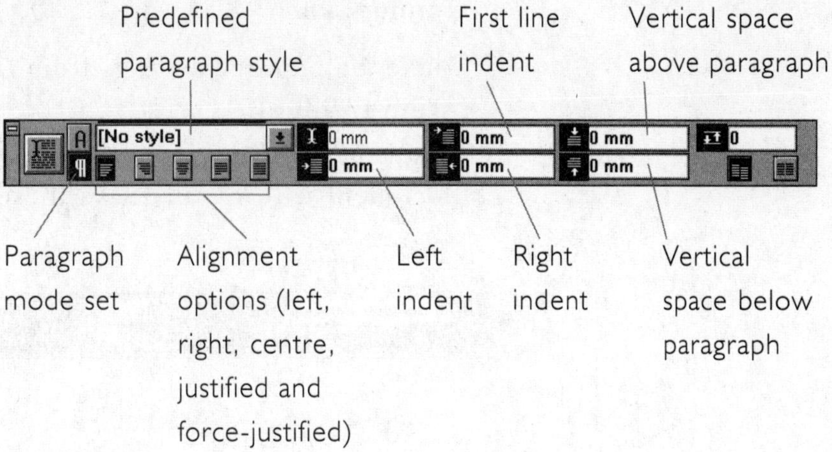

Examples of Paragraph Settings

This text has a space below paragraph of 5mm. It is left aligned with a first line indent of 10mm. This paragraph uses centre alignment.	This text is justified. This means that space is adjusted between words/letters so that each line begins and ends at the same place, apart from this final line. Force justification affects all lines in the paragraph.

Menu Options

Individual settings may also be made using the Type menu. Note that some of these options have keyboard shortcuts listed.

For more information about predefined paragraph styles, see Chapter 11, "Style Sheets".

Default Text Settings

Setting Document Defaults

1. Make sure that no text is selected, and no insertion point active. The best way to do this is to click on the pointer tool.
2. Make the required settings from the Control palette or Type menu.
3. From now on all new text created in the current document will initially have these new attributes.

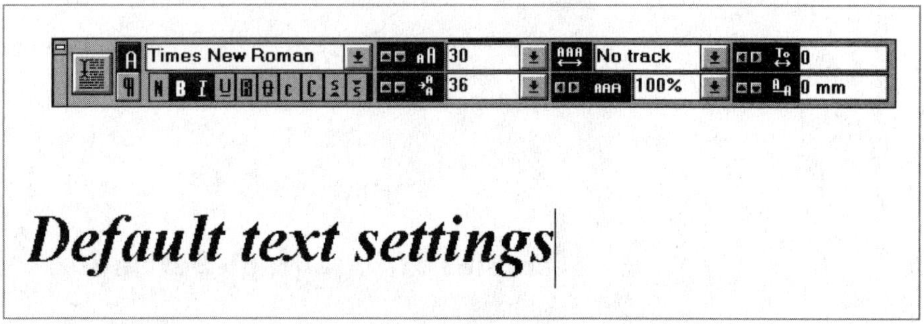

Setting PageMaker Global Text Defaults

1. Close all documents.
2. Make the required text settings. These are automatically saved in the PageMaker CNF file (see the topic "Defaults" in Chapter 3).

Working with Blocks of Text

If you click on your text with the pointer tool, it will be treated as a single PageMaker element: a text block. This can be moved or resized without altering the attributes of the text within.

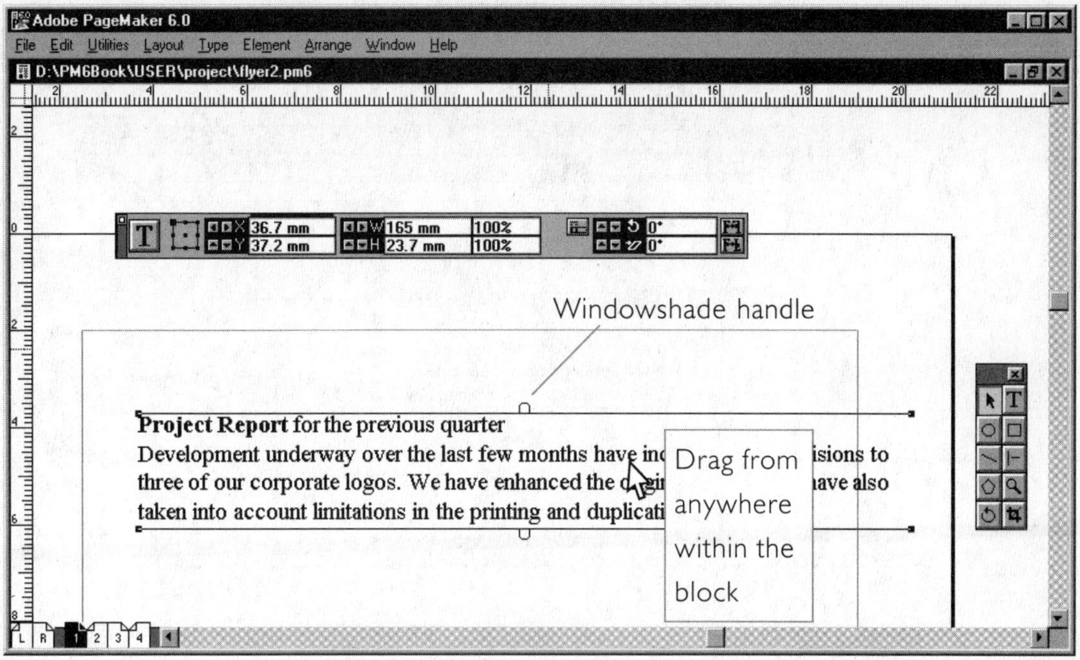

Moving a Text Block

You cannot alter the text attributes with the pointer, only the text tool. Making text attribute changes with the pointer tool active will instead alter the document defaults.

1. Select with the pointer tool.
2. Drag from anywhere within the block (avoid the handles).

Text blocks have two extra handles known as windowshades. These are normally blank but are sometimes used to indicate text which is continued to or from another block.

Resizing Text Blocks

This can be done either by dragging on the object's handles or via the Control palette:

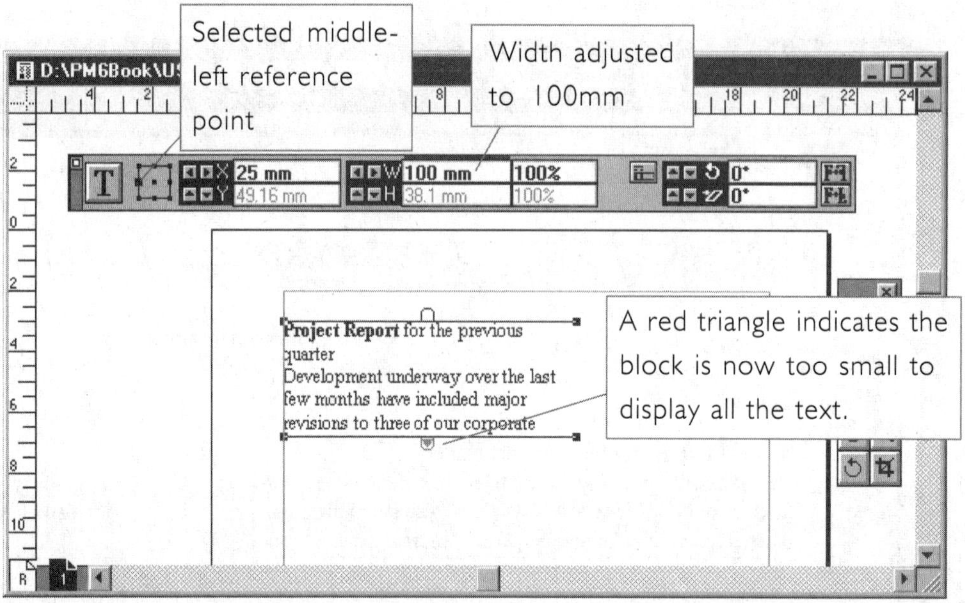
D:\PM6Book\U
Selected middle-left reference point
Width adjusted to 100mm
25 mm
49.16 mm
100 mm
38.1 mm
100%
100%
0°
0°
Project Report for the previous quarter
Development underway over the last few months have included major revisions to three of our corporate
A red triangle indicates the block is now too small to display all the text.

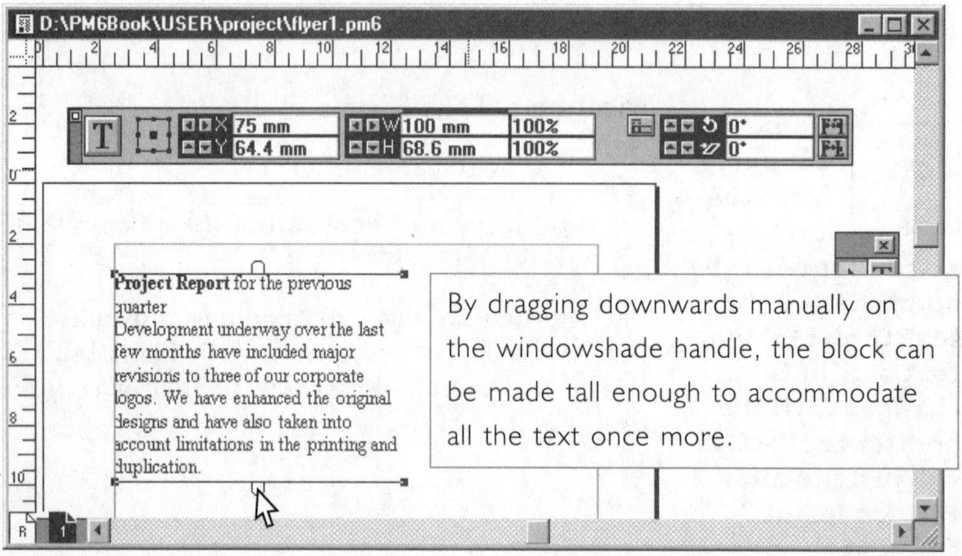
D:\PM6Book\USER\project\flyer1.pm6
75 mm
64.4 mm
100 mm
68.6 mm
100%
100%
0°
0°
Project Report for the previous quarter
Development underway over the last few months have included major revisions to three of our corporate logos. We have enhanced the original designs and have also taken into account limitations in the printing and duplication.
By dragging downwards manually on the windowshade handle, the block can be made tall enough to accommodate all the text once more.

More Advanced Text Effects

Kerning

If all characters are evenly spaced out, some combinations of letters give the illusion of too much horizontal space:

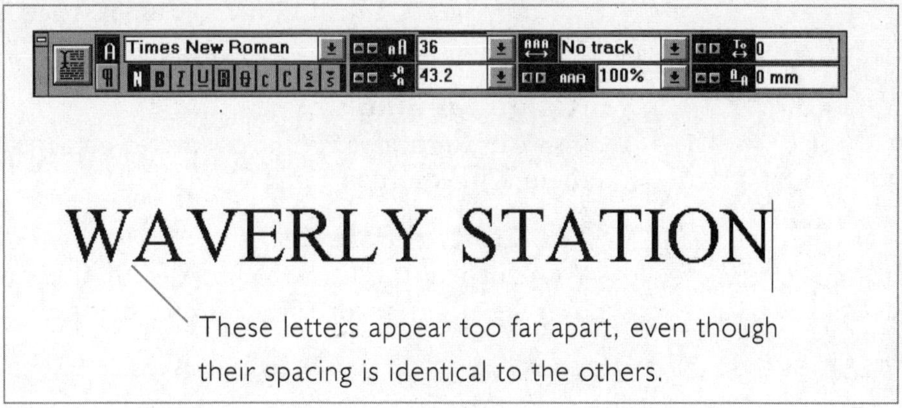
Times New Roman
36
No track
0
43.2
100%
0 mm
WAVERLY STATION
These letters appear too far apart, even though their spacing is identical to the others.

PageMaker recognises these pairs of characters automatically, and will adjust accordingly. This is known as automatic pair kerning (accessed by selecting Paragraph, Spacing from the Type menu).

WAVERLY STATION
Space adjusted automatically

Kerning can also be carried out manually:

1. Click an insertion point (using the text tool) between the characters to be kerned.
2. Type **Control** and **Backspace** to kern the characters together. **Control**, **Shift** and **Backspace** will move them further apart.

Range Kerning

You can kern a range of characters by firstly selecting them with the text tool.

The Control Palette

You can use the Control palette for full numeric control over kerning, as in the example below:

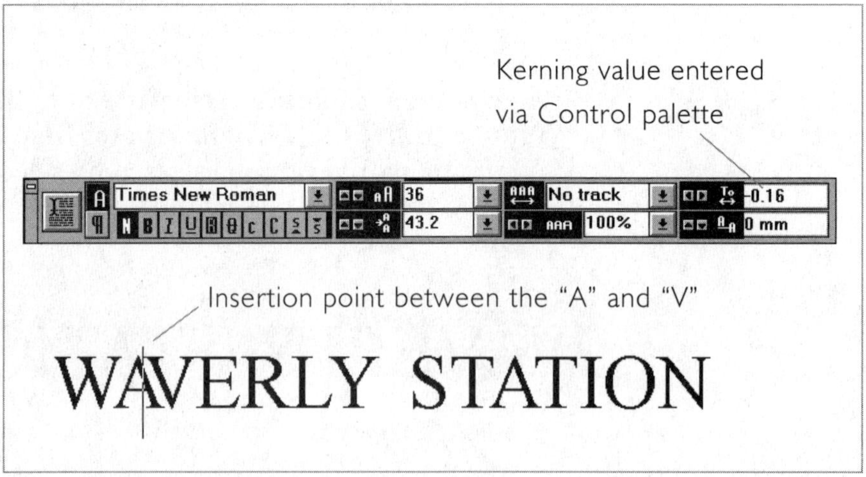

Tracking

This is similar to kerning in that it deals with the horizontal space between letters.

Tracking is a paragraph-level attribute which takes note of the font and the size of the text to which it applies. PageMaker has five intelligent tracking algorithms, ranging from **Very Tight** through **Normal** to **Very Loose**.

Tracking can be applied either from the Type menu or the Control palette:

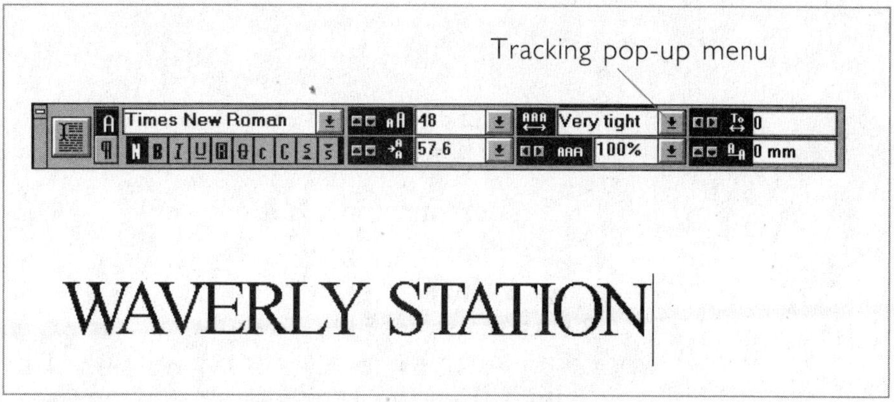

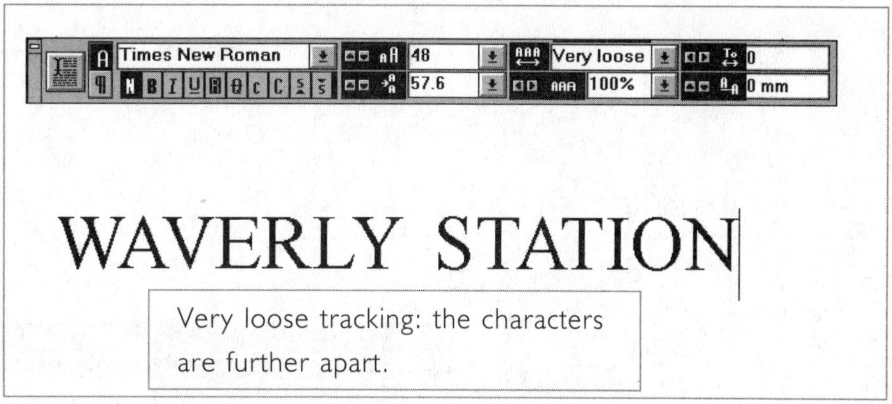

In general, tracking keeps big characters closer together – since spacing is much more noticeable at large point sizes.

Shift Baseline

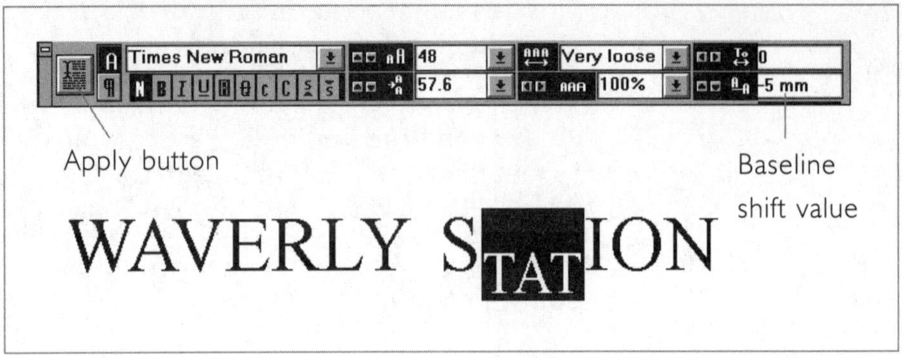

1. Select the required characters with the text tool.
2. Enter the baseline shift value into the Control palette. A negative value indicates a shift downwards.
3. Click the Apply button.

Set Width

This scales text horizontally by a given percentage, without altering its vertical point size. This can be done either from the Type menu or by the Control palette as a character-level attribute:

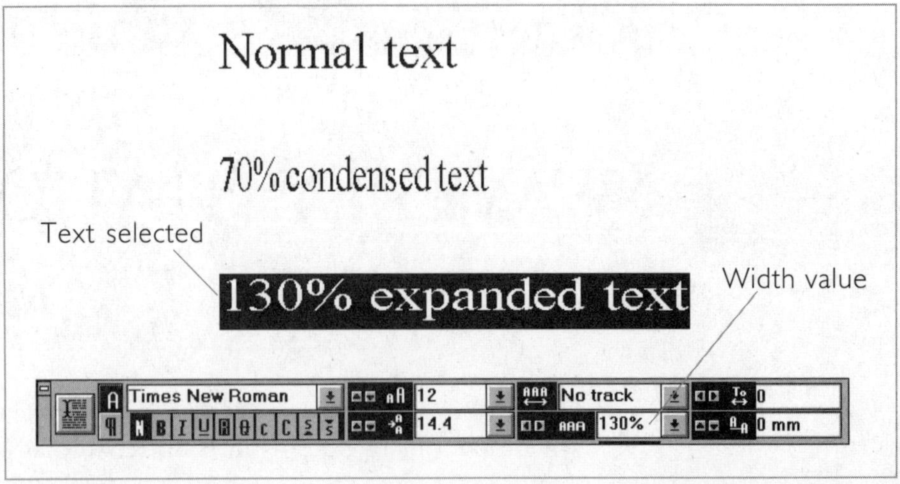

CHAPTER SIX

Transformations

This chapter takes you through different transformations which can be applied to graphic and text elements. Some, like cropping, only apply to imported graphic items.

Covers

Skewing 76

Reflecting 76

Cropping and Resizing with the Control Palette 77

Combining Effects 78

Rotating with the Control Palette 79

Locking Elements 80

Skewing

Text and graphic objects can be skewed about a reference point to give them a twisted effect:

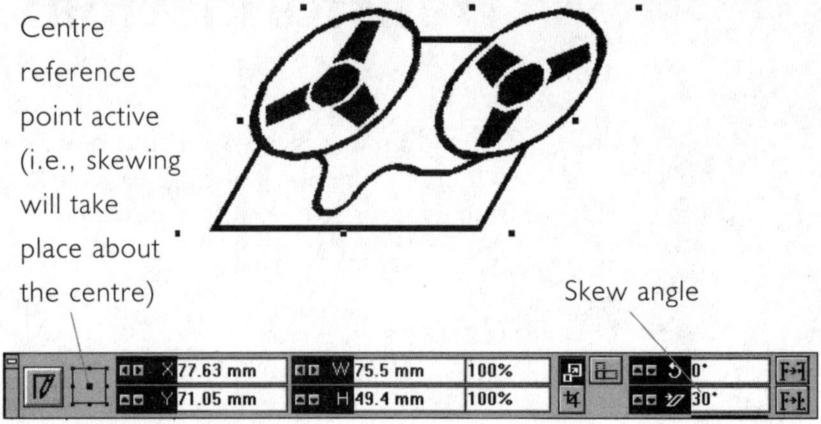

You can return any element to its original state by choosing Remove Transformation from the Arrange menu in PageMaker 6 (or the Element menu in PageMaker 5).

1. Select the object and reference point.
2. Enter the skew angle and click the Apply button.

Reflecting

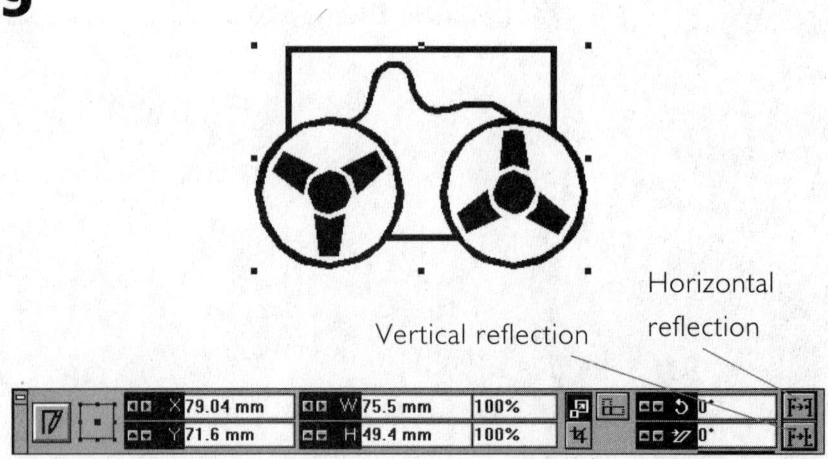

1. Select the object and reference point.
2. Click on either the horizontal or vertical reflection icon.

Cropping and Resizing with the Control Palette

Graphic images can be cropped and resized very precisely using the Control palette, as follows:

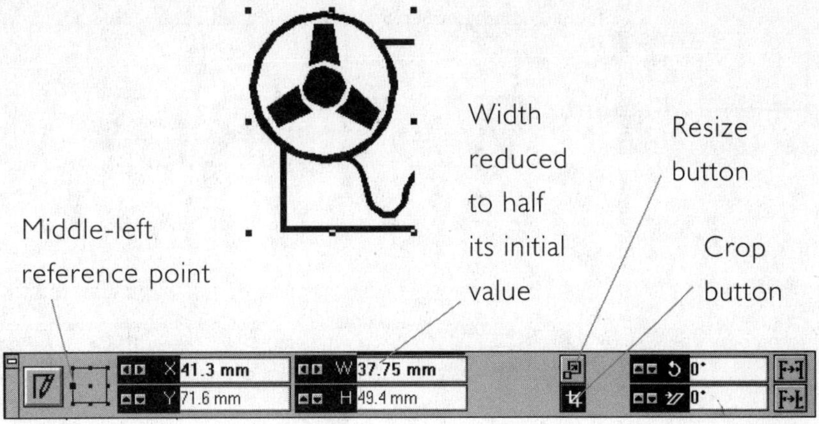

1. Select the element and choose a reference point. In this example we are using the middle-left object handle.

2. Select the crop or resize button. You can now either adjust the reference point's coordinates, or edit the overall width/height of the object. The element will be cropped or resized to accommodate the changes. In this case we have cropped the image, adjusting the width to exactly half its previous value.

Combining Effects

The transformations discussed on the previous pages can be combined to produce impressive effects, as in the example below.

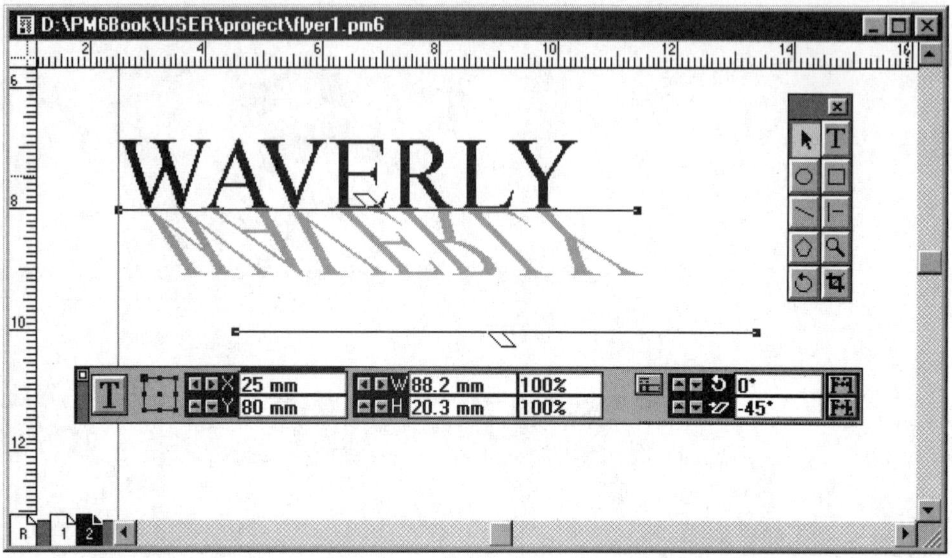

In the above example the following steps were taken.

1. The text block was selected, then **Copy** and **Paste** (from the Edit menu) were chosen.
2. The copy was vertically reflected using the icon in the Control palette.
3. It was then skewed minus 45 degrees about its top left corner.
4. A 30% grey colour was applied using the Colour palette (see Chapter 12).
5. The transformed element was positioned accordingly.

Rotating with the Control Palette

1. Make sure the Control palette is active (Window menu).
2. Select the element for rotation.

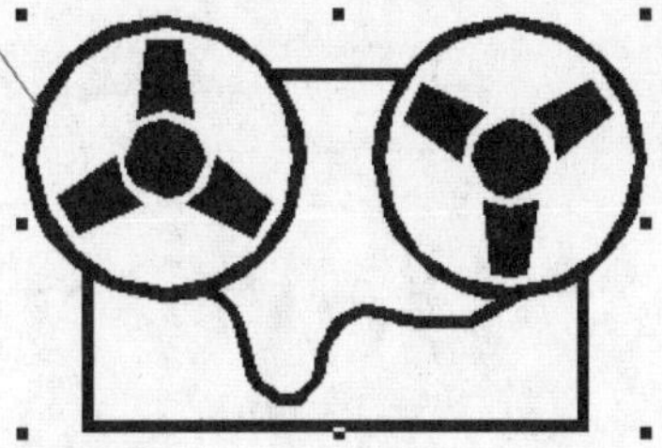

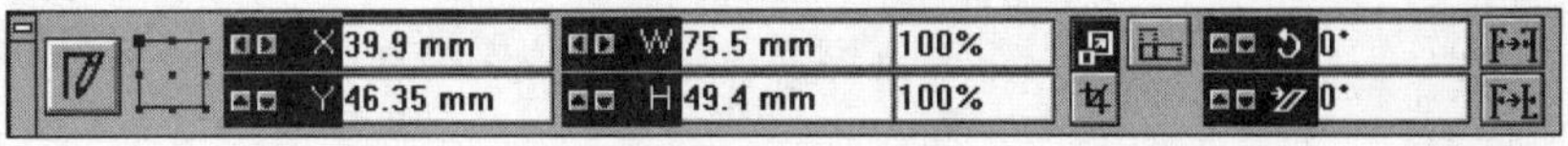

3. Choose the reference point (in this example we shall rotate the object about its centre).

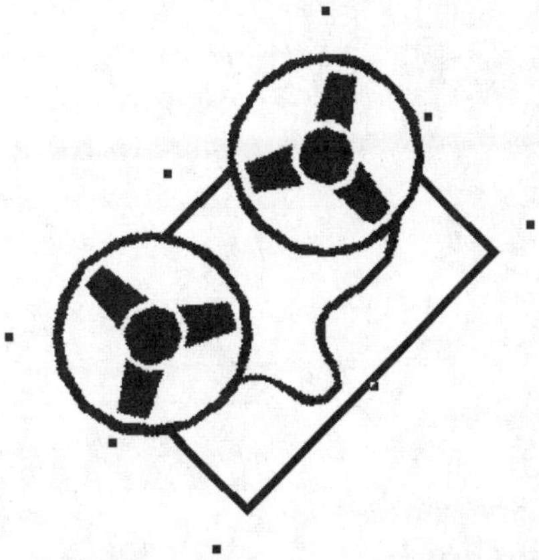

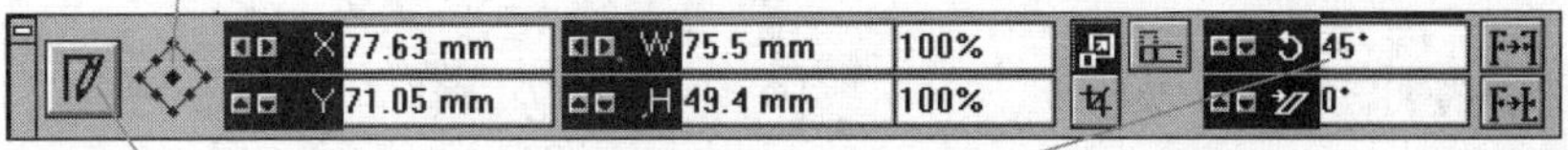

4. Enter the angle of rotation and then click the Apply button.

Locking Elements (PageMaker version 6 or above)

If you have PageMaker version 6 or above then you can use the Lock Position feature to fix elements in a certain position on the page.

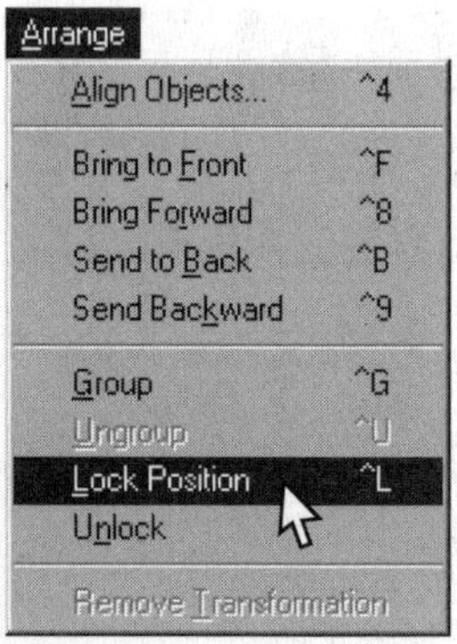

1. Select the elements to be locked.
2. Choose **Lock Position** from the Arrange menu.

The elements are now immovable. If you want to change their position or size, or if you want to delete them, then you must firstly select them, then choose **Unlock** from the Arrange menu.

The light grey handles indicate that these elements are locked.

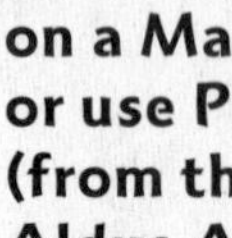

The best way to protect an element if you're using PageMaker 5 or below is to place it on a Master page, or use PS-Group (from the Utilities/ Aldus Additions menu) to attach it to something else.

CHAPTER SEVEN

Importing Text

This chapter shows you how to import text files prepared in another package such as a word-processor. Once it has been brought in, the text behaves exactly as if it was created with PageMaker.

Covers

Placing Text 82

Threaded Text 84

Manipulating Threaded Text Blocks 86

Autoflow 88

Placing Text

This is exactly the same as importing graphics:

1. Choose **Place** from the File menu. The Place dialog box will appear.

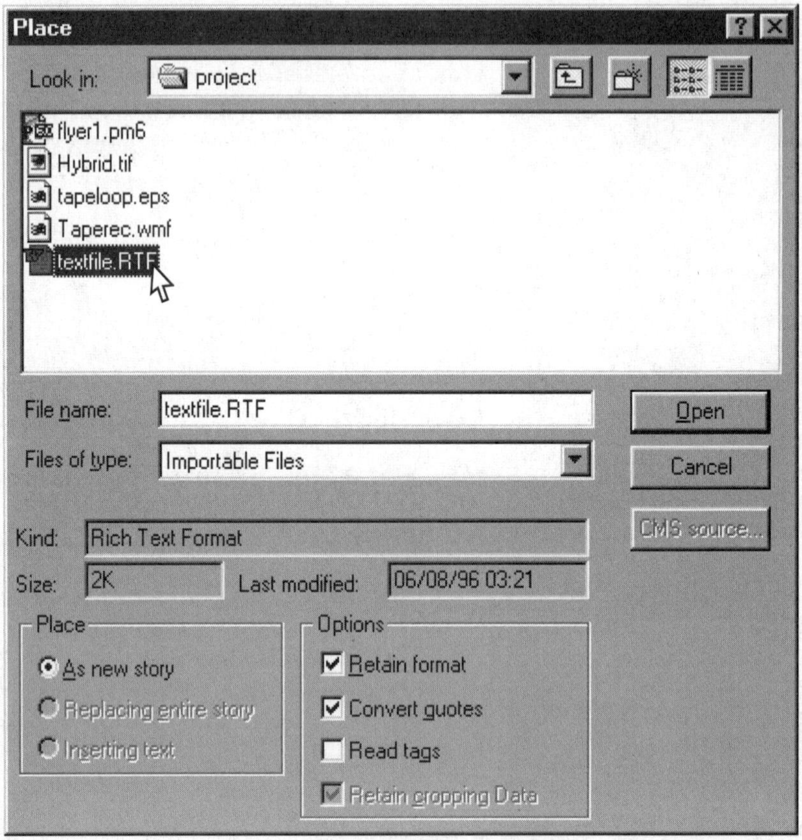

2. Locate the file to be placed by using the directory box or by typing the path in the File name box.

3. Either enter the file name or select the required file from the directory box and click **OK**.

4. PageMaker will return to layout view – your pointer will be a loaded text icon. Click somewhere inside the page margins (or where you wish the top-left corner of the text block to be). The text will flow onto the page.

Text Place symbol (loaded icon)

When importing text, PageMaker only ever works with its own private copy of the original file. This allows you to freely edit the placed text without disturbing the source document.

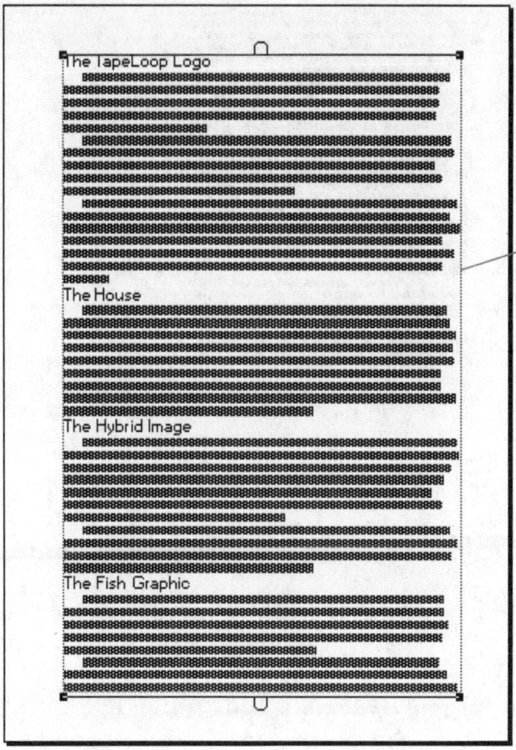

The text will normally flow within the page margins.

HANDY TIP

If you click and drag with the loaded text icon you can pre-draw the text box into which the story will be placed.

Threaded Text

A small red triangle in the lower windowshade handle indicates that there is more text than can be currently displayed in the text box.

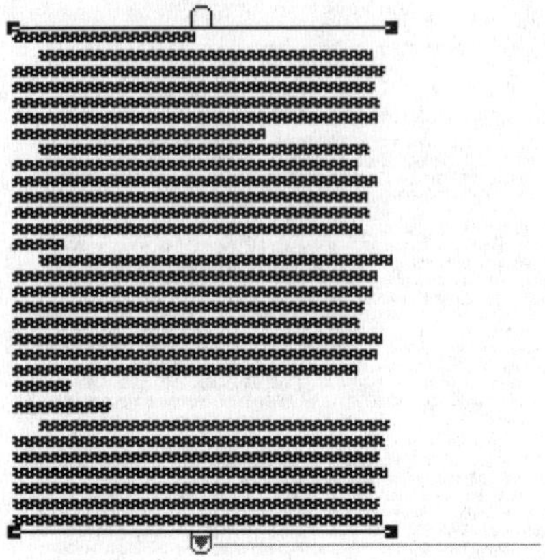

Red triangle indicating more text to be placed

To remedy this you can:

a) Increase the block size by dragging on a handle.

b) Decrease the size of the text using the Control palette or Type menu.

c) Create an additional text box (or boxes) into which the story may be continued.

To Thread Text Into Another Block

1. Click once directly on the red triangle using the pointer tool. The pointer will turn into the loaded text icon once more, giving you the opportunity to place a second text block.

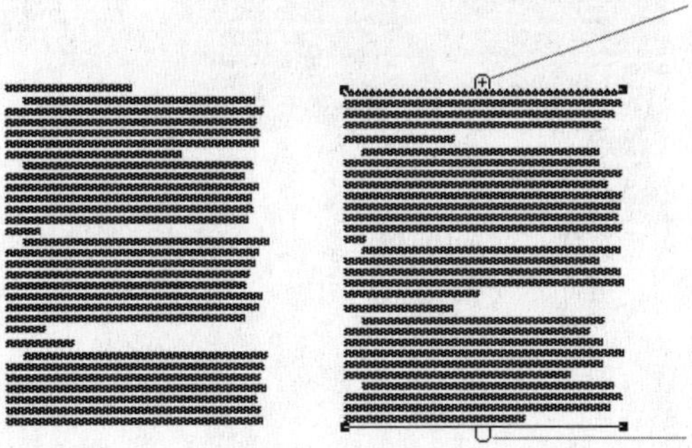

The small + symbol in the top windowshade handle indicates that the story has been continued from a previous block of text
An empty handle indicates the end of the story

2. Click to place the second block. There is still only one story, but it is now threaded through two text blocks.

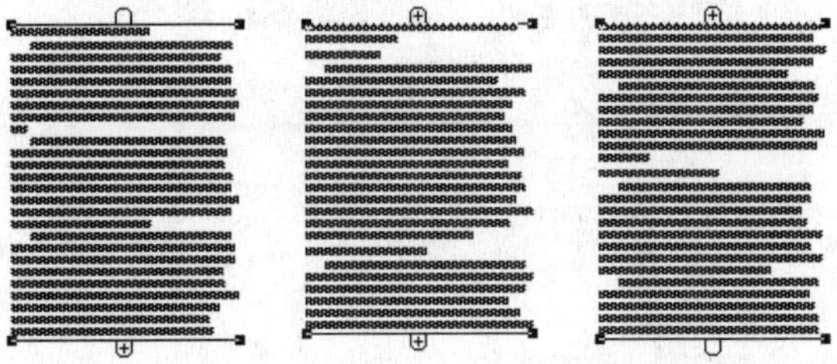

You can use this technique to thread a story through three or more text blocks. The + symbols in the windowshade handles remind you that the blocks are linked.

Selecting with the Text Tool

1. Click anywhere inside a block with the text tool.
2. Choose **Select All** from the Edit menu. The text in all of the threaded blocks will be selected.

Manipulating Threaded Text Blocks

To change the proportion of text held by any of a number of threaded text blocks, drag up or down on the windowshade handles.

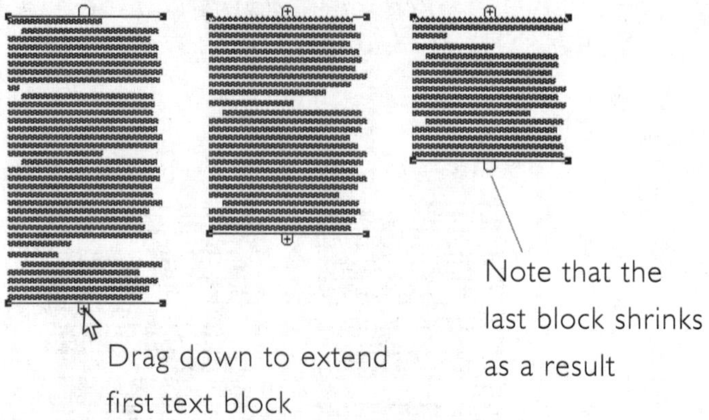

Note that the last block shrinks as a result

As long as these blocks are linked by threaded text, changing one will affect the others.

Closing a Text Block

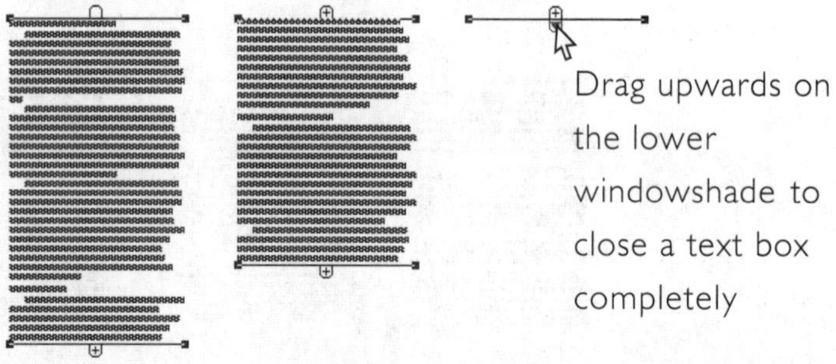

Drag upwards on the lower windowshade to close a text box completely

If you completely close a threaded text block (by dragging on a handle with the pointer tool), the text itself will not be destroyed – instead it will flow into the next block.

If the closed block was the last in the story, the previous block will contain a red triangle in its lower windowshade handle, giving you the chance to re-place the text.

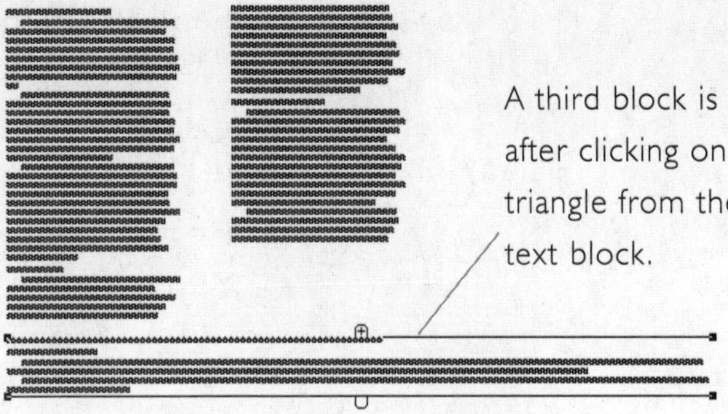

A third block is re-created after clicking on the red triangle from the previous text block.

REMEMBER **Text is often threaded through blocks on consecutive pages.**

You can reflow text at any point:

1. Click on a + sign on one of the existing blocks. The loaded text icon will appear, which gives you the opportunity to place the text from that point onwards in the story (note this will affect later text blocks which currently form part of the story).
2. Click or click-drag to place the remaining text. You can abort this action by clicking on the pointer tool.

HANDY TIP **To "de-thread" a text block, select it with the pointer tool, choose Cut (Edit menu), then Paste. The block will return as an independent text element.**

Summary of Terms

A complete *story* may be imported using the Place command, and may occupy several threaded text blocks.

A text block has *windowshade* handles, which give an indication as to how the text is threaded.

An empty windowshade handle denotes the end of a story.

A red triangle reminds you that there is more text still to be placed.

A plus sign (+) indicates that the story is continued to/from another existing text block.

Autoflow

1 Make sure that the Autoflow option is active (there should be a tick next to its entry on the Layout menu).

2 Go to the File menu, and place a text file in the normal way. This time your loaded text icon will look like this:

3 Locate the position for the first text block and click once. PageMaker will place this block and then automatically generate all the additional text blocks according to the margins and column guides which are present. New pages will be created if required.

Keyboard Shortcuts:

Normal manual textflow (default setting).

Autoflow: hold down the **Control** key.

Semi-automatic flow: hold down **Control** and **Shift** together. With this option you still need to click to position each text block, but it is not necessary to click each red triangle.

CHAPTER EIGHT

Master Pages

Master pages offer you a very effective way of setting up and controlling the overall design of your documents. This chapter shows you how they work, and also how to set up regular or irregular text column guides.

Covers

Master Pages 90
Multiple Master Pages 92
Column Guides 93

Master Pages

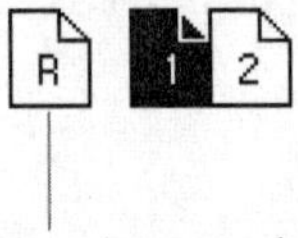

Master page icon

In a single-sided document, the page icon labelled **R** represents the document's Master page. In a double-sided document there are two Master pages labelled **L** and **R** (representing Left and Right pages).

Any elements placed on a Master page will normally appear on all the other pages as a fixed background.

This helps to set up a consistent design for your document.

1. Click on the **R** Master page icon.
2. Add some text or graphic elements to the page.

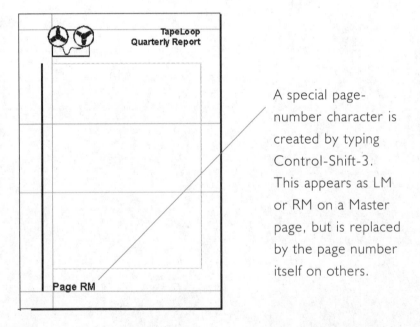

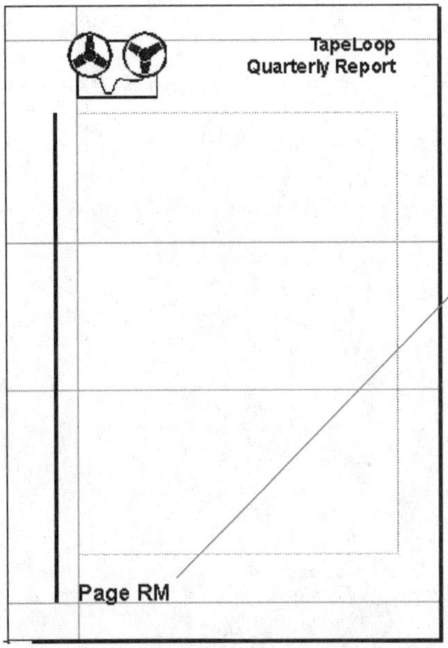

A special page-number character is created by typing Control-Shift-3. This appears as LM or RM on a Master page, but is replaced by the page number itself on others.

Move to the numbered pages in your document. If your document is single-sided, then all pages will use the Master design as their background. If the document is double-sided, then left and right pages will take their design from the **L** and **R** Master pages respectively.

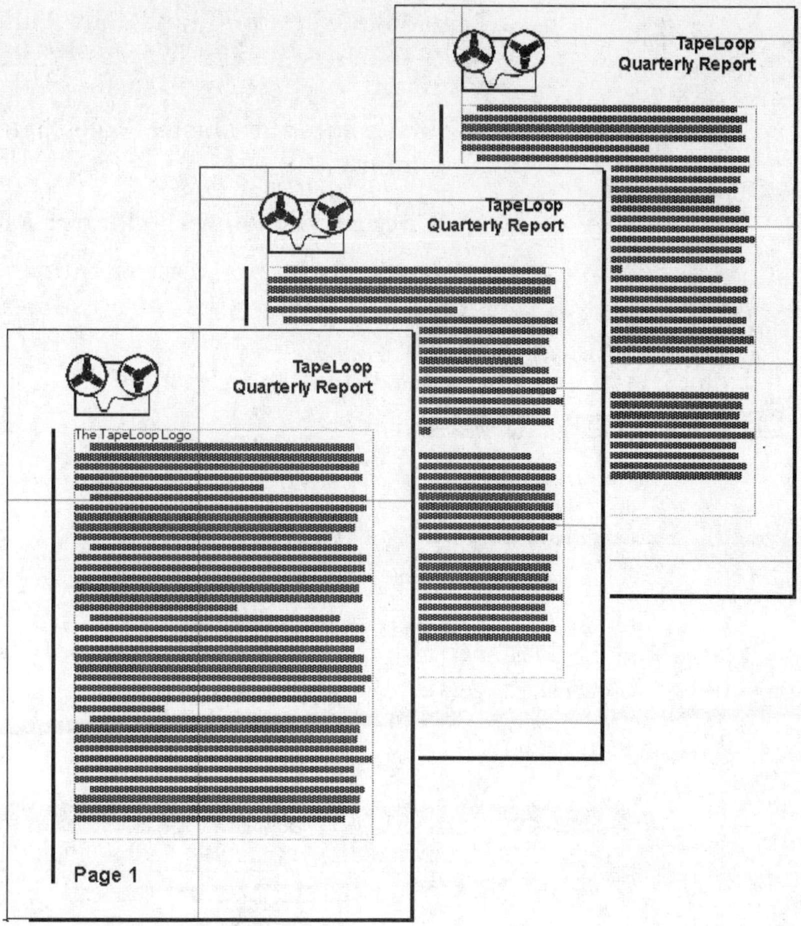

On individual document pages, you can switch off the Master items by clicking on **Display Master Items** in the Layout menu to remove the tick.

Although Master elements are fixed (non-editable) on other pages, you can edit guidelines from a Master page. If you change them, however, you can reset them to their original state with **Copy Master Guides** (also from the Layout menu).

Multiple Master Pages **(PageMaker version 6 or above)**

PageMaker version 6 (and above) allows you to work with more than one design for Master pages.

1. Make sure the Master Pages palette is active (Window menu).

2. Click here to view the Master Page pop-up menu.

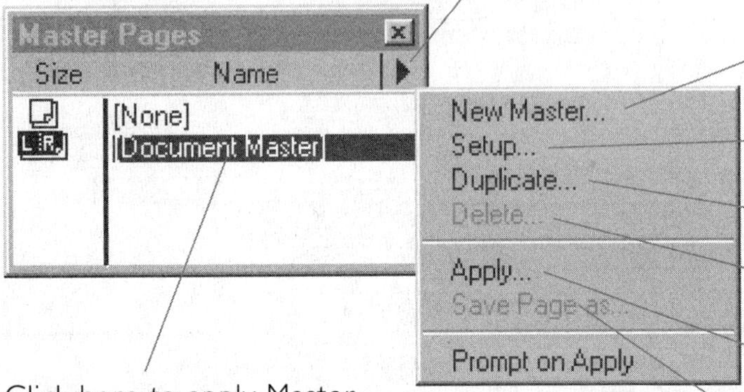

Sets up new Masters from scratch

Changes setup of current Masters

Duplicates current Masters

Deletes Masters

Applies Masters to specified range of pages

Saves a copy of current page(s) as a new Master

Click here to apply Master page design to current page(s).

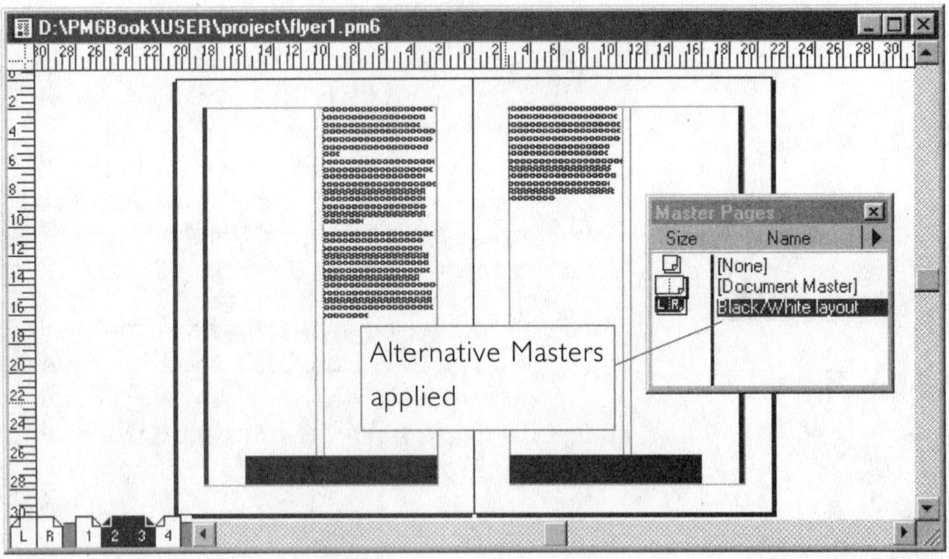

Column Guides

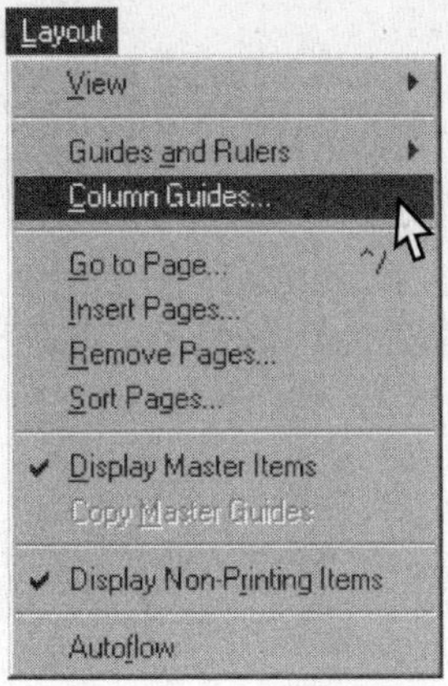

You can instruct PageMaker to automatically format pages with multiple columns of text.

1 Choose **Column Guides...** from the Layout menu. The following dialog box will appear:

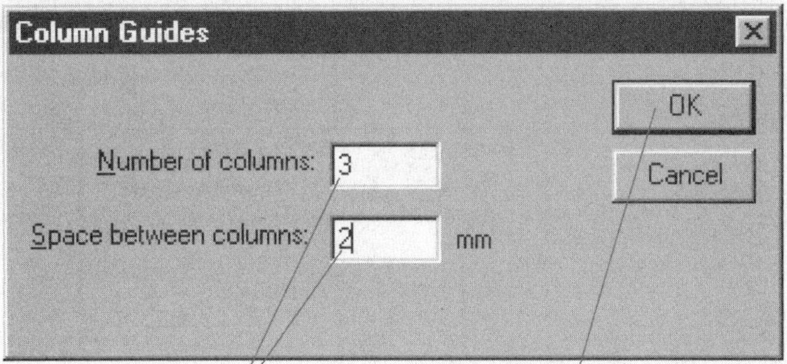

2 Enter the number of columns required and the space between them.

3 Click **OK**.

When you return to the page these dark blue guides will appear. They are magnetic (like other guides). Furthermore, when placing text you will find that it flows into a column rather than completely over the page.

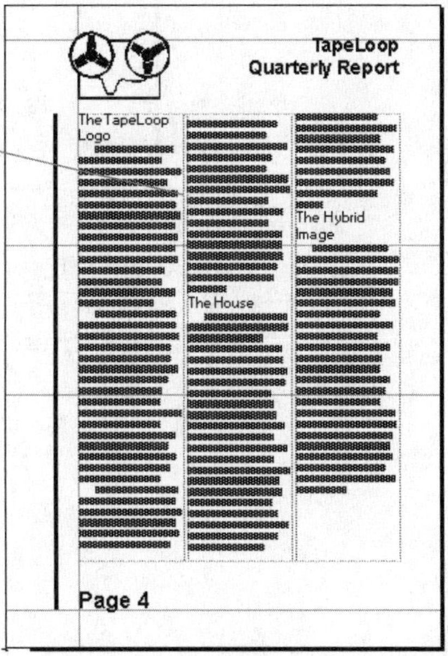

Irregular Columns

1. Create the required number of columns using the previous method. They will initially be of equal width.

2. Manually drag the blue column boundaries left or right using the pointer tool. It may help to have the Control palette active, as you will be able to read off the Y coordinate as you move.

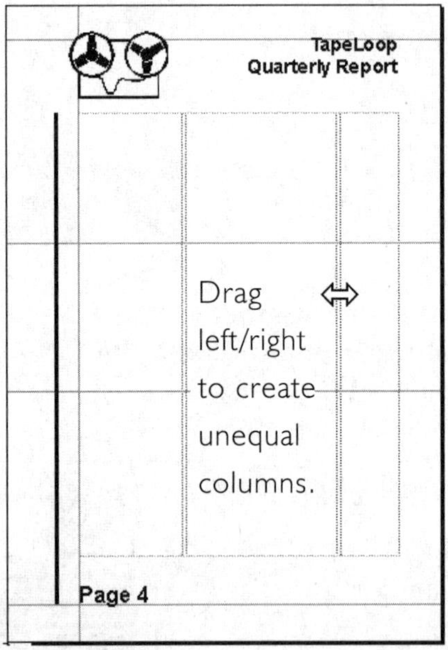

You would normally create the guides and columns on the Master page(s). This lets you set up a consistent layout all the way through the document.

CHAPTER NINE

Working with Large Amounts of Text

This chapter takes you through a range of PageMaker features designed to make working with large amounts of text much easier. In particular we'll look at controls which save you from too much manual resizing and repositioning of text blocks as you try to shuffle headings and main stories into their correct places.

Covers

Type Specifications 96

Paragraph Specifications 97

Widows and Orphans 98

The Keep With Next Command 100

Column and Page Breaks 101

Paragraph Rules 102

Indents/Tabs 104

Hyphenation 107

Inline Graphics 108

Text Wrap 110

The Guide Manager 112

Type Specifications

Virtually all the text effects found in the Control palette are also accessible from the Type menu:

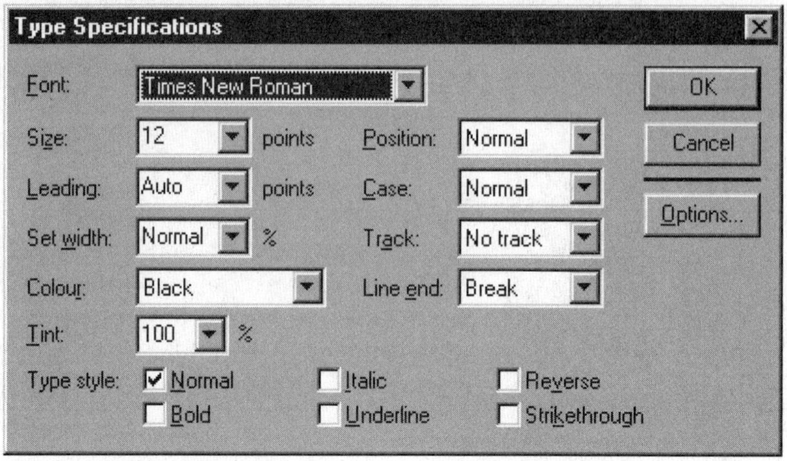

1. Select the text you want to change.
2. Choose **Type Specs** from the Type menu. Virtually all the character-level text attributes are present.
3. The **Options** button allows you to customise the SMALL CAPS size as well as Super/Subscript.

Paragraph Specifications

Paragraph Specifications

Indents:

Left [0] mm
First [0] mm
Right [0] mm

Paragraph space:

Before [0] mm
After [0] mm

OK
Cancel
Rules...
Spacing...

Alignment: [Left ▼] Dictionary: [UK English ▼]

Options:

☐ Keep lines together
☐ Column break before
☐ Page break before
☐ Include in table of contents

☐ Keep with next [0] lines
☐ Widow control [0] lines
☐ Orphan control [0] lines

| Either click an insertion point within the paragraph you want to change, or select multiple paragraphs with the text tool.

2 Choose **Paragraph...** from the Type menu.

3 All the paragraph-level attributes can be accessed from this dialog box, e.g. space above/below, indents, alignment. The other attributes will be discussed later in this chapter.

Dictionary

Your PageMaker installation will include UK dictionaries, but you can also purchase additional dictionary files. These are used for spell-checking and hyphenation purposes. From this dialog box you can specify the dictionary to be used for each paragraph.

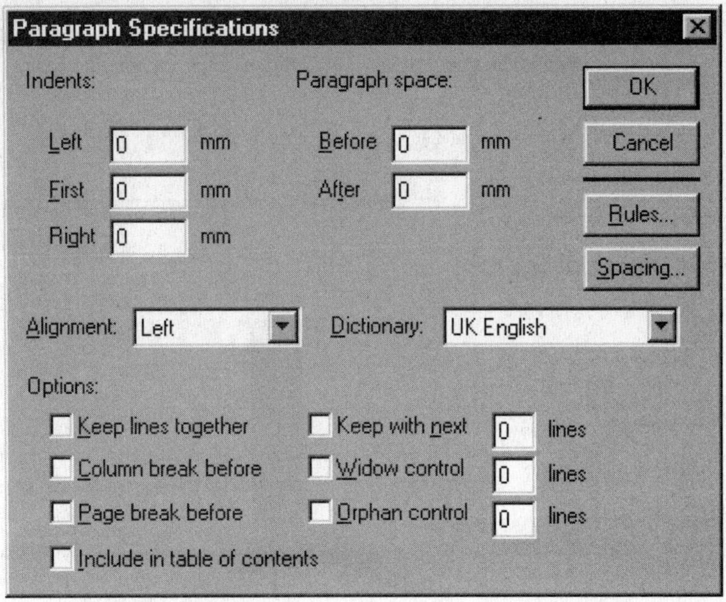

Widows and Orphans

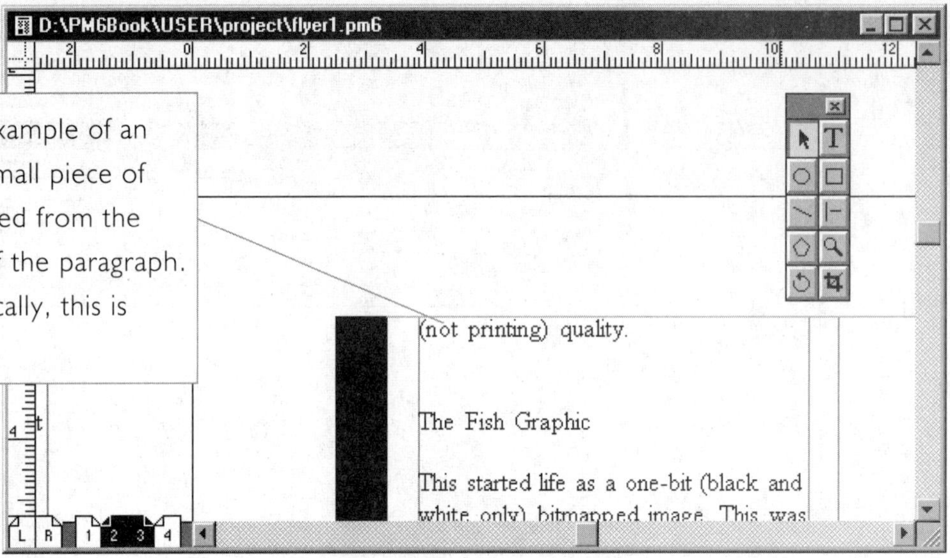

This is an example of an orphan, a small piece of text separated from the main part of the paragraph. Typographically, this is undesirable.

In the example below, we are using the Paragraph Specifications dialog box (select **Paragraph...** from the Type menu) to set orphan size automatically to a minimum of 3 lines:

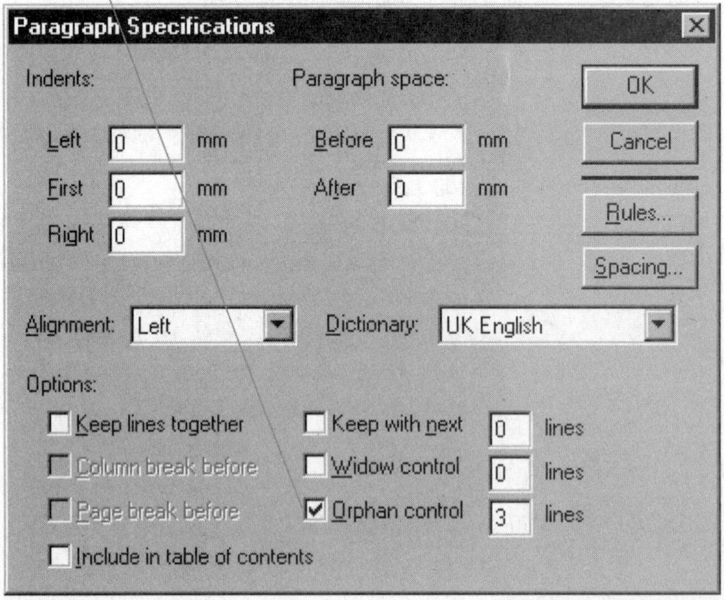

PageMaker will now automatically readjust text blocks so that no orphans of less than 3 lines appear:

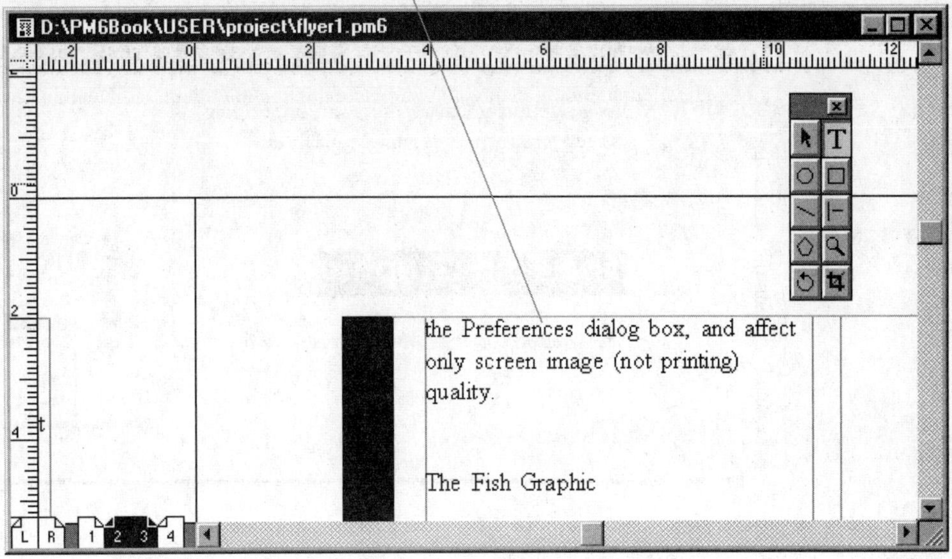
D:\PM6Book\USER\project\flyer1.pm6
the Preferences dialog box, and affect
only screen image (not printing)
quality.
The Fish Graphic

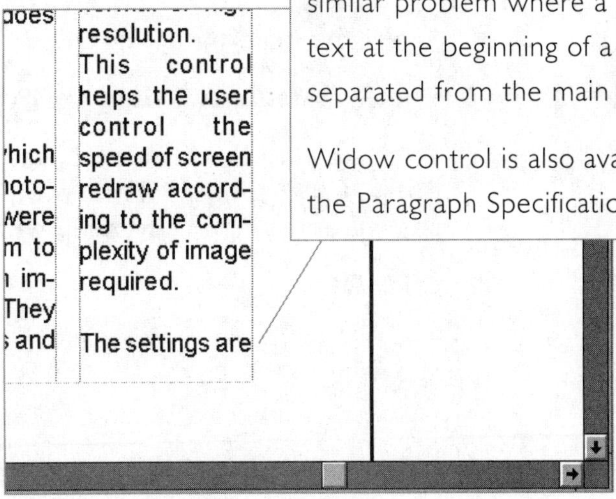
resolution.
This control helps the user control the speed of screen redraw according to the complexity of image required.
The settings are

This is an example of a widow, a similar problem where a small piece of text at the beginning of a paragraph is separated from the main text.

Widow control is also available from the Paragraph Specifications dialog box.

The Keep With Next Command

Sometimes we want to make sure that a paragraph such as a heading is kept with the next few lines, to avoid the following problem:

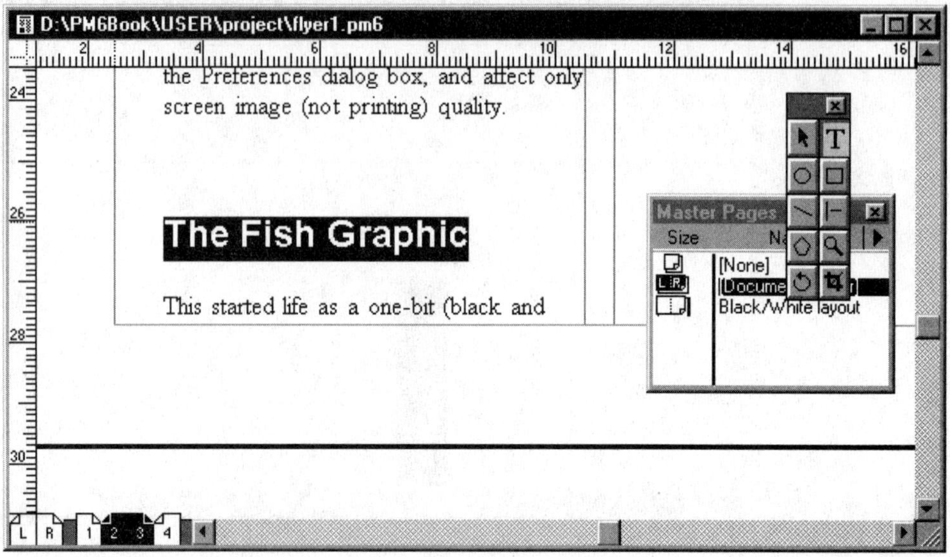
D:\PM6Book\USER\project\flyer1.pm6
the Preferences dialog box, and affect only
screen image (not printing) quality.
The Fish Graphic
This started life as a one-bit (black and
Master Pages
Size
[None]
Black/White layout

The **Keep with next** feature is used to do this, as follows:

1. Select the heading paragraph.
2. Choose **Paragraph...** from the Type menu.
3. To make sure the heading is kept with the next three lines of text (i.e. not broken over two columns or pages), enter “3” in the **Keep with next** box.
4. Click **OK**.

Column and Page Breaks

Sometimes we wish to ensure that there is always a column or page break before certain text paragraphs. In the example below we have set all three headings to include a column break, so each starts at the top of its own block:

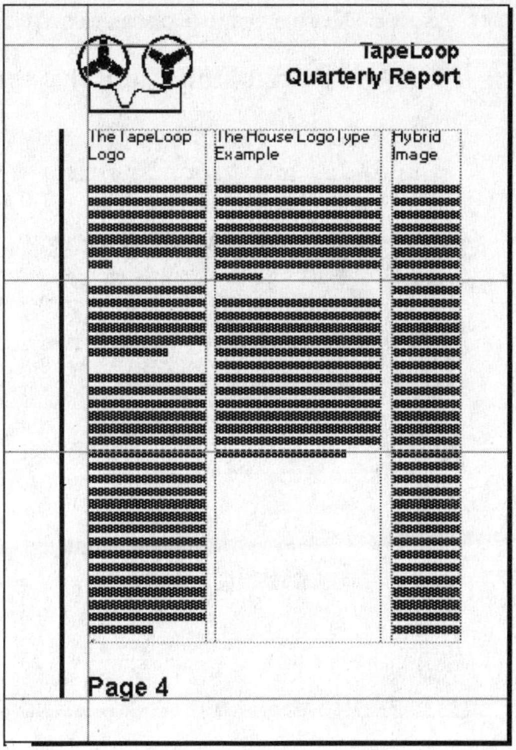

HANDY TIP See Chapter 11, "Style Sheets", for a more automatic way of setting these attributes to multiple headings.

1. Select the heading paragraph.
2. Choose **Paragraph...** from the Type menu.
3. Set **Column break before**.
4. Click **OK**.
5. Repeat for the other headings. From now on, no matter how you move or edit the text, PageMaker will always adjust the blocks so that each heading appears at the top of a column.

Paragraph Rules

Paragraph rules are lines directly above or below a paragraph. Unlike normal horizontal lines, they are attached to the text itself.

Creating

1. Select the required paragraph with the text tool.
2. Choose **Paragraph...** from the Type menu.
3. Click on the **Rules** button. Enter the required details in the dialog box which appears:

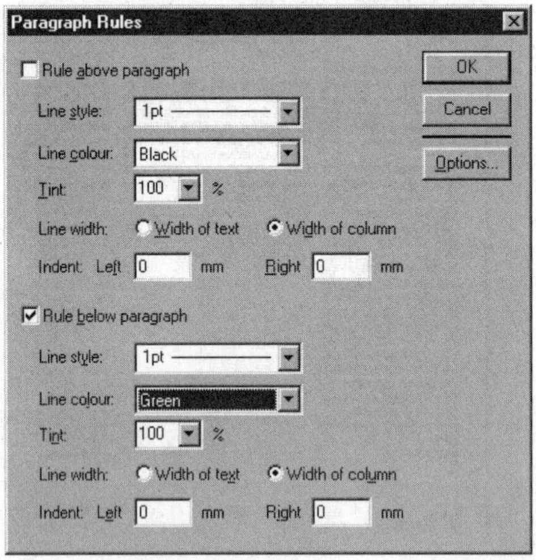

Here we are setting a 1-point green line to appear below the selected paragraph.

Although the measurement system is currently millimetres, you can enter other units into most dialog boxes. Points and picas are specified as in the following example: 3p6 represents 3 picas and 6 points (note 1 pica = 12 points).

4. Clicking on the **Options** button will allow you to specify how far above/below the baseline the rule should appear:

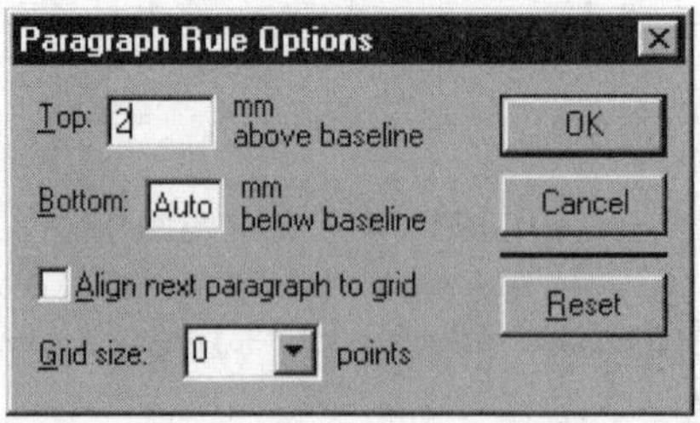

5. Click **OK** in each of the open dialog boxes to set the rules.

In the following example, these paragraph settings have been applied to the three centred headings:

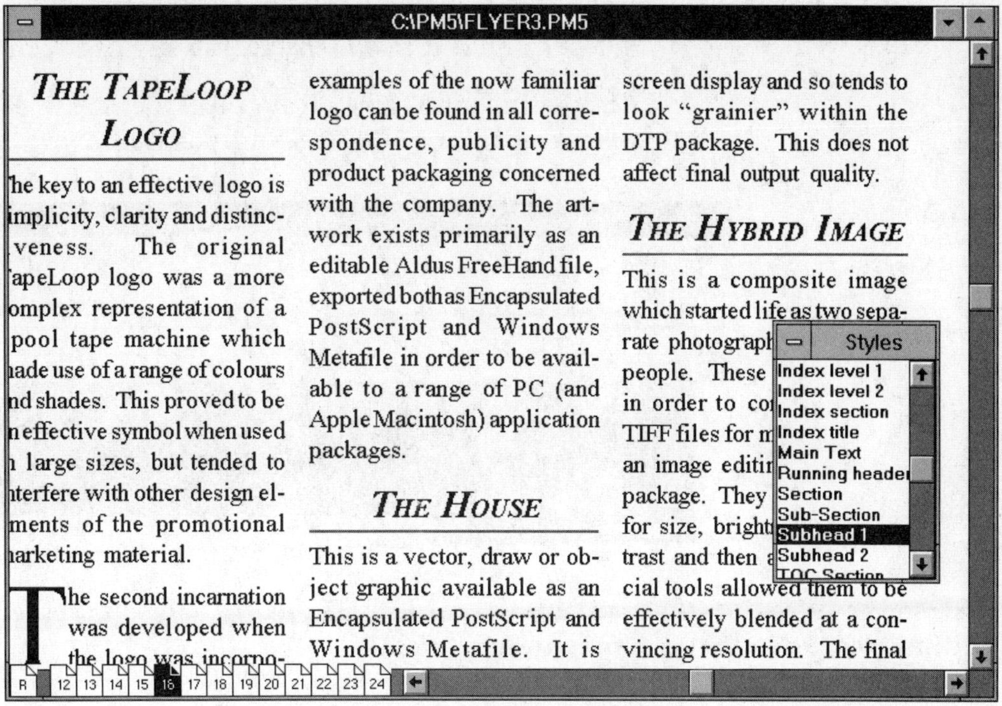
C:\PM5\FLYER3.PM5
THE TAPELOOP LOGO
he key to an effective logo is implicity, clarity and distinc- veness. The original apeLoop logo was a more omplex representation of a pool tape machine which ade use of a range of colours nd shades. This proved to be n effective symbol when used large sizes, but tended to terfere with other design el- ments of the promotional arketing material.
The second incarnation was developed when
examples of the now familiar logo can be found in all corre- spondence, publicity and product packaging concerned with the company. The art- work exists primarily as an editable Aldus FreeHand file, exported both as Encapsulated PostScript and Windows Metafile in order to be avail- able to a range of PC (and Apple Macintosh) application packages.
THE HOUSE
This is a vector, draw or ob- ject graphic available as an Encapsulated PostScript and Windows Metafile. It is
screen display and so tends to look "grainier" within the DTP package. This does not affect final output quality.
THE HYBRID IMAGE
This is a composite image which started life as two sepa- rate photograph people. These in order to co TIFF files for m an image editi package. They for size, bright trast and then cial tools allowed them to be effectively blended at a con- vincing resolution. The final
Styles
Index level 1
Index level 2
Index section
Index title
Main Text
Running heade
Section
Sub-Section
Subhead 1
Subhead 2
R 12 13 14 15 16 17 18 19 20 21 22 23 24

If this text is moved or edited, the paragraph rules will move too, so that they are always in the correct position.

Usually, paragraph rules are used as part of a style definition. See Chapter 11, "Style Sheets", for more information.

Indents/Tabs

When entering text, the **Tab** key will move the insertion point to the next specified horizontal tab position. It is useful to be able to specify your own tabulation:

1. Select some text in which the **Tab** key has been used.
2. Choose **Indents/Tabs...** from the Type menu. The following ruler will appear in position above the text:

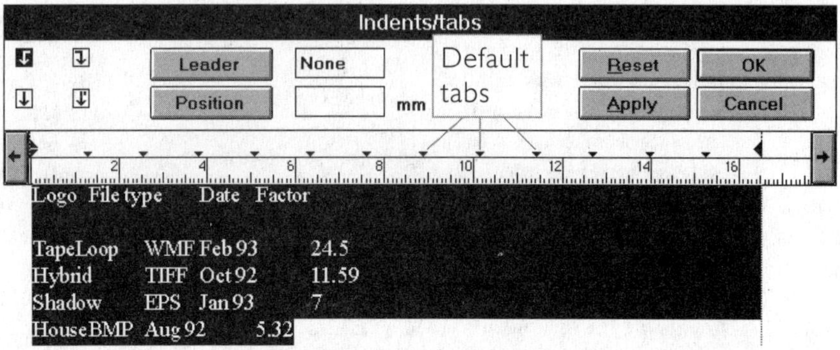

In the above example, the **Tab** key had been pressed once in between each item.

3. Click once above the ruler to create your own tab marker. You can then select the type of tab from the four tab icons.

Tab icons (clockwise from top): left-aligned, right-aligned, decimal and centred.

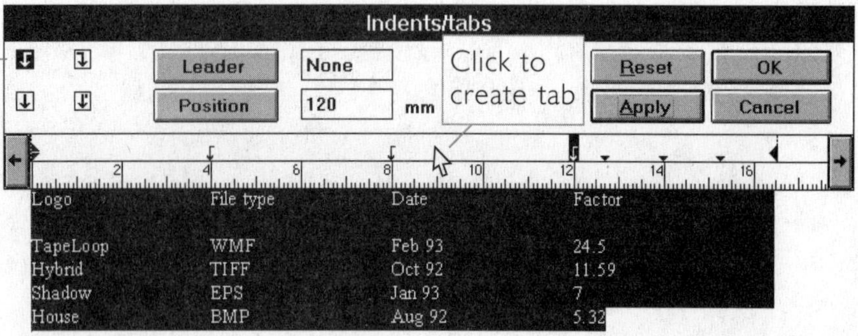

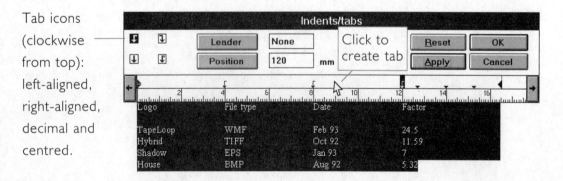

4. To see changes in the text without quitting the dialog box, click the **Apply** button.

In the previous example we created three left-aligned tabs at 4 cm intervals. To move a tab, simply drag its icon left or right. To delete a tab drag it back down into the ruler (it will disappear).

Setting Leaders

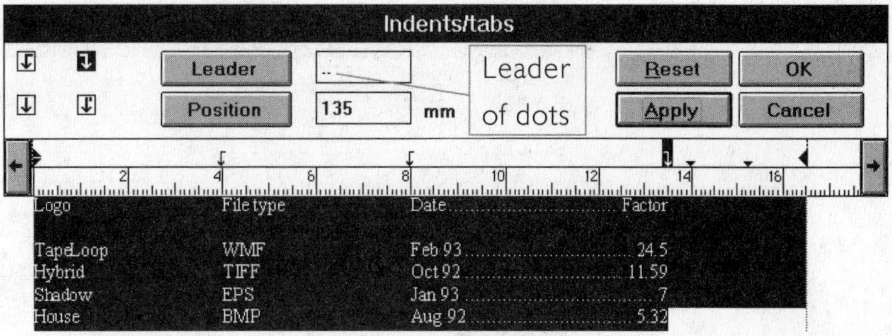

1. Select a tab by clicking directly on it.
2. Choose a suitable symbol from the **Leader** pop-up menu.
3. Click **Apply**.

In the above example, we have set a leader of dots which fill the space leading up to the third tab position.

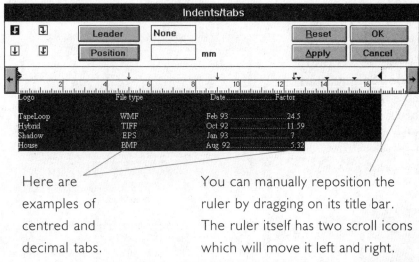

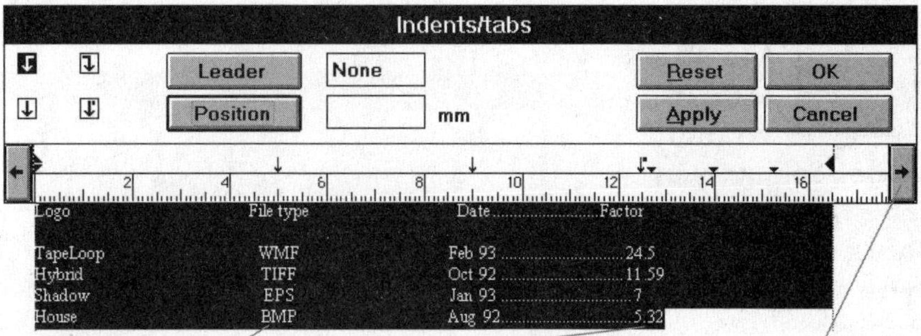

Here are examples of centred and decimal tabs.

You can manually reposition the ruler by dragging on its title bar. The ruler itself has two scroll icons which will move it left and right.

Setting Indents

The larger triangles at the sides of the ruler represent the left and right indents. (The left indent is split into first and subsequent paragraph lines.) Although these are normally controlled numerically in the Paragraph Specifications dialog box, you can move them here manually by dragging.

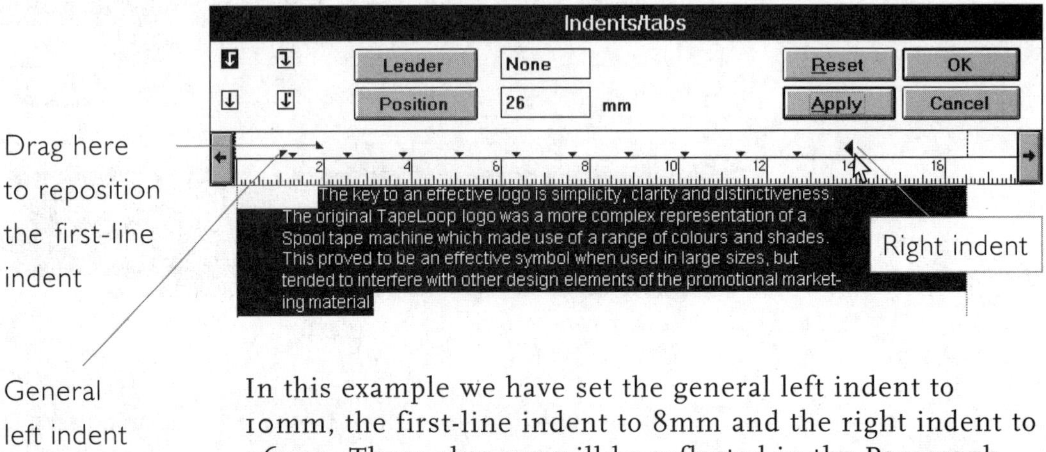
Indents/tabs
Leader
None
Reset
OK
Position
26
mm
Apply
Cancel
The key to an effective logo is simplicity, clarity and distinctiveness.
The original TapeLoop logo was a more complex representation of a
Spool tape machine which made use of a range of colours and shades.
This proved to be an effective symbol when used in large sizes, but
tended to interfere with other design elements of the promotional market-
ing material.
Drag here to reposition the first-line indent
Right indent
General left indent

In this example we have set the general left indent to 10mm, the first-line indent to 8mm and the right indent to 26mm. These changes will be reflected in the Paragraph Specifications dialog box.

By entering measurements in the box provided, and using the pop-up menu marked **Position**, you can add, delete and move tabs numerically rather than manually.

HANDY TIP

To move the left-indent triangle independently of the first-line indent, hold down Shift as you drag with the mouse.

Hyphenation

Manual hyphenation involves the user typing a special code (Control+hyphen) when entering text. This sets a possible hyphen position within a word.

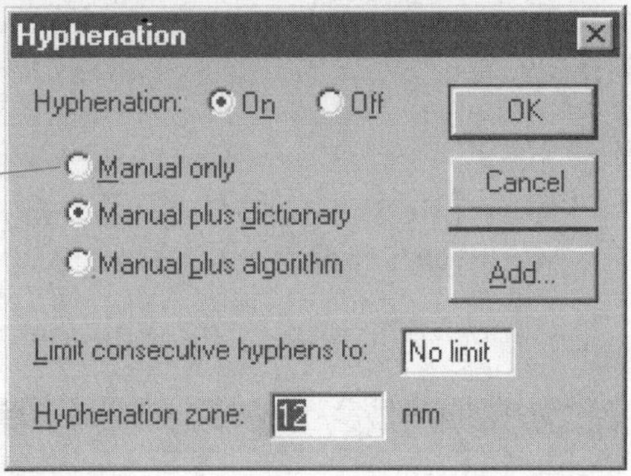

1. Select the text you wish to change with the text tool.
2. Choose **Hyphenation...** from the Type menu.

As well as switching hyphenation on and off, you can control the degree of hyphenation:

Limit consecutive hyphens to: will allow you to set a limit to the number of consecutive lines which can end with hyphens.

Hyphenation zone: is the width of text at the end of a line which PageMaker will consider for hyphenation.

PageMaker uses a hyphenation dictionary which contains markers within words at places where it is allowable to create a break.

Adding to the Dictionary

1. Select the word.

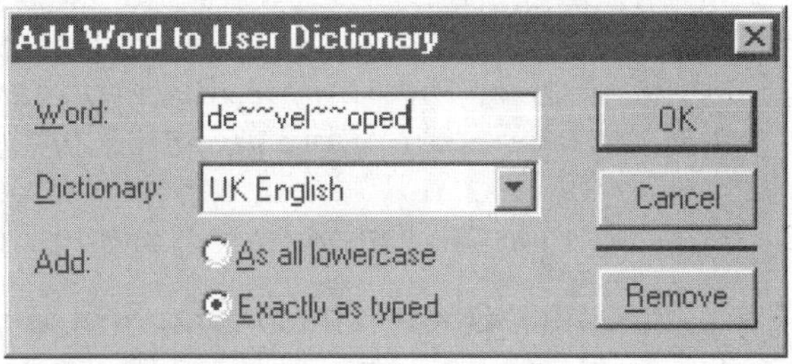

2. Choose **Hyphenation** from the Type menu and click **Add**.

3. Type the word using the tilde (~) to indicate possible hyphens. One tilde represents the most preferential break, two is less preferential and so on.

REMEMBER

If a word is not present in PageMaker's hyphenation dictionary, it will use an intelligent algorithm to "guess" suitable positions for hyphens.

Inline Graphics

These are graphic elements which (like paragraph rules) are treated as part of a text block.

Placing

1. With the text tool, place an insertion point where you want the graphic to appear.
2. Choose **Place** from the File menu.

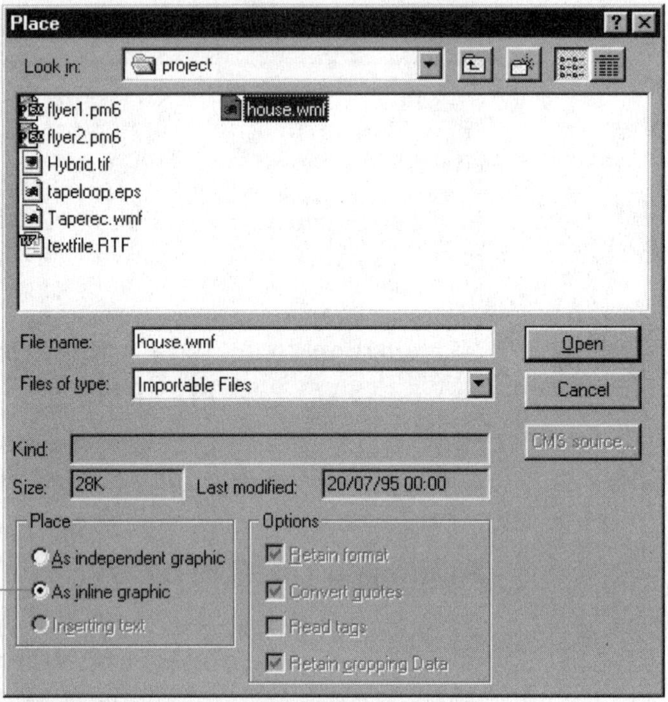

Note the option to place as an inline graphic

3. Choose the graphic file, making sure the option to place as an inline graphic is active. If it is greyed out there is no insertion point active in your document, so you will need to repeat steps 1 and 2.
4. Click **Open**. The graphic will appear as part of the text. It can still be resized with the pointer tool, but to all other intents and purposes it is treated as a large text character. This is very useful if you want an illustration to be kept with a certain piece of text even after radical editing at later stages.

Inline Graphic Example

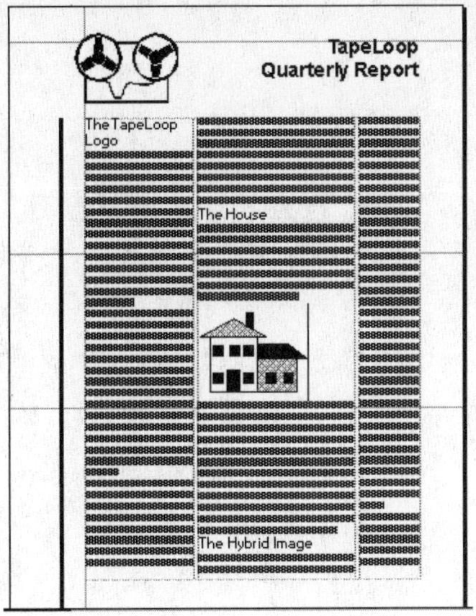

Note the example on the left. A paragraph at the top of the first column was deleted to produce the example on the right. Note how the inline graphic moves with the text...

Note that text effects such as centre alignment are also available for inline graphics.

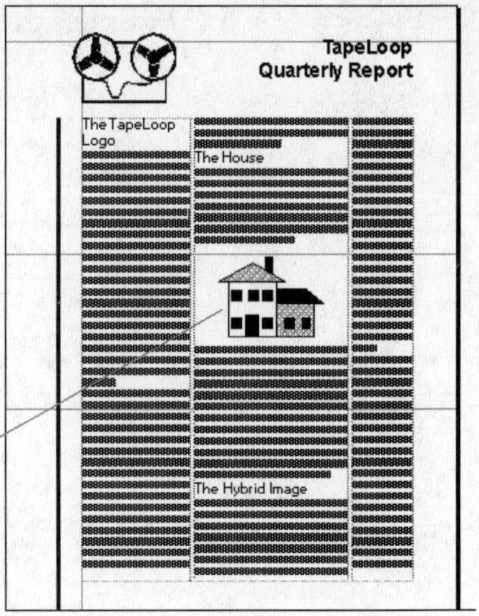

Changing an Inline Graphic to a Normal Graphic

1. Select the element with the pointer tool.
2. From the Edit menu, choose **Cut**, then **Paste**.

The graphic will return as a normal element, free from the text block.

Changing a Normal Graphic to an Inline Graphic

1. Select the element with the pointer tool.
2. Choose **Cut** from the Edit menu.
3. Select the text tool and create an insertion point at the desired location within a text block.
4. Choose **Paste**.

The graphic will appear as part of the text block.

Text Wrap

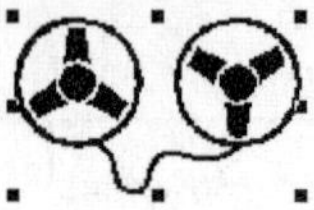

This graphic has no wrap selected.

This is used to prevent graphics and text from overlapping each other. It is applied to a graphic element to create a text-exclusion boundary.

Regular Wrap

1 Select the graphic.

2 Choose **Text Wrap...** from the Element menu. The following dialog box will appear:

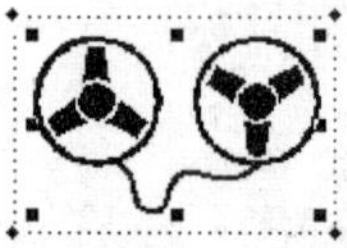

This graphic has a text-wrap boundary (represented by the dotted line).

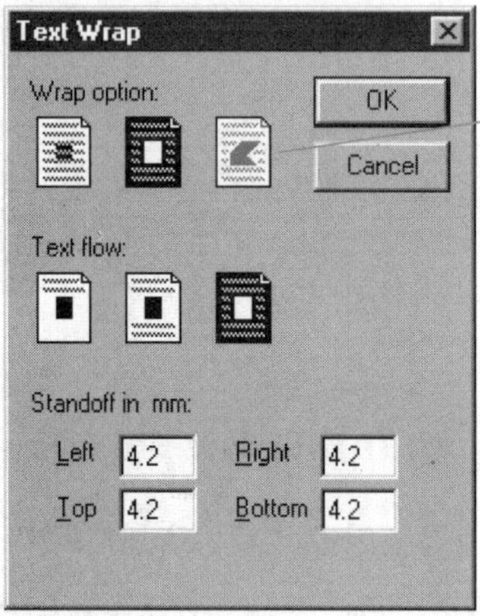

The three wrap options (from left to right) are:

- No wrap (normal)
- Regular wrap
- Irregular wrap

You can also choose whether you want text to flow above, above and below, or all around the graphic element.

3 Currently, **No wrap** is selected. Click on the second option, which allows text to wrap around a regular (rectangular) object.

4 Select the type of text flow required, usually the third option (text flowing all around the graphic).

5 Enter the standoff distance for each side. Click **OK**.

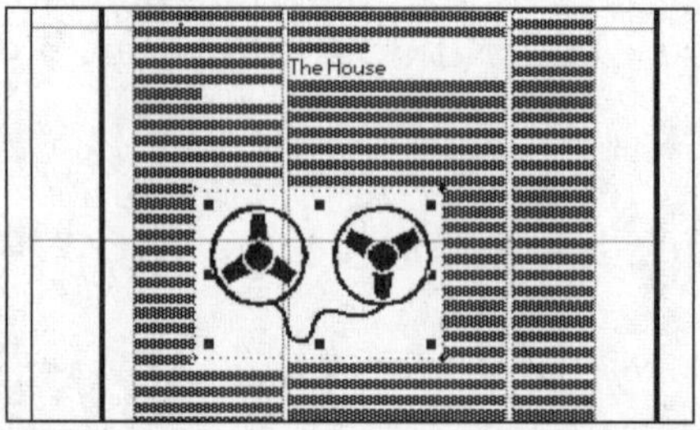

If you now move the graphic over some text, the text will reflow around it at the specified distance.

Irregular Wrap

You can create an irregular text wrap by manually editing the exclusion zone around a regularly wrapped graphic.

1. As before, create a regular wrap around the graphic.
2. Zoom in so that you can see the dotted line clearly. The line joins small diamond-shaped handles, which can be manually dragged about with the pointer tool.

To create a new "handle", click on a vacant part of the dotted line.

To edit the boundary into an irregular shape, drag one of the handles.

To delete a handle, simply drag it into its neighbour.

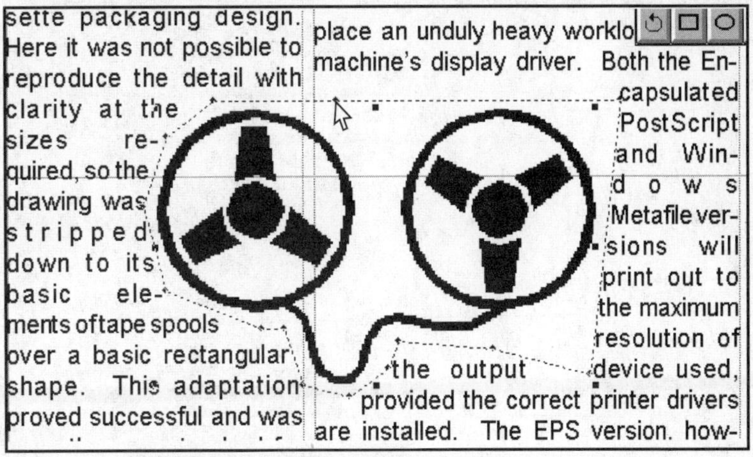

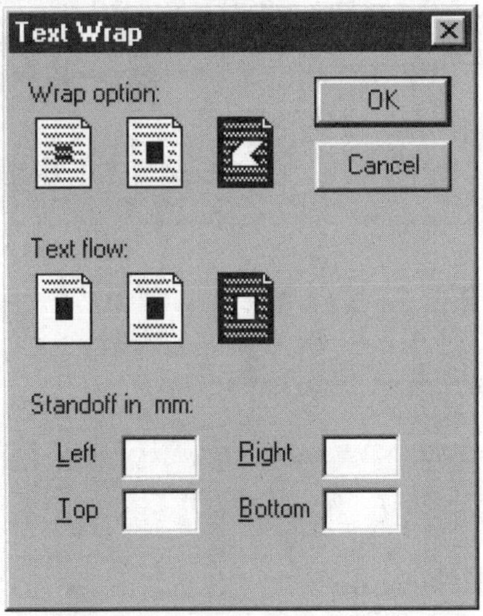

If you now return to the Text Wrap dialog box, you will see that the irregular wrap option (previously greyed out), is now active.

HANDY TIP

If screen redraw is slow during editing of the boundary, hold down the spacebar. The text will not reflow until you release.

The Guide Manager (PageMaker version 6 or above)

The Guide Manager is one of the most useful Plug-ins to ship with PageMaker version 6 (and above). It helps you to set up and easily access regular systems of guidelines from any document.

1 Choose **Guide Manager** from the Utilities menu, PageMaker Plug-ins submenu...

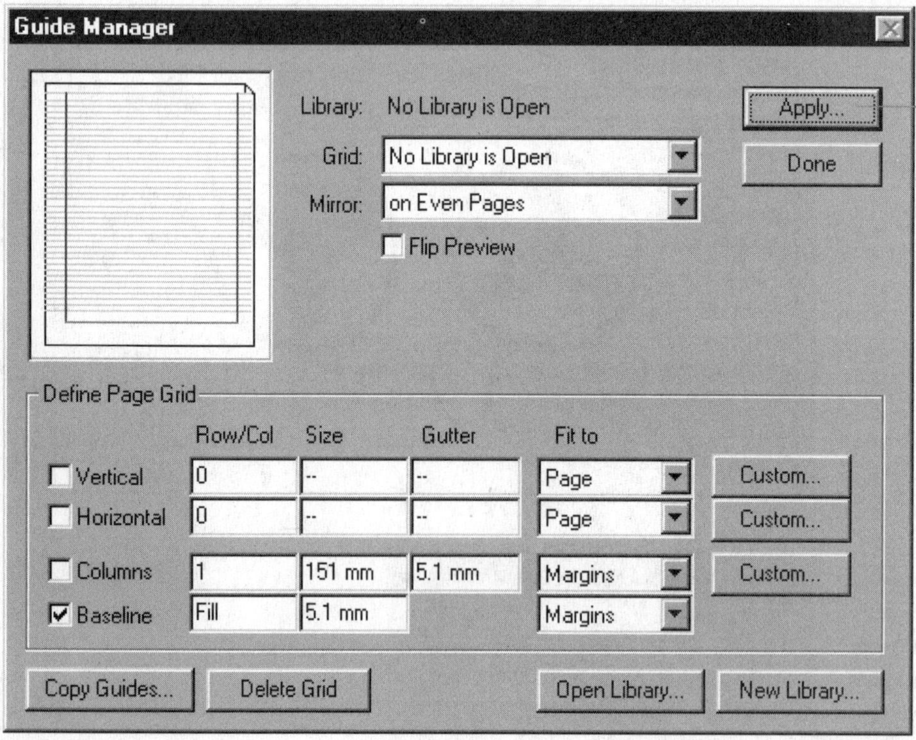

Click Apply to use the current guide system of any of your document's pages.

2 Click on **New Library** to start a new library of guidelines, or **Open Library** to access a library which has already been saved.

3 Select **New Grid** from the Grid pop-up.

4 Enter the appropriate settings for **Define Page Grid.**

5 Click **Done**.

CHAPTER TEN

The Story Editor

The Story Editor offers you a different view of the text contained in your document. It provides a quick way of editing and navigating around large stories, as well as word-processing features such as a Spelling Checker and Search/Replace facilities.

Covers

Using the Story Editor **114**

The Spelling Checker **115**

Find and Change **116**

Story and Layout Views **118**

Using the Story Editor

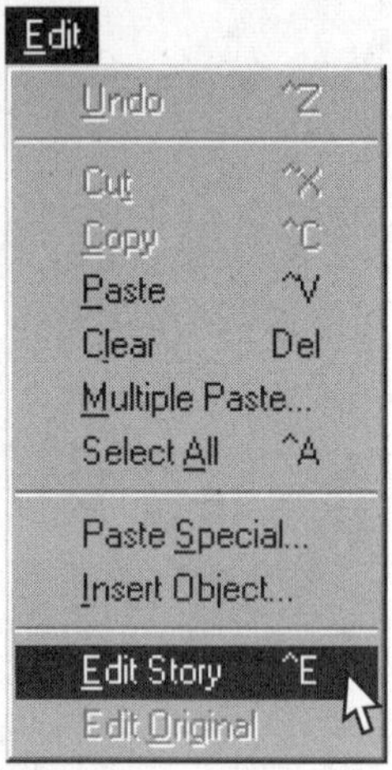

The Story Editor provides you with a simplified view of text, with an entire story in one window (even if it is split into many text blocks in normal layout view).

Starting Up

1. Select the text to be edited.
2. Choose **Edit Story** from the Edit menu.

For convenience and fast editing purposes, the story is displayed in one font and one size. The subtler text effects are not shown.

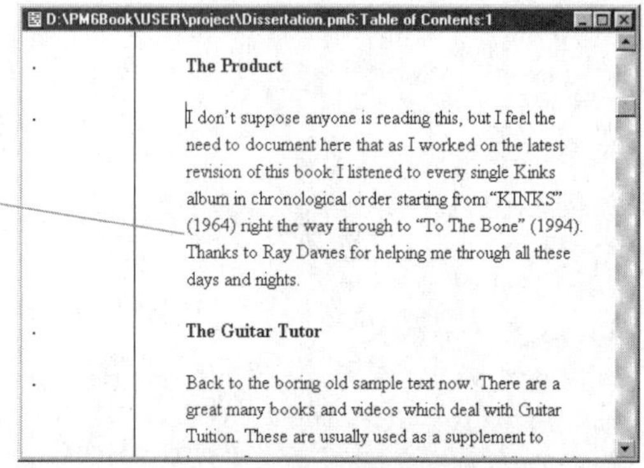

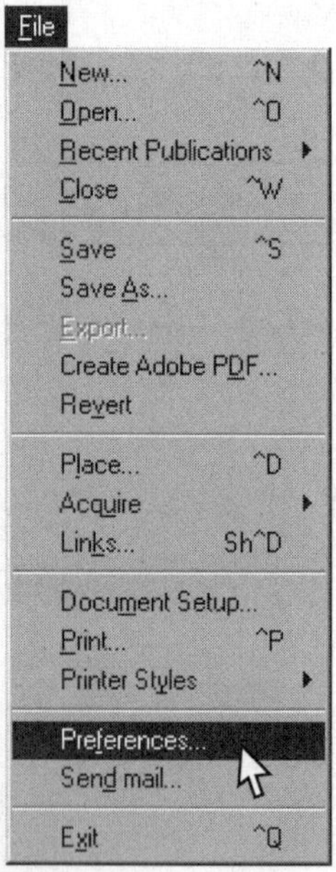

If you choose Preferences from the File menu, and click on the More button, you will be able to change the Story Editor font and point size.

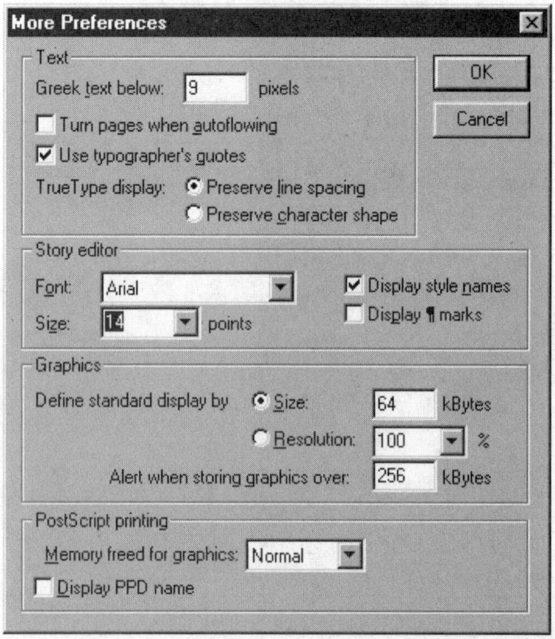

HANDY TIP

You can also call up the Preferences dialog by double-clicking directly on the pointer tool.

The Spelling Checker

PageMaker allows you to take some of the pain out of proof-reading your text by providing a Spelling Checker which will query any word it finds that does not match an entry in its extensive dictionary. To use this feature, open the Story Editor as described opposite, then do the following:

1 Choose **Spelling...** from the Utilities menu. The following dialog box will appear:

REMEMBER **The dictionary PageMaker uses will depend on the setting made in the Paragraph Specifications dialog box (select Paragraph... from the Type menu).**

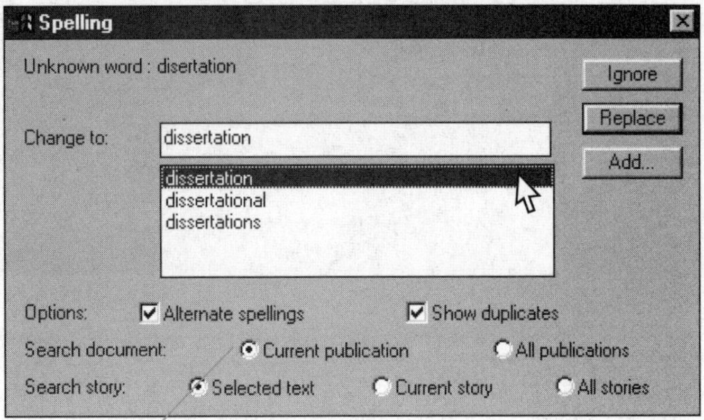

2 Choose whether you want to check the entire document, the current story, or just a sample of text which you have selected.

HANDY TIP **Another way to call up the Story Editor is to triple-click on a text block with the pointer tool.**

3 Click the **Start** button.

PageMaker will warn you of any words it cannot locate in its dictionary. If the word is indeed incorrect then you have the choice to re-enter it or choose from a selection of closest matches in the dictionary. If the word is correct (e.g. a proper noun) then you can instruct PageMaker either to ignore this occurrence or to add it to the user section of the dictionary.

The Spelling Checker will also warn you about duplicate words (a common typing mistake), and possible capitalisation errors.

4 When the spell check is complete, close the Spelling window to return to the main part of the Story Editor.

Find and Change

These are both options in the Utilities menu. You can search a story for specific text or attributes, and automatically replace any instances with different words or effects. From the Story Editor, do the following:

1. Choose **Change...** from the Utilities menu.

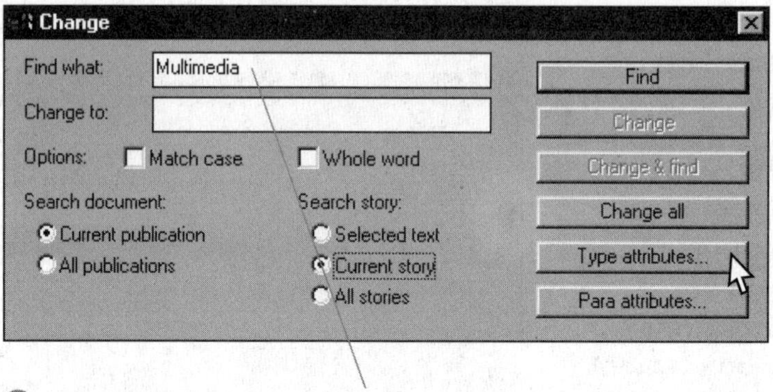

2. You can now enter the search text, and text which will replace this. You can also search/replace on the basis of attributes by clicking one of the Attributes buttons. In this example we shall look for all instances of the word "Multimedia", changing them to Bold.

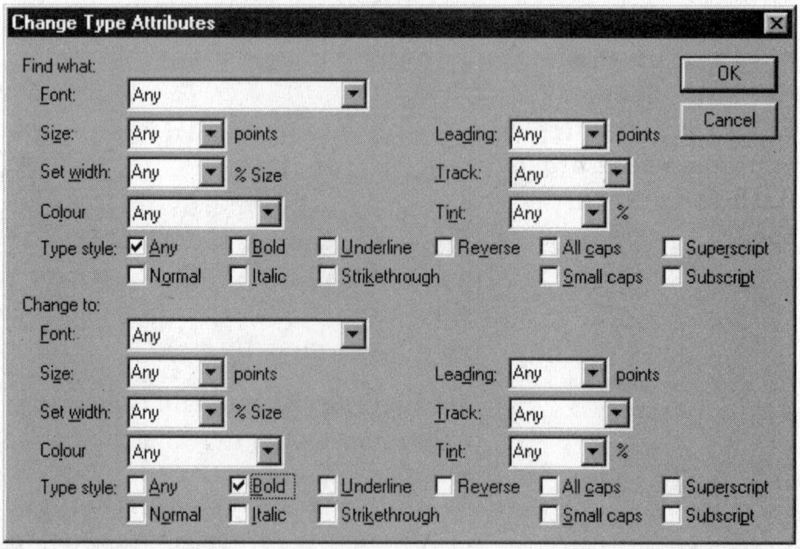

3. You can manually step through the search (using the **Find next** and **Change** buttons) or click on **Change all** to instruct PageMaker to carry out the task automatically.

4. When finished, close the Change window to return to the main Story view. The result can be seen below:

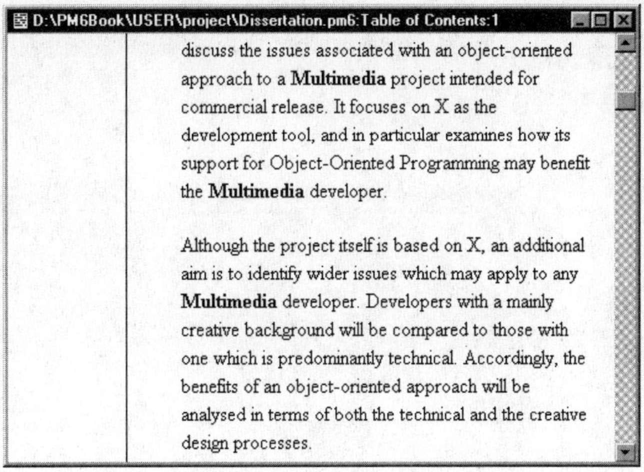
D:\PM6Book\USER\project\Dissertation.pm6:Table of Contents:1

discuss the issues associated with an object-oriented approach to a **Multimedia** project intended for commercial release. It focuses on X as the development tool, and in particular examines how its support for Object-Oriented Programming may benefit the **Multimedia** developer.

Although the project itself is based on X, an additional aim is to identify wider issues which may apply to any **Multimedia** developer. Developers with a mainly creative background will be compared to those with one which is predominantly technical. Accordingly, the benefits of an object-oriented approach will be analysed in terms of both the technical and the creative design processes.

The **Find** function works in exactly the same way (but without the facility to replace text). It is also possible to search/replace using the following metacharacters:

Wildcard character	^?	Registermark symbol	^r
Carriage return	^p	Caret	^^
Line break	^n	White space	^w
Tab	^t	Thin space	^<
Discretionary (soft) hyphen	^-	Non-breaking space	^s
Non-breaking hyphen	^~	En space	^>
Computer-inserted hyphen	^c	Em space	^m
In-line graphic marker	^g	En dash	^=
Index marker	^;	Em dash	^_
Page # marker	^3	Non-breaking slash	^/
Bullet	^8	Single open quote	^[
Copyright symbol	^2	Single close quote	^]
Section marker	^6	Double open quote	^{
Paragraph marker	^7	Double close quote	^}

(The ^ symbol means you should press Shift + 6.)

Story and Layout Views

REMEMBER **Invoking the Story Editor with no text selected will open up a new story. You will be asked to place this on leaving the Story Editor.**

You can return to Layout view (pages and Pasteboard) from the Edit menu, or by closing down the Story window.

In PageMaker you can operate many story windows which can be arranged, minimised, maximised or resized in the normal way.

In the example below we have several documents open simultaneously: their layout windows have been minimised so that we can easily choose which document or story to select.

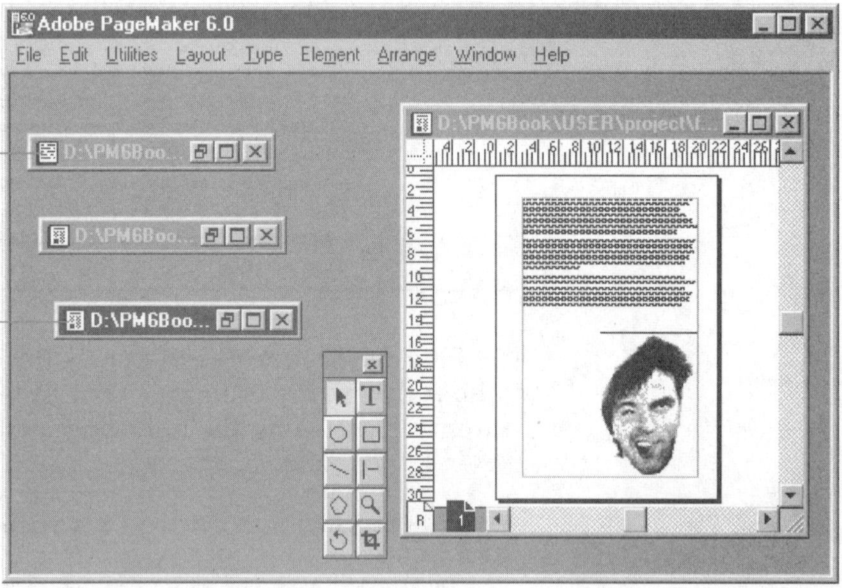

REMEMBER **In the Story Editor you still have access to the Type menu, and with it the full range of PageMaker text effects. Remember however that you will not see many of the changes until you return to Layout view.**

Display Invisible Characters

1. From Story view open the Story menu.

Note the option to display normally invisible characters in the Story Editor. It is often useful to be able to distinguish visually between spaces, tabs and return characters. (You can also set this from **File/Preferences.../More...**)

CHAPTER ELEVEN

Style Sheets

Although many people find it possible to avoid the use of styles altogether, they provide an extremely effective way of controlling the design and formatting of headings and main text. As well as allowing you to make drastic changes to a document at any stage in the design process, styles can help you to ensure that the overall look and feel of your publications remain consistent.

Covers

Paragraph Styles 120

Using Styles 121

Changing a Style 122

Style by Example 123

Styles in the Story Editor 124

Copying Styles From Another Document 124

Paragraph Styles

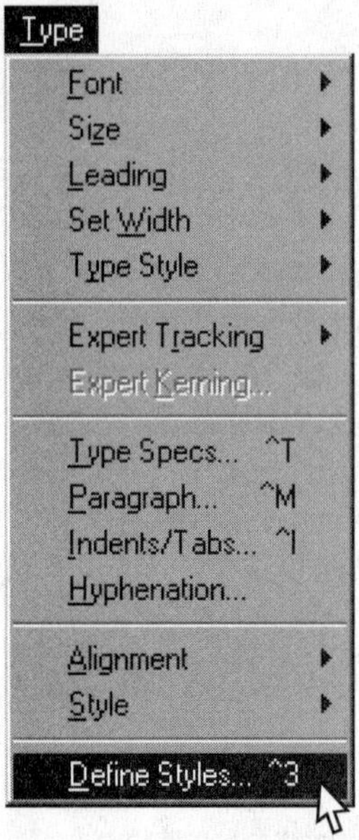

Styles allow you to save a complete set of text attributes under a single name, which you can then use quickly and easily throughout your documents.

Defining a Style

1 Choose **Define Styles...** from the Type menu. The following dialog box will appear:

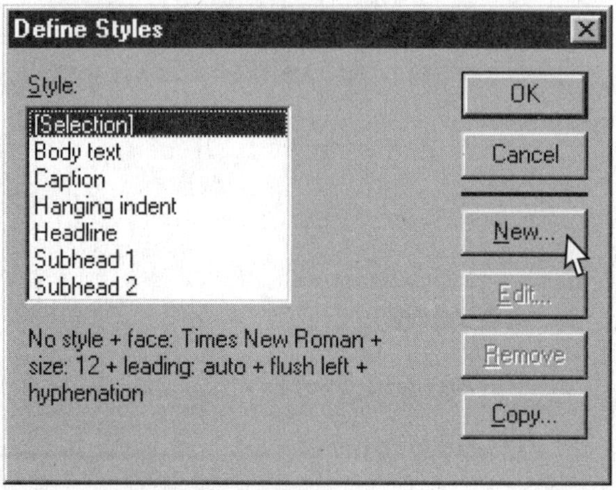

2 Click on **New...** to create a new style.

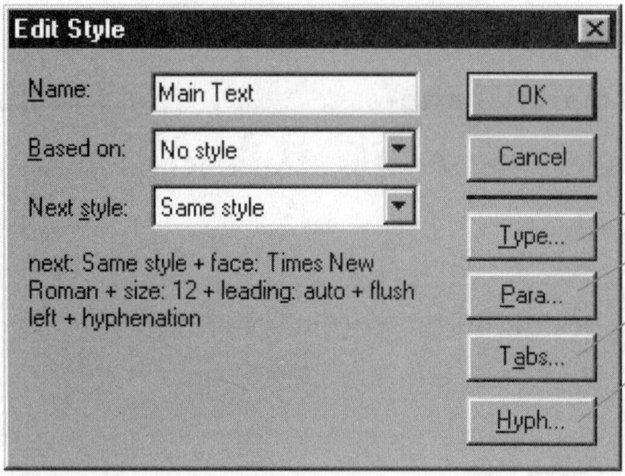

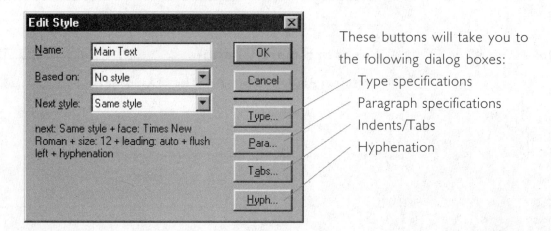

These buttons will take you to the following dialog boxes:

Type specifications
Paragraph specifications
Indents/Tabs
Hyphenation

3 Enter a name for the style, then use the **Type...**, **Para...**, **Tabs...** and **Hyph...** buttons to set the text attributes.

4 Click **OK** when you have finished.

Using Styles

1. Make sure the Styles palette is active (Window menu).
2. With the text tool, select or click inside the paragraph you want to change.
3. Click on the appropriate style in the palette. The style, along with all its attributes, will be applied to the text. In this example, the style Subhead1 has been applied to all subheadings on the page:

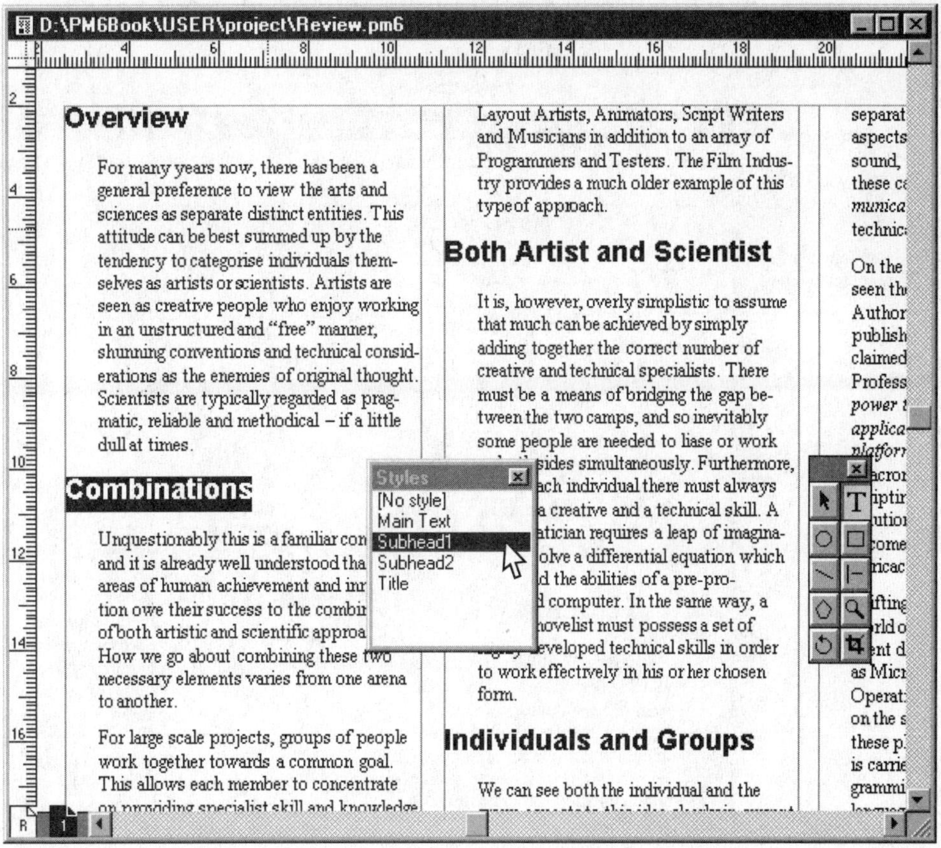
D:\PM6Book\USER\project\Review.pm6
Overview
For many years now, there has been a general preference to view the arts and sciences as separate distinct entities. This attitude can be best summed up by the tendency to categorise individuals themselves as artists or scientists. Artists are seen as creative people who enjoy working in an unstructured and "free" manner, shunning conventions and technical considerations as the enemies of original thought. Scientists are typically regarded as pragmatic, reliable and methodical – if a little dull at times.
Combinations
Styles
[No style]
Main Text
Subhead1
Subhead2
Title
Layout Artists, Animators, Script Writers and Musicians in addition to an array of Programmers and Testers. The Film Industry provides a much older example of this type of approach.
Both Artist and Scientist
It is, however, overly simplistic to assume that much can be achieved by simply adding together the correct number of creative and technical specialists. There must be a means of bridging the gap between the two camps, and so inevitably some people are needed to liase or work
Individuals and Groups
We can see both the individual and the
necessary elements varies from one arena to another.
For large scale projects, groups of people work together towards a common goal. This allows each member to concentrate
to work effectively in his or her chosen form.

Changing a Style

HANDY TIP **A shortcut to the Edit Style dialog box is to hold down the Control key and click directly on the style name within the palette.**

1. Choose **Define Styles...** from the Type menu.
2. Click on the style you wish to change, then on the **Edit...** button.
3. Make the changes to the attributes. If you hold down Shift when clicking **OK**, PageMaker will exit from all dialog boxes (even if you are several levels inside).

PageMaker remembers the style applied to each paragraph, so in this example all the Subhead1 paragraphs change instantly.

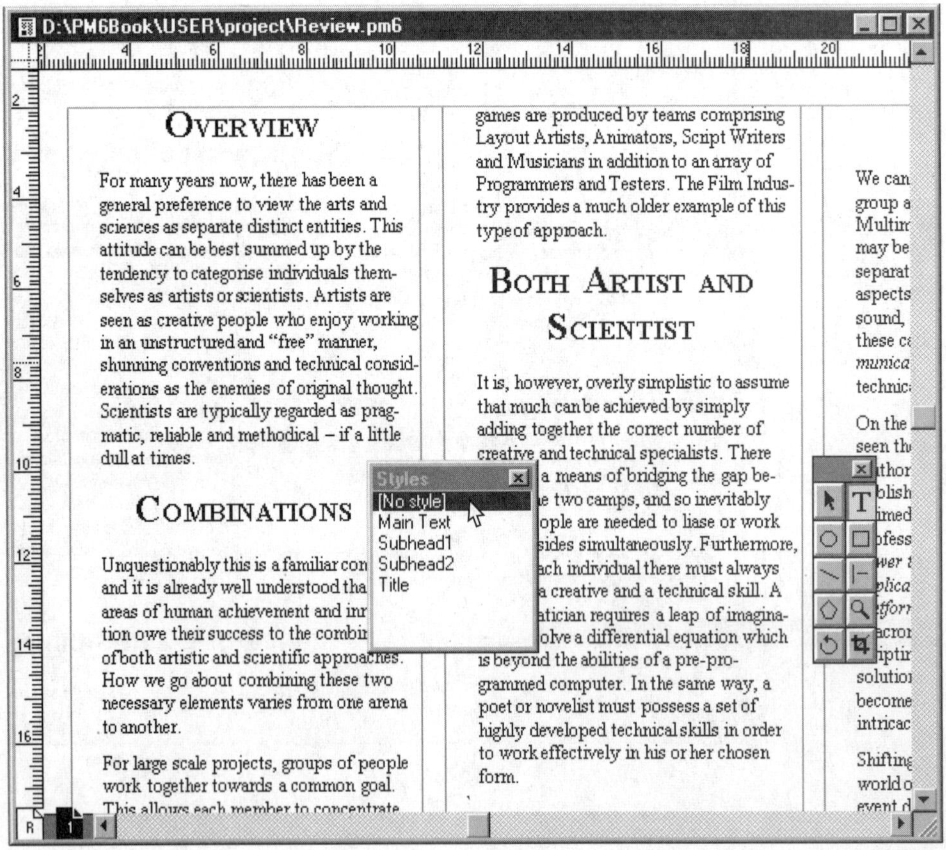
D:\PM6Book\USER\project\Review.pm6
OVERVIEW
For many years now, there has been a general preference to view the arts and sciences as separate distinct entities. This attitude can be best summed up by the tendency to categorise individuals themselves as artists or scientists. Artists are seen as creative people who enjoy working in an unstructured and "free" manner, shunning conventions and technical considerations as the enemies of original thought. Scientists are typically regarded as pragmatic, reliable and methodical – if a little dull at times.
COMBINATIONS
How we go about combining these two necessary elements varies from one arena to another.
For large scale projects, groups of people work together towards a common goal.
games are produced by teams comprising Layout Artists, Animators, Script Writers and Musicians in addition to an array of Programmers and Testers. The Film Industry provides a much older example of this type of approach.
BOTH ARTIST AND SCIENTIST
It is, however, overly simplistic to assume that much can be achieved by simply adding together the correct number of creative and technical specialists. There
is beyond the abilities of a pre-programmed computer. In the same way, a poet or novelist must possess a set of highly developed technical skills in order to work effectively in his or her chosen form.
Styles
[No style]
Main Text
Subhead1
Subhead2
Title

Style by Example

Sometimes it is useful to be able to experiment with text effects directly on the page, so that you can test out ideas before deciding on the exact attributes for your styles. Once you have done this, you can sample the text to automatically create a style definition.

Let us assume that you have a specimen piece of text which already has all the attributes you would like to build into a style.

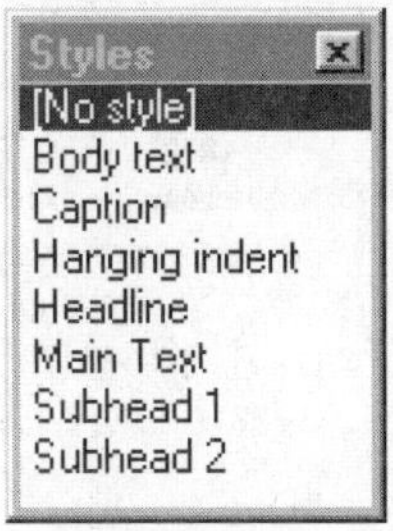

1 Select part of the text. Note that **[No style]** is highlighted in the Styles palette.

2 Choose **Define Styles...** from the Type menu.

3 Making sure that **[Selection]** is active, click on **New.**

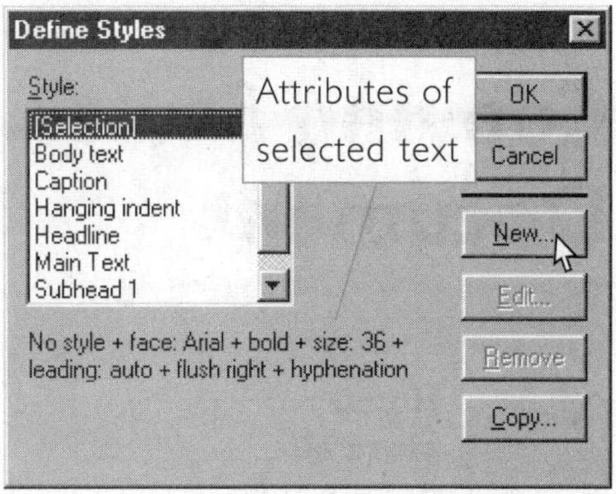

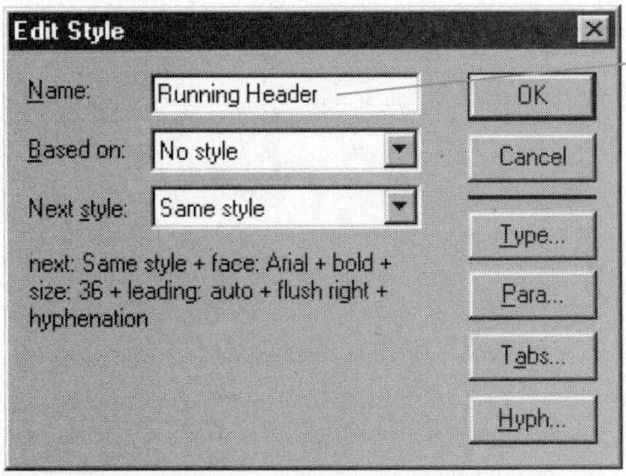

4 Enter a name for the style. All the attributes of the selected text are already present, so there is no more work to be done. Hold down Shift and click **OK** to return to the page.

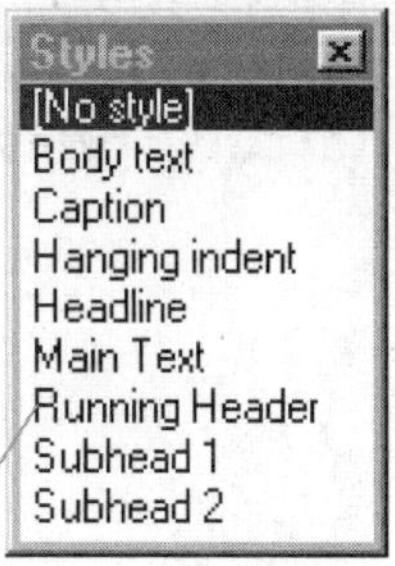

The new style now appears in the palette

Styles in the Story Editor

You can also use the Style palette in the Story Editor. Because many text effects do not show up in a Story window, style names appear in the margin to help you keep track of current settings.

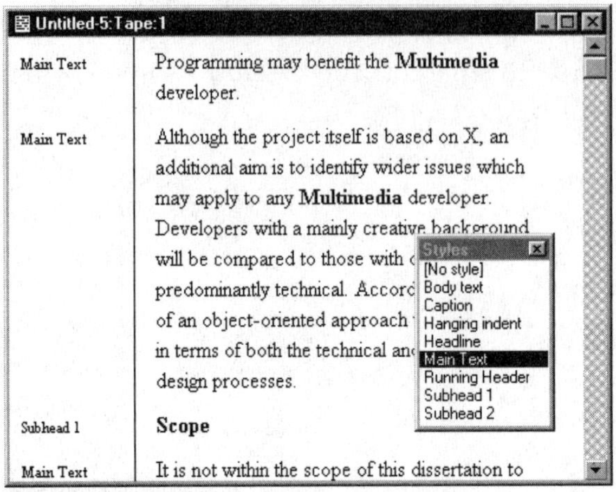

Untitled-5:Tape:1
Main Text
Programming may benefit the Multimedia developer.
Main Text
Although the project itself is based on X, an additional aim is to identify wider issues which may apply to any Multimedia developer. Developers with a mainly creative background will be compared to those with a predominantly technical. Accord of an object-oriented approach in terms of both the technical and design processes.
Styles
[No style]
Body text
Caption
Hanging indent
Headline
Main Text
Running Header
Subhead 1
Subhead 2
Subhead 1
Scope
Main Text
It is not within the scope of this dissertation to

The facility to display style names in the margin of a Story window can be turned on and off from the More Preferences dialog box.

To reach this choose Preferences from the File menu, then click More.

Copying Styles From Another Document

1. Choose **Define Styles...** from the Type menu and click on the **Copy** button.
2. Locate the document and click **OK**.

If this document uses the same style names, you will be asked if you wish to overwrite existing styles.

If you close all documents you can change the global default styles.

CHAPTER TWELVE

Long Document Features

This chapter shows you how to set up an automatic Table of Contents and Index for your document. It also explains how to group together a series of PageMaker files as a "Book" publication. Additionally, the Colour palette and Print Dialog are covered.

Covers

The Book Command 126

Table of Contents 127

Rebuilding the Table of Contents 129

Making Index Entries 130

More Complex Entries 131

Creating the Index 134

Indexing with the Story Editor 136

The Colour Palette 137

Links 138

The Print Dialog 138

The Book Command

When working with a long publication, it is common practice to divide it amongst several PageMaker documents. You can still treat these as a single publication using the Book command.

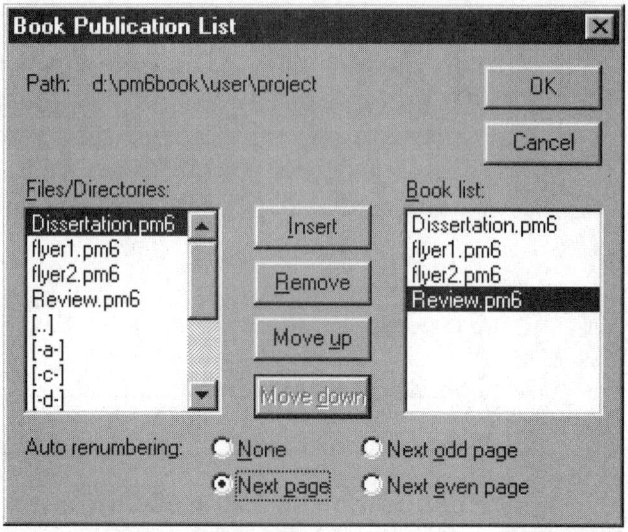

HANDY TIP

Choosing auto renumbering will cause PageMaker to open all other chapter files and modify their page numbers.

1. Choose **Book...** from the Utilities menu.
2. Locate each component file, using the **Insert** button to add them to the Book list.
3. Use the **Move up** and **Move down** buttons to assemble the "chapters" in the correct order.
4. Select the appropriate type of page numbering. Click **OK**.

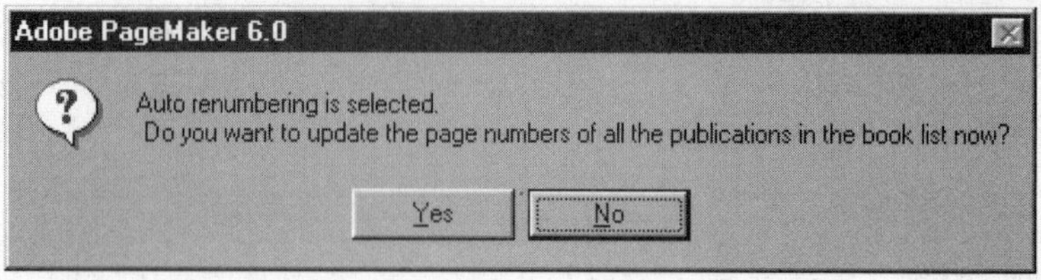

Although the individual files are still separate, there are features (such as printing, table of contents generation, and indexing) which can operate over the entire book.

Table of Contents

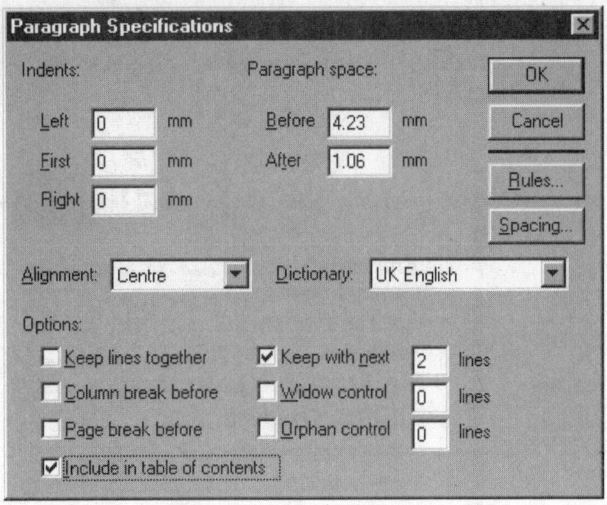

At the bottom left corner of the Paragraph Specifications dialog box (select **Paragraph...** from the Type menu), there is an option **Include in table of contents**.

Normally this option is set as part of the definition of heading or subheading styles of text (see Chapter 11 "Style Sheets").

Creating a Table of Contents

1. Set the **Include in table of contents** attribute for your heading styles, and also for individual paragraphs if necessary.

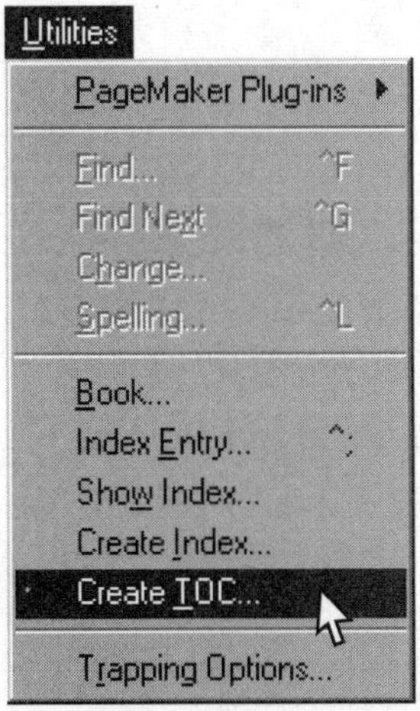

2. Choose **Create TOC...** from the Utilities menu.

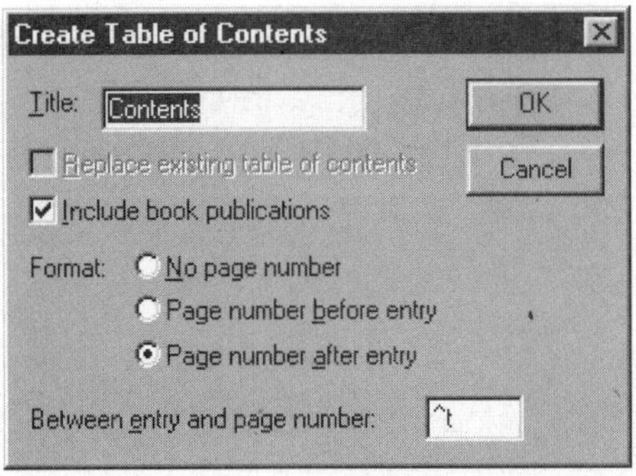

From this dialog box you can specify the TOC Title, as well as the format for the page references. Note that a TOC can be compiled for a complete book list.

When PageMaker is ready, it will display a text place symbol, allowing you to place the TOC on a suitable page:

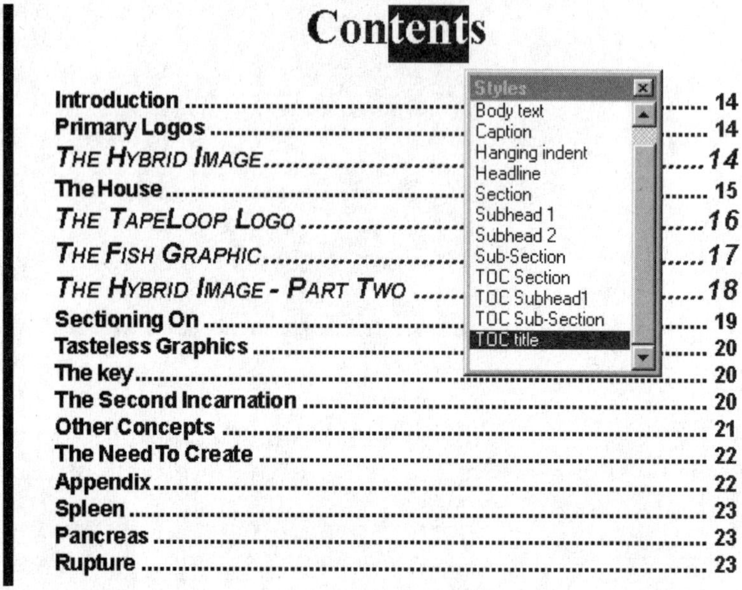

If you look in the Styles palette, you will see that new styles are created for each type of TOC entry. For example, the word "Contents" at the top of the table uses the style TOC title.

In the above example, three PageMaker styles had the **Include in table of contents** attribute set. PageMaker located all instances of these and included them in the Contents page. It also created three new styles corresponding to these, plus TOC title.

You are obviously free to edit and format this new table in any way you wish, but if you make the changes by editing these new styles, then it will be easy to rebuild the TOC.

You will need to rebuild the TOC should you add any new entries, edit the main document text, or change the page numbering.

Rebuilding the Table of Contents

By altering the TOC styles you can radically reformat the Contents page:

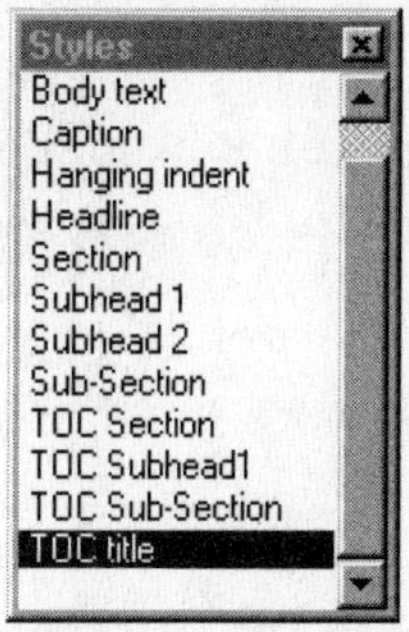

In this example, we renumbered the pages in our document, so needed to recreate the TOC...

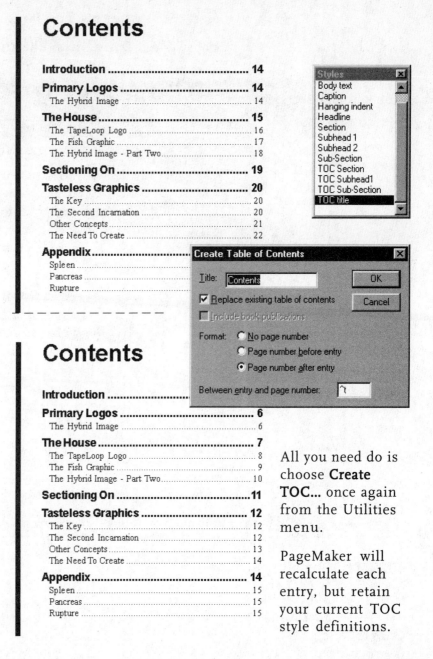

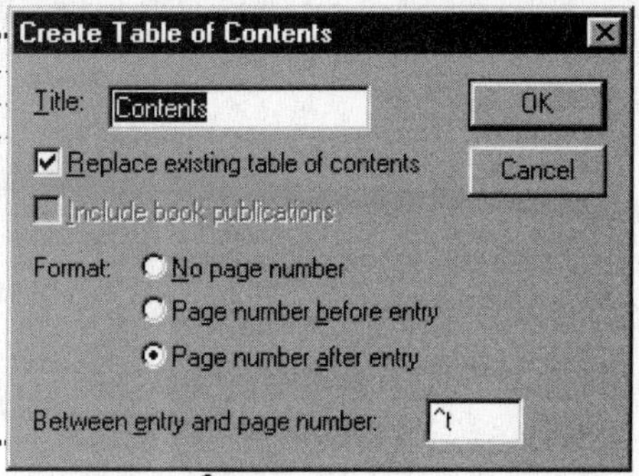

Contents

Introduction .. 14
Primary Logos 14
The Hybrid Image 14
The House ... 15
The TapeLoop Logo 16
The Fish Graphic 17
The Hybrid Image - Part Two...................... 18
Sectioning On .. 19
Tasteless Graphics 20
The Key ... 20
The Second Incarnation 20
Other Concepts ... 21
The Need To Create 22
Appendix..
Spleen ...
Pancreas ..
Rupture ...

Styles
Body text
Caption
Hanging indent
Headline
Section
Subhead 1
Subhead 2
Sub-Section
TOC Section
TOC Subhead1
TOC Sub-Section
TOC title

Contents

Introduction ..
Primary Logos ... 6
The Hybrid Image 6
The House ... 7
The TapeLoop Logo 8
The Fish Graphic 9
The Hybrid Image - Part Two...................... 10
Sectioning On ..11
Tasteless Graphics 12
The Key ... 12
The Second Incarnation 12
Other Concepts ... 13
The Need To Create 14
Appendix.. 14
Spleen ... 15
Pancreas .. 15
Rupture ... 15

Create Table of Contents

Title: Contents

☑ Replace existing table of contents

☐ Include book publications

Format: ◯ No page number
◯ Page number before entry
◉ Page number after entry

Between entry and page number: ^t

OK Cancel

All you need do is choose **Create TOC...** once again from the Utilities menu.

PageMaker will recalculate each entry, but retain your current TOC style definitions.

Making Index Entries

To create an index entry, do the following using either Layout or Story view:

1. Select the relevant word or phrase with the text tool.
2. Choose **Index Entry...** from the Utilities menu.

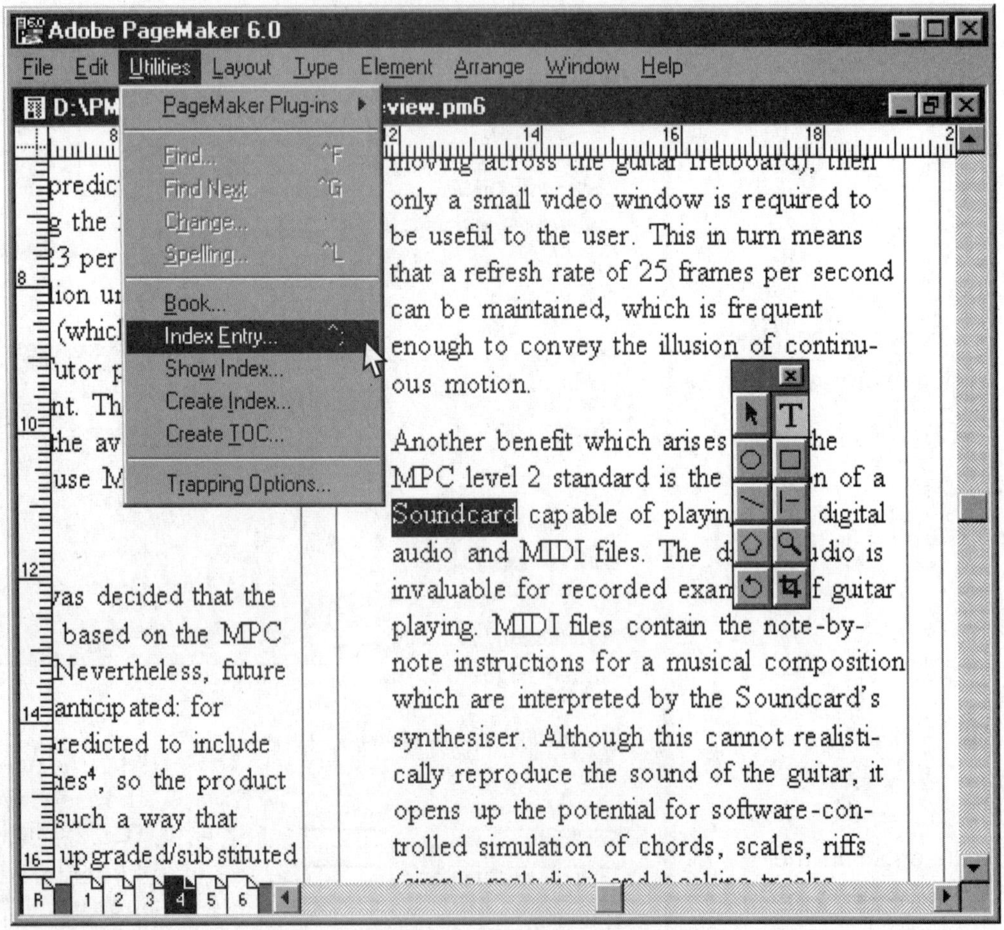
Adobe PageMaker 6.0
File Edit Utilities Layout Type Element Arrange Window Help
PageMaker Plug-ins
Find... ^F
Find Next ^G
Change...
Spelling... ^L
Book...
Index Entry... ^;
Show Index...
Create Index...
Create TOC...
Trapping Options...
only a small video window is required to be useful to the user. This in turn means that a refresh rate of 25 frames per second can be maintained, which is frequent enough to convey the illusion of continuous motion.
Another benefit which arises the MPC level 2 standard is the n of a Soundcard capable of playin digital audio and MIDI files. The d dio is invaluable for recorded exam f guitar playing. MIDI files contain the note-by-note instructions for a musical composition which are interpreted by the Soundcard's synthesiser. Although this cannot realistically reproduce the sound of the guitar, it opens up the potential for software-controlled simulation of chords, scales, riffs

HANDY TIP

The Index Entry keyboard shortcut is Control and ; (semicolon).

The Add Index Entry dialog appears, as below:

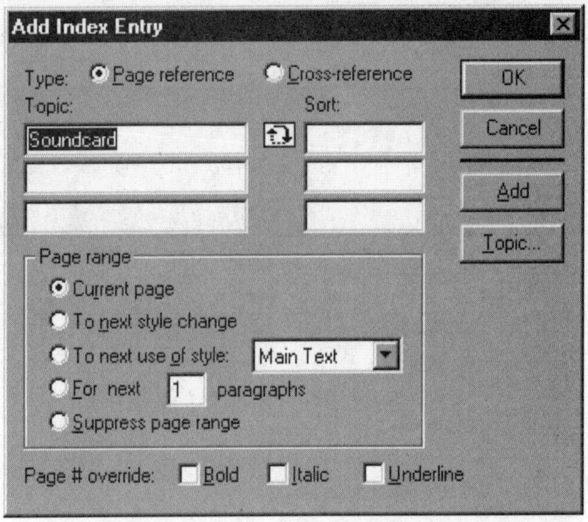

To see how these entries finally appear, look over the example index on page 135.

3 For a simple index entry accepting the default settings, simply click **OK**. PageMaker will set up an index entry which keeps track of the selected text.

More Complex Entries

Sorting Entries Manually

Use the **Sort** box to override the sort preferences:

In this example, the "Digital audio" entry will appear in the index under A rather than D.

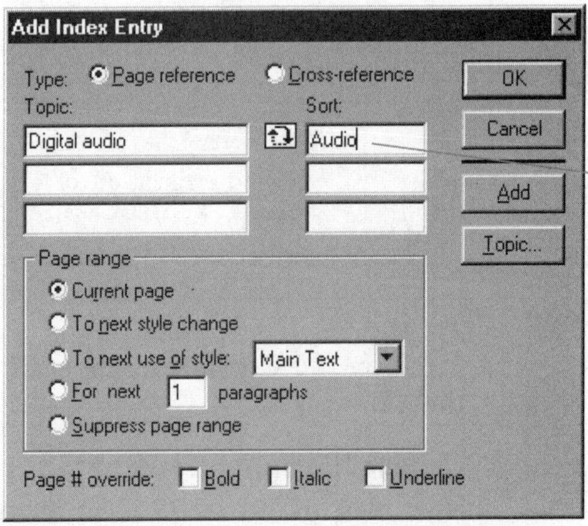

"Audio" entered manually

Subtopics

You can make an entry part of a more major index topic, or subdivide it into subtopics (to a maximum of three levels):

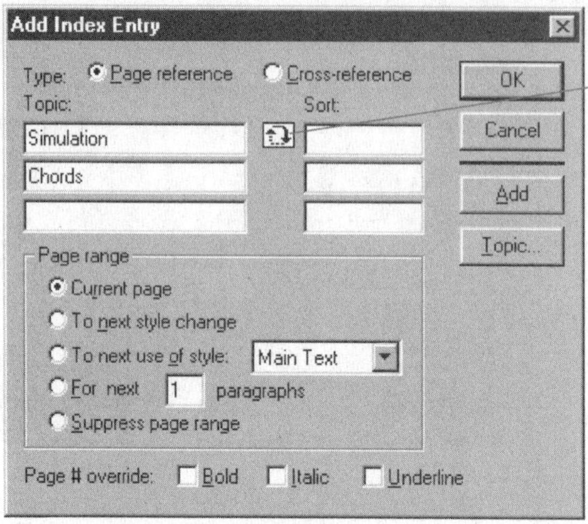

This button moves the text in the topic boxes down one level. The text in the lowest box moves back to the top.

Creating a Cross-reference

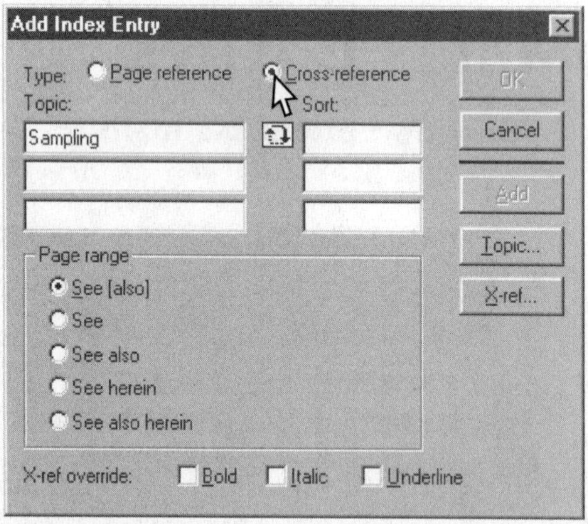

1. Click on the **Cross-reference** radio button at the top of the dialog box.
2. Choose the appropriate option: e.g., “See [also]” will add “also” if the entry has a page reference.

3 Click on the **X-ref** button.

The following dialog box will appear:

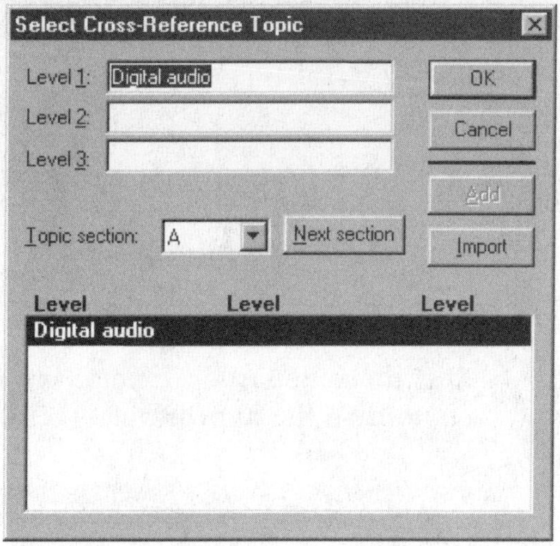

4 Select the initial letter of the required topic using the **Topic section** pop-up menu, or click on the **Next section** button. A list of the existing entries will be displayed.

5 Locate and select the topic to which you wish to cross-reference, then click **OK**.

Specifying a Range of Pages

Sometimes it is desirable to include a range of pages, rather than a single page reference next to an entry:

Here PageMaker will track a range of pages starting at the index entry, and ending at the next occurrence of text in the style "Main Text".

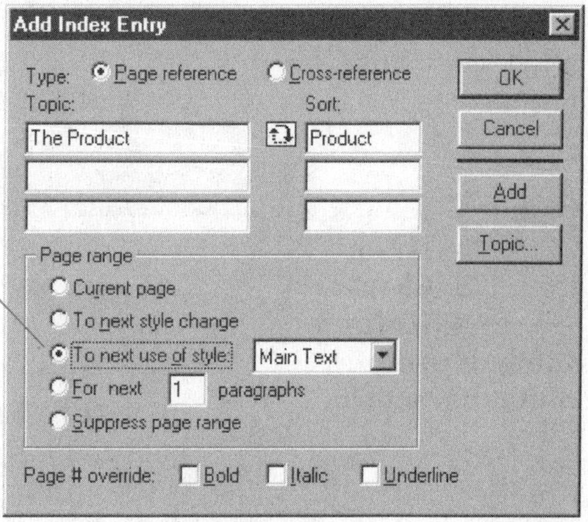

Creating the Index

REMEMBER

An index is normally compiled across a book list. If you haven't already assigned a book list to the file that is to hold your index, follow the procedure outlined on page 126.

To create an index, open the file that you want to contain it (or create a new one using File>New), then do the following:

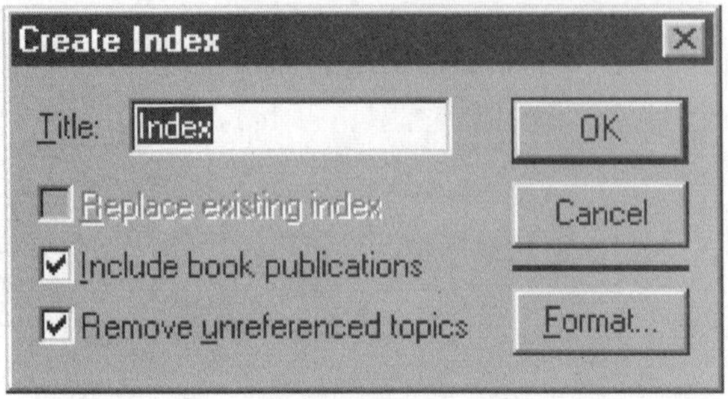

1 Choose **Create Index...** from the Utilities menu.

2 Edit the index title if necessary. Click on **Format...** to customise the appearance of the index.

Metacharacters are used in these format boxes. For example, the "Between page #s" box contains a comma and the metacharacter representing an en space (a space the width of the letter "n").

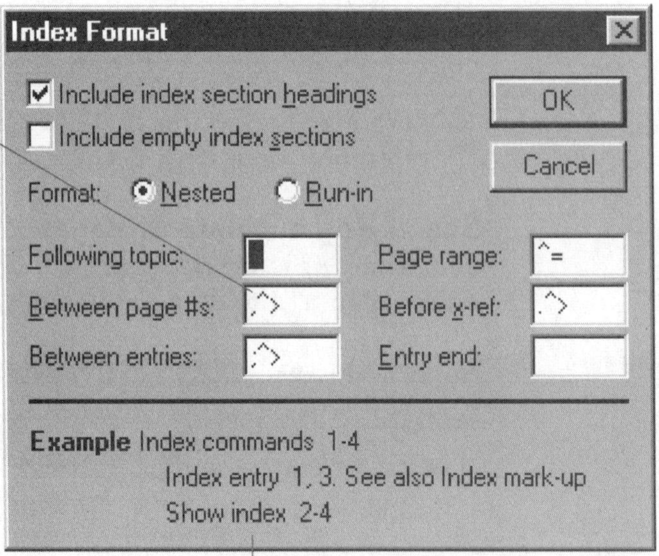

The example index text automatically changes to reflect any changes you make to the format.

HANDY TIP

See page 117 in Chapter 10 for a table of useful metacharacters.

3 Click **OK**. PageMaker will look through all book publications for index entries. When it is ready, you will be presented with a loaded text icon.

4 Find a suitable place for the index and click. The new index story will flow onto the page.

Example Index

Here is a short sample of an index generated by PageMaker, using some of the entries made on the preceding pages.

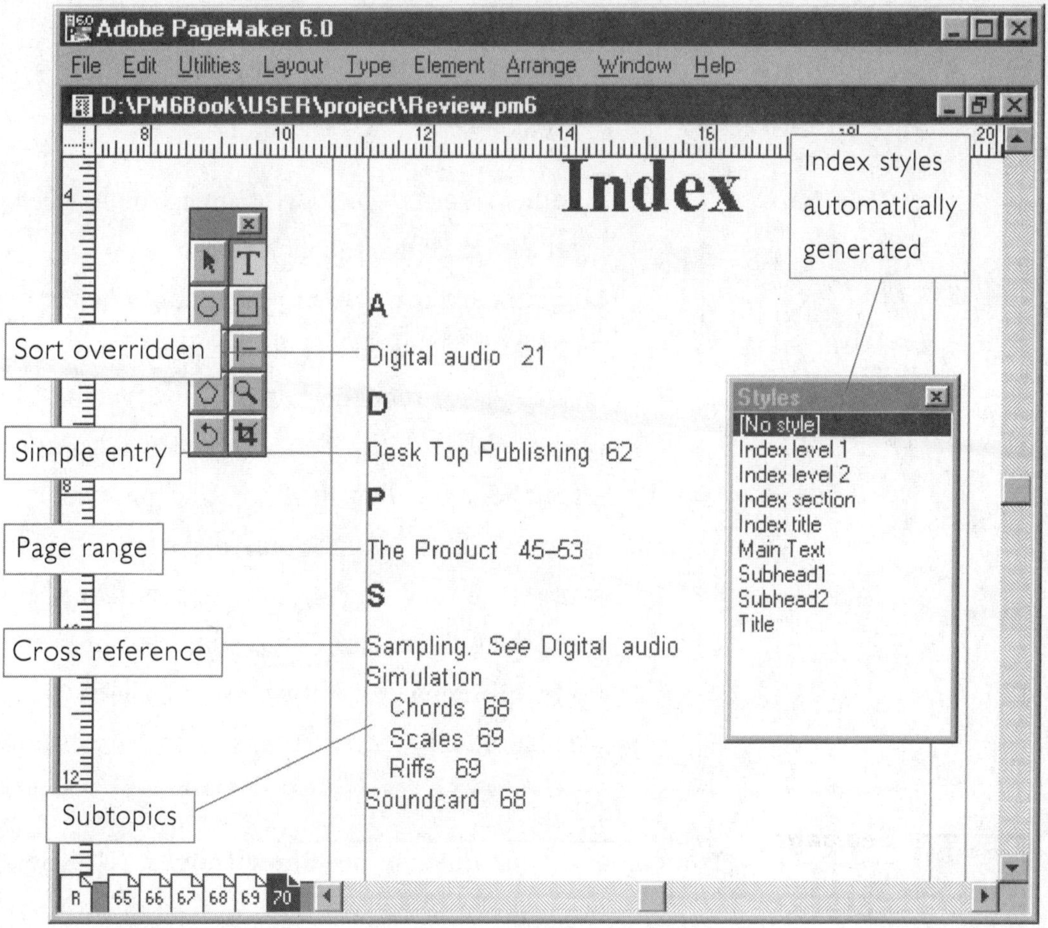

Indexing with the Story Editor

In the Story Editor, index markers show up as inverse diamond shapes.

You can search and replace using the index marker metacharacter (^;).

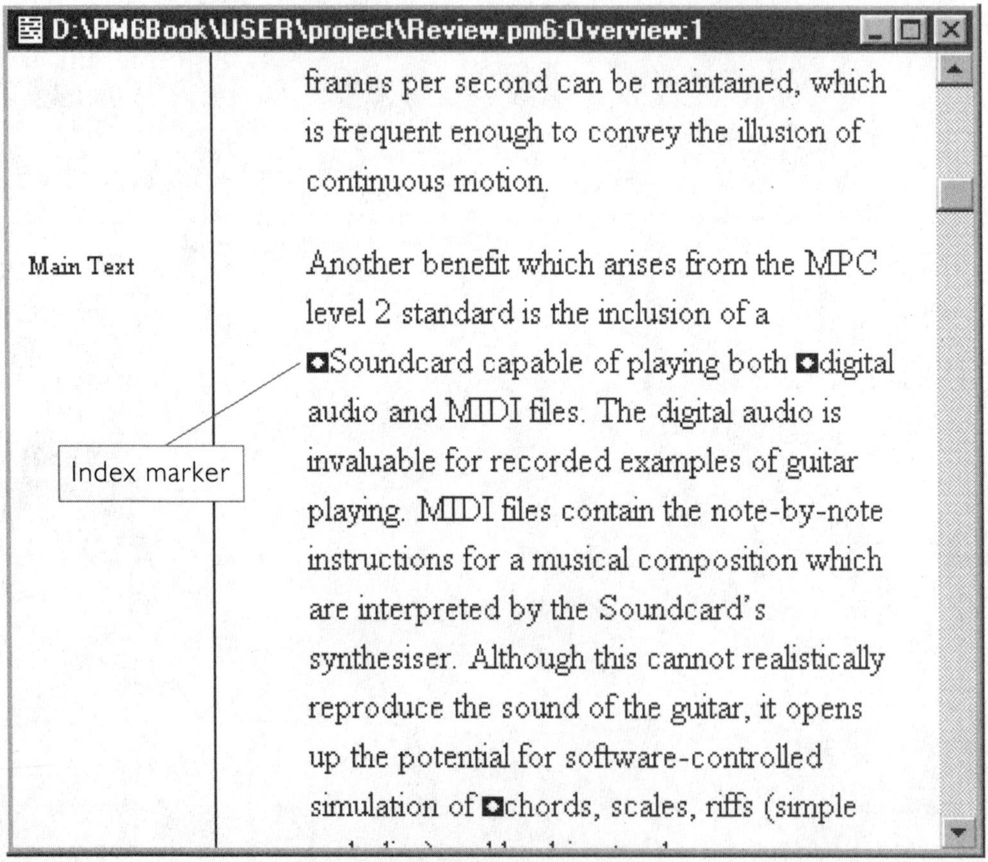
D:\PM6Book\USER\project\Review.pm6:Overview:1
frames per second can be maintained, which is frequent enough to convey the illusion of continuous motion.
Main Text
Another benefit which arises from the MPC level 2 standard is the inclusion of a Soundcard capable of playing both digital audio and MIDI files. The digital audio is invaluable for recorded examples of guitar playing. MIDI files contain the note-by-note instructions for a musical composition which are interpreted by the Soundcard's synthesiser. Although this cannot realistically reproduce the sound of the guitar, it opens up the potential for software-controlled simulation of chords, scales, riffs (simple
Index marker

You can edit your index using **Show Index...** (Utilities menu).

Rebuilding is the same as for Tables of Contents.

The Colour Palette

To change the colour of elements, do the following:

1. Make sure the Colours palette is active (Window menu).
2. Select one or more elements whose colour you want to change.

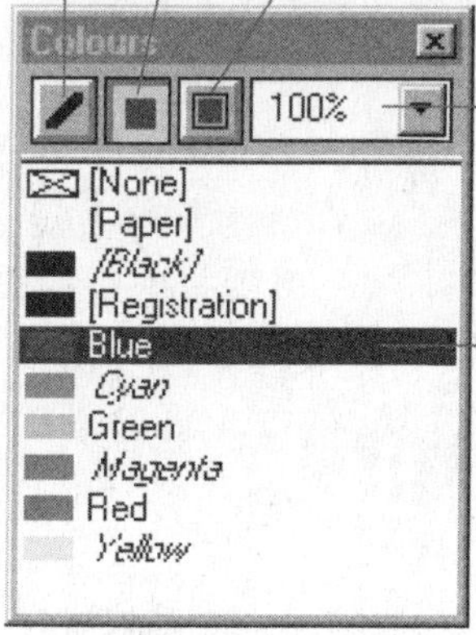

3. Choose line, fill or both from the Colour palette.
4. Select the colour.

Defining and Editing Colours

To edit an existing colour, hold down the Control key and click on its entry in the Colours palette.

To create and edit a new colour, Control-click on [None] in the Colour palette.

In either case the following dialog appears:

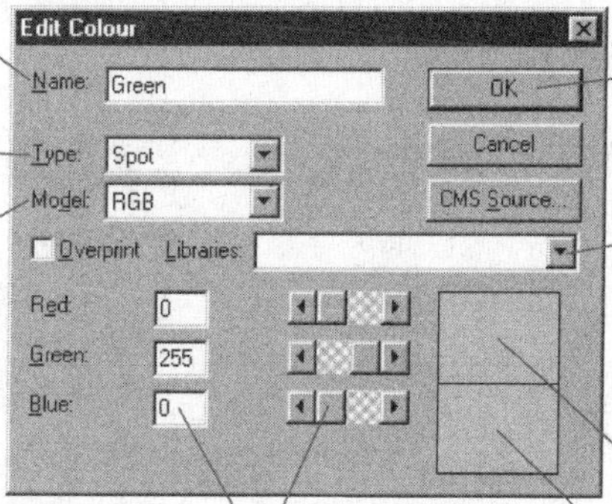

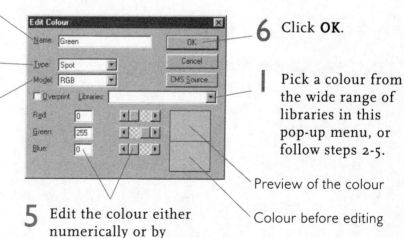

1. Pick a colour from the wide range of libraries in this pop-up menu, or follow steps 2-5.
2. Enter the colour name here.
3. Choose colour type from Spot, Process or Tint.
4. Select colour model from RGB, CMYK or HLS.
5. Edit the colour either numerically or by adjusting the slider bars.
6. Click **OK**.

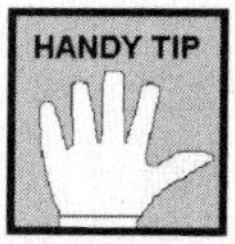

You can create, edit, delete and copy colours by choosing Define Colours... from the Element menu.

Links

The Links dialog box gives you information about all items of text and graphics which have been placed into your document. To display it, choose **Links...** from the File menu, then click **OK** when you're done.

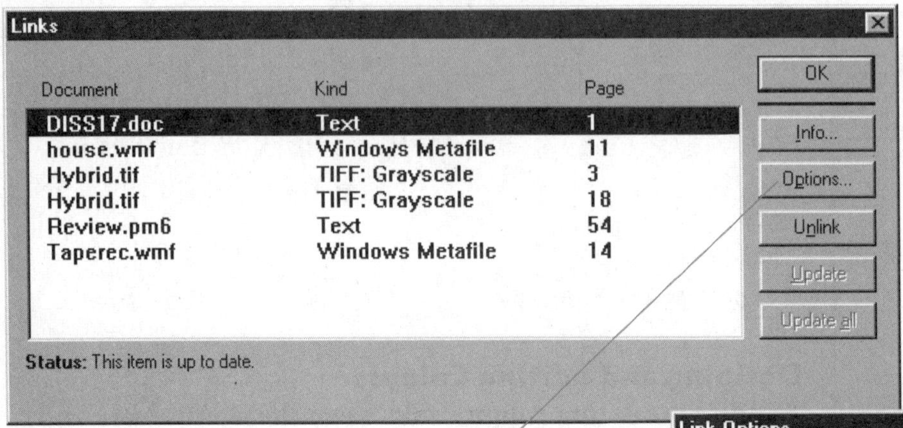

PageMaker keeps track of all imported elements, remembering their file type, size, location and date modified.

Click here to access the options for each linked file.

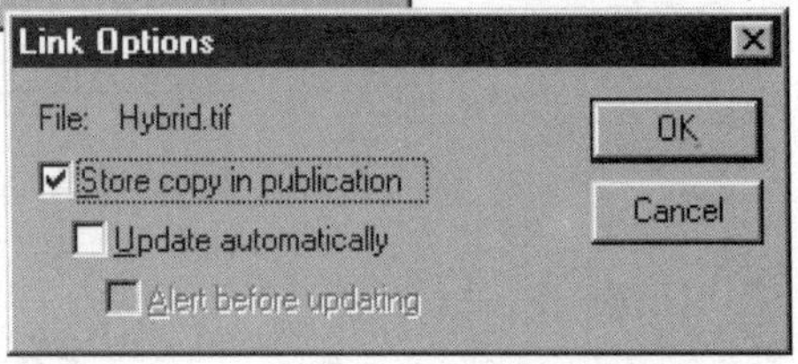

The Print Dialog

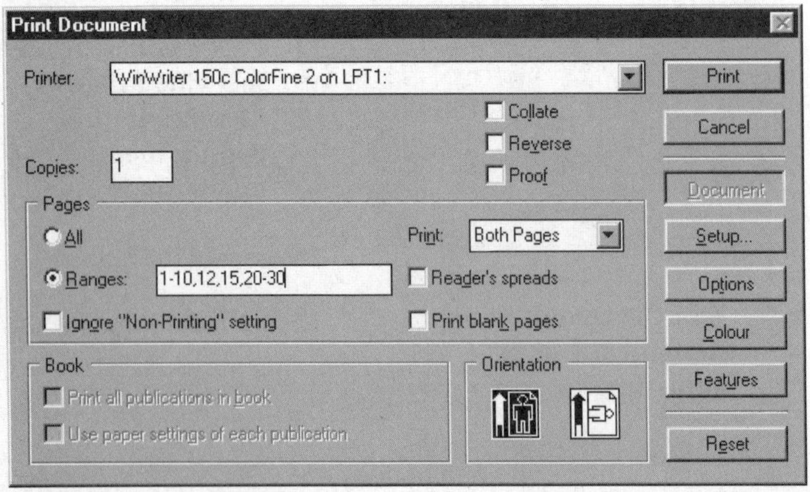

The Print dialog (choose **Print** from the File menu) allows you to access a wide range of print options.

PageMaker can print a selection of pages. In this case we are about to print pages 1 to 10 inclusive, page 12, page 15 and pages 20 to 30 inclusive.

CHAPTER THIRTEEN

Utilities

PageMaker contains a wealth of utilities (which can be added to via the Plug-ins sub-menu). This chapter introduces you to a few of these, as well as some more integral features such as the Library palette and the facility to compress TIFF files.

Covers

The Table Editor 140

The Library Palette 142

Sorting Pages 143

HTML Author 143

Create PDF 143

Open Template 144

Compressing TIFF Files 144

The Table Editor

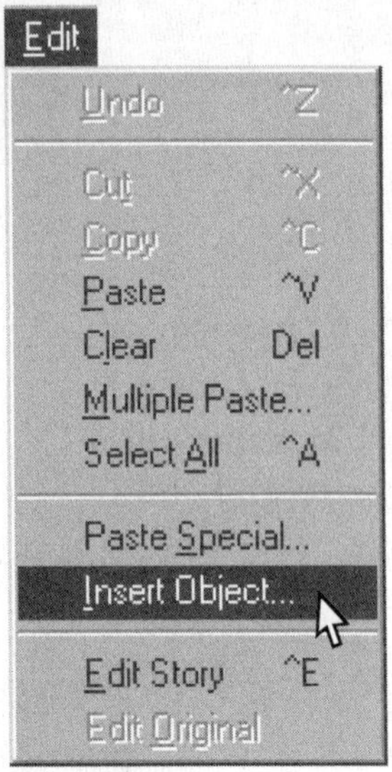

This is a separate Application program designed to help you create tables of text for use in PageMaker.

1. To activate the Table Editor from within PageMaker, choose **Insert Object** from the Edit menu.

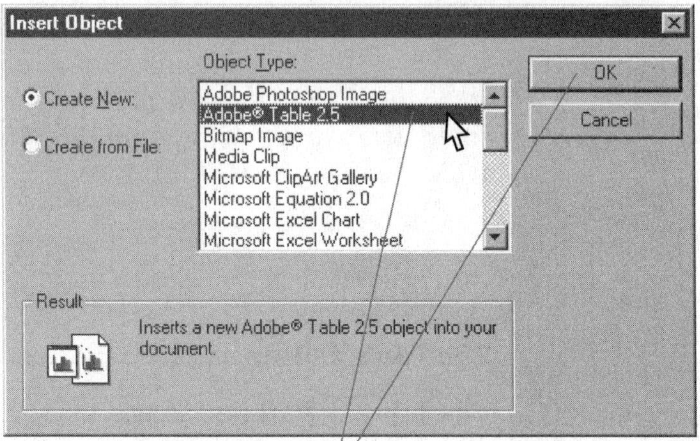

You can also run the Table Editor program independently, from the Windows 95 Start menu, or the Windows 3.1 Program or File Manager.

2. Select the **Adobe Table** object type and click **OK**.
3. Select the appropriate Table setup options, then click **OK**. You can return to this at any time from the Table Editor's File menu.

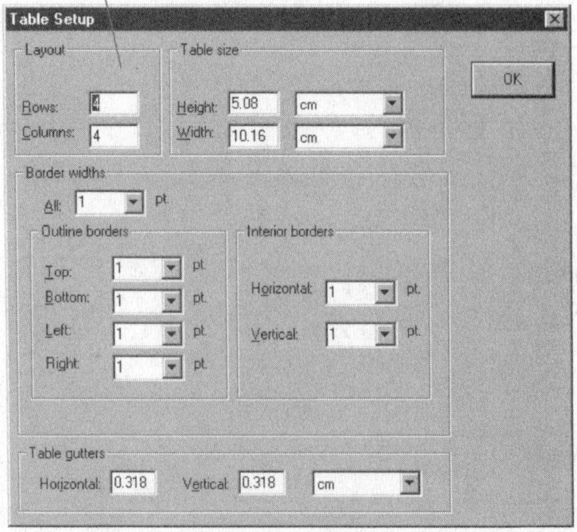

...contd

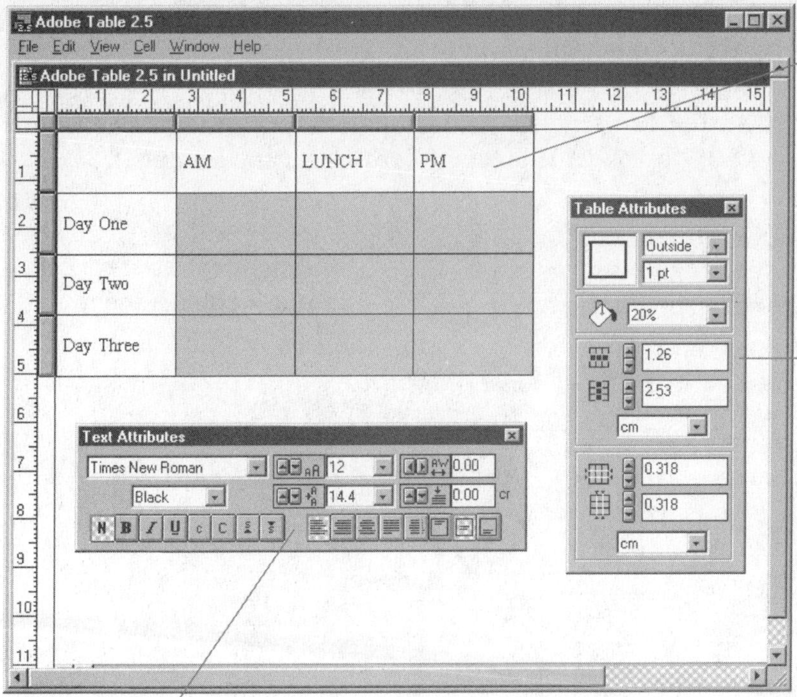

4 Enter the text of your table in the appropriate cells, just as you would in a spreadsheet package.

You can use this palette to change cell attributes such as line, fill and dimensions.

This palette controls text formatting. You can also choose Type and Paragraph Specs from the Edit menu.

5 When you are happy with your table, close the Table Editor by selecting the **Exit** command from the File menu. You are returned to PageMaker, and the table appears in your document for you to position and resize.

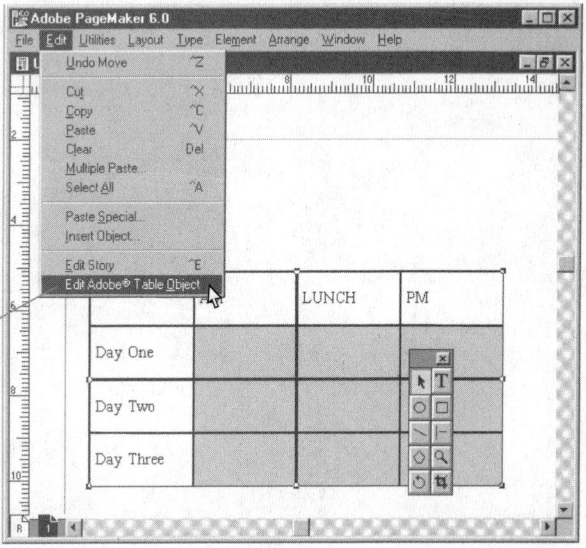

To edit the table subsequently, select it then choose Edit Adobe® Table Object from the Edit menu.

The Library Palette

If there are no libraries to open, then enter a name to create a new library after attempting to activate the Library palette.

This palette can be used to store commonly required PageMaker elements.

1. Make sure that the **Library** palette option is active (Window menu). The current library will appear.

Click here to add the selected item to the current library.

Click here to access the library options menu.

To retrieve a copy of an item from the library, simply drag it onto the page or Pasteboard.

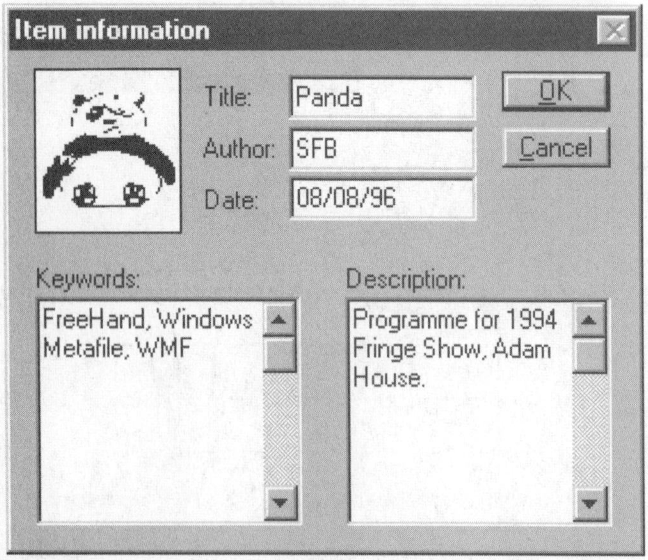

If you double-click on a library item you can enter information such as Title, Author, Date and Description.

Keywords can be used as a basis for a search operation activated from the library options menu.

Sorting Pages

When re-ordering a publication, bear in mind any stories which run over several pages.

The **Sort Pages** feature, present as a plug-in Addition in PageMaker 5, can be accessed directly from the Layout menu in PageMaker 6 and above.

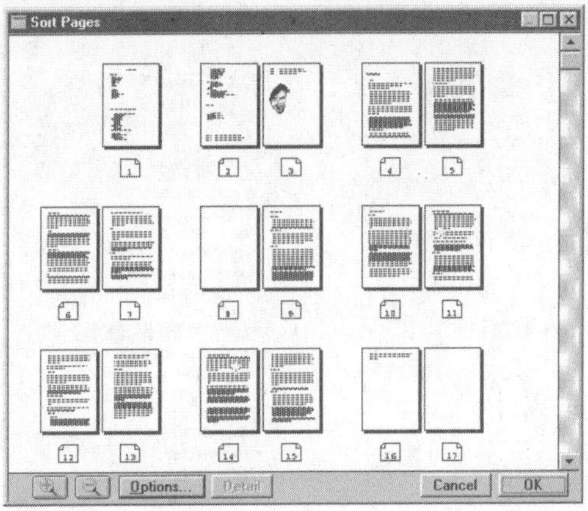

It allows you to easily re-order the pages in your document, simply by dragging the page thumbnail images around within the window.

HTML Author (PageMaker version 6 or above)

HTML, or HyperText Markup Language is a file format which is used for defining World Wide Web pages on the Internet.

The HTML Author is a new Plug-in feature introduced with PageMaker 6. It firstly scans your document for conformance to the HTML specification, and then presents you with a range of tools for setting up your Web pages.

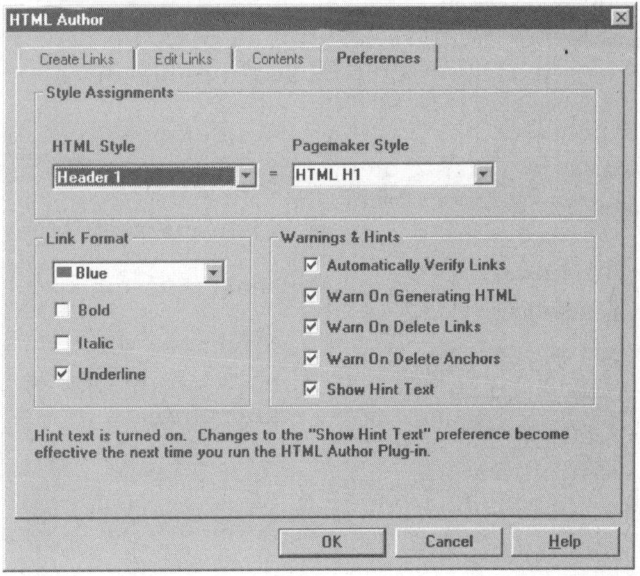

Create PDF

PDF is Adobe's Portable Document Format, which allows the Adobe Acrobat reader to access PDF files with hyperlinks. The **Create Adobe PDF...** command (File menu) allows you to export your PageMaker document in PDF form.

Open Template

This Plug-in automatically generates Template PageMaker documents which you can adapt for your own use.

1. Select **Open template** (Utilities menu, PageMaker Plug-ins submenu).
2. Choose a design and page size.
3. Click **OK**. A new untitled document will be generated.

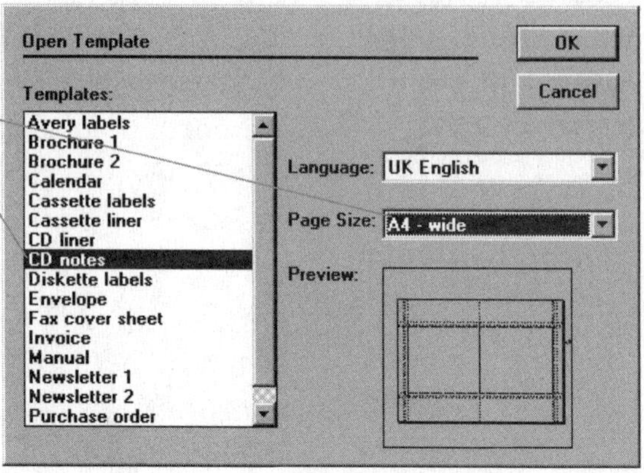

Compressing TIFF Files

TIFF files can take up a lot of space on disk and within a document, depending on their size, resolution and number of colours/grey levels.

PageMaker has built-in LZW (Lempel-Ziv & Welch) TIFF compression, which works by making a compressed copy of the file without changing the original.

> To avoid name clashes PageMaker adds a suffix to the compressed copy it creates: (_P or _D for moderate compression, and _L or _M for maximum compression).

1. Choose **Place...** from the File menu.

For moderate compression:

2. Select the file then hold down **Control** and **Alt** as you click **OK**. Keep these keys held down for a few seconds afterwards.

For maximum compression:

3. As above, but hold down **Control**, **Shift** and **Alt**.

Name	Size (bytes)
hybrid.tif	185520
hybrid_d.tif	37412
hybrid_m.tif	35322

The compression efficiency will depend on the contents of the graphic. In this example the original was compressed to less than a fifth of its original size.

CHAPTER FOURTEEN

Tips and Techniques

As well as learning the features of PageMaker, it is important to spend time contemplating your general work methods. We have already seen that using Style sheets can help you to work in a more organised and efficient fashion.

In this chapter we'll look at creating and using template documents, copying between documents, how to insert special characters into your documents using keyboard combinations, and general ways of improving your overall design skills. Finally, there are a few tips on how to use this book to its best effect if you have an Apple Macintosh.

Covers

Template Documents **146**

Using a Template **147**

Creating Your Own Template **149**

Copying From One Document to Another **150**

Special Keyboard Characters **151**

Using PageMaker on the Mac **152**

Template Documents

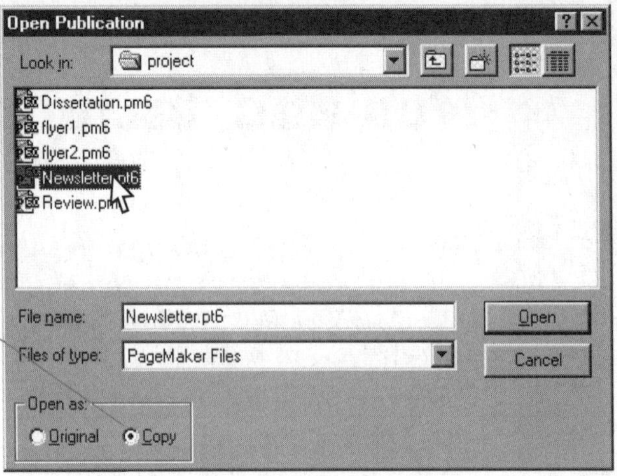

Note the default option to open an untitled copy. You can override this if you wish to edit the original file.

A PageMaker 6 template document has a PT6, rather than a PM6 extension. PageMaker will by default open a copy (rather than the original) of a template when **Open** is chosen from the File menu.

Dummy text

Dummy graphic box

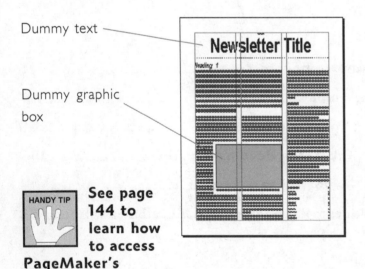

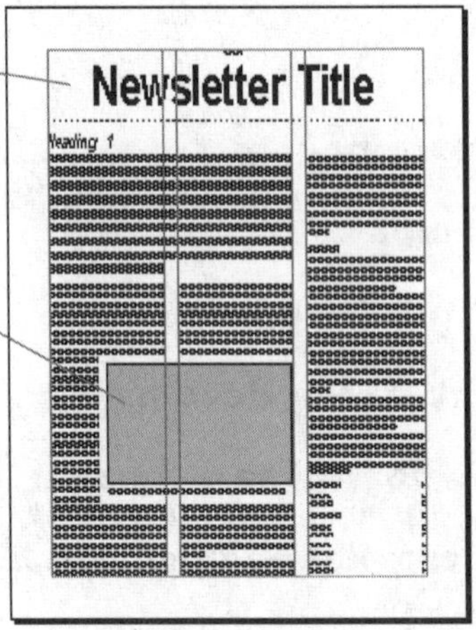

A template is actually an ordinary PageMaker document. It has normally been designed as a blueprint, a specimen for you to adapt to your own needs.

This template is a newsletter created using dummy text and FPO (for position only) graphic boxes.

HANDY TIP

See page 144 to learn how to access PageMaker's automatic templates.

Using a Template

Once you have opened a copy of a template, you can edit it just as you would a document you had created from scratch, replacing text and graphic objects as you see fit.

The original text was selected and then overtyped, retaining all of its original attributes.

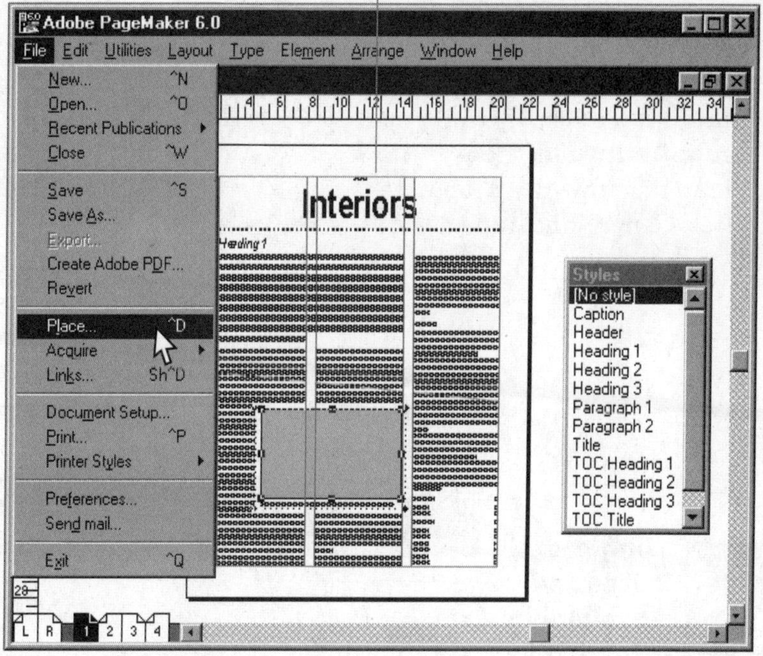

Retyping Text

Retype any small pieces of dummy text by selecting first with the text tool. The original text attributes will remain as you overtype.

Replacing Graphic Elements

1 Select a dummy graphic with the pointer tool.

2 Choose **Place** from the File menu.

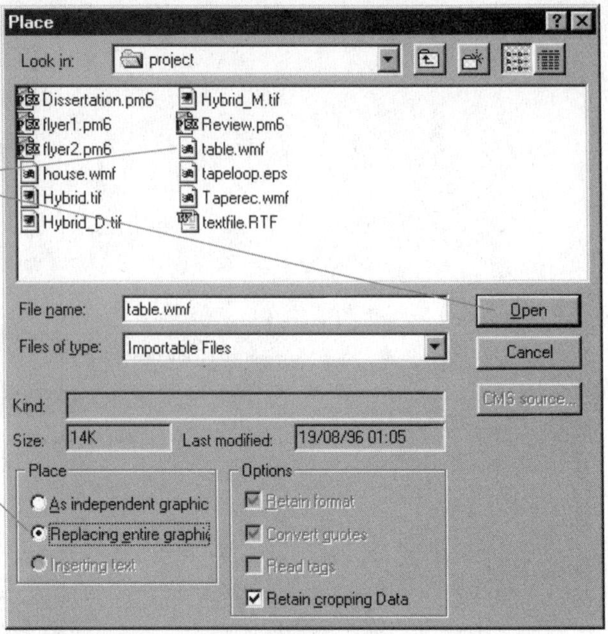

4 Select the new file and click **Open**.

3 From the Place dialog box, make sure that the **Replacing entire graphic** option is active. If it is greyed out then there is no element currently selected – click Cancel and repeat steps 1 and 2.

The imported element will replace the original, retaining its position, size and text wrap properties:

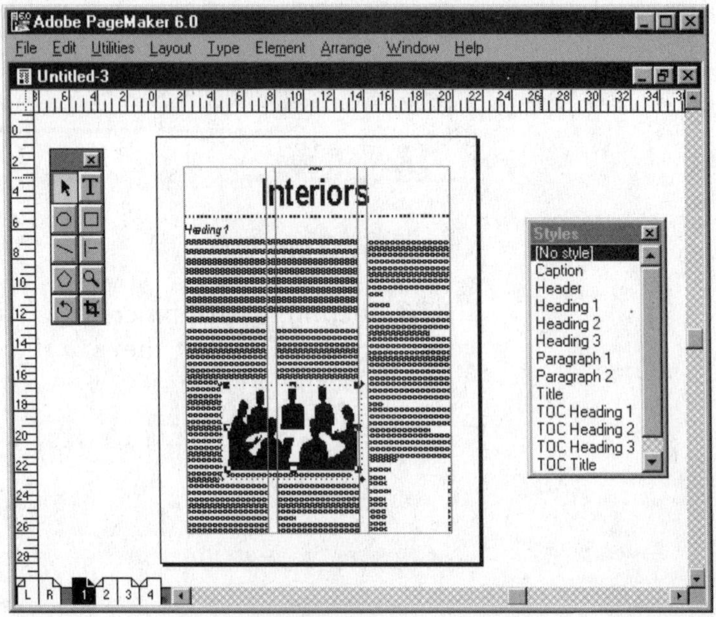

HANDY TIP

Single or threaded text blocks can also be replaced using this method.

Creating Your Own Template

If you need to produce a consistent series of documents (e.g. reports where the contents vary from month to month but the design remains the same), then it is a good idea to create a template:

1. Create the PageMaker document in the normal way. It is usual to use dummy text and grey boxes for graphics to be replaced.
2. Choose **Save** from the File menu.

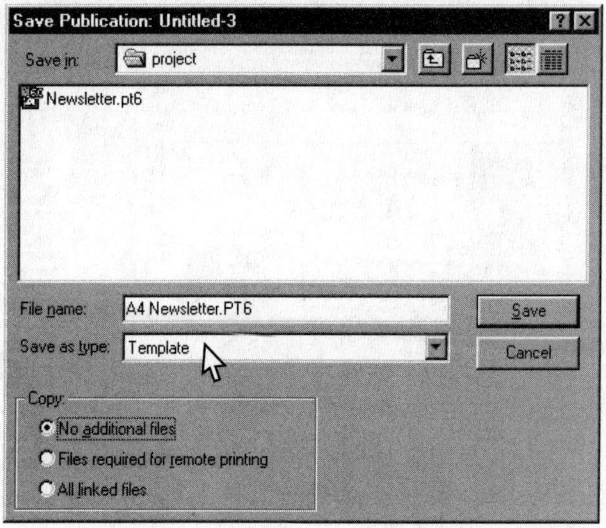

3. Select the **Template** option in the **Save as type** box.
4. Click **Save**.

A PT6 document will be created. Another advantage of using templates is that they can be used by someone with minimal design/typography experience, since that part of the document-generation process has already been completed by the template designer.

Copying From One Document to Another

You can copy objects from one PageMaker document to another without using the Clipboard, simply by dragging an element over into an adjacent window:

1. Open both documents in turn (File menu).
2. Choose **Tile** from the Window menu:

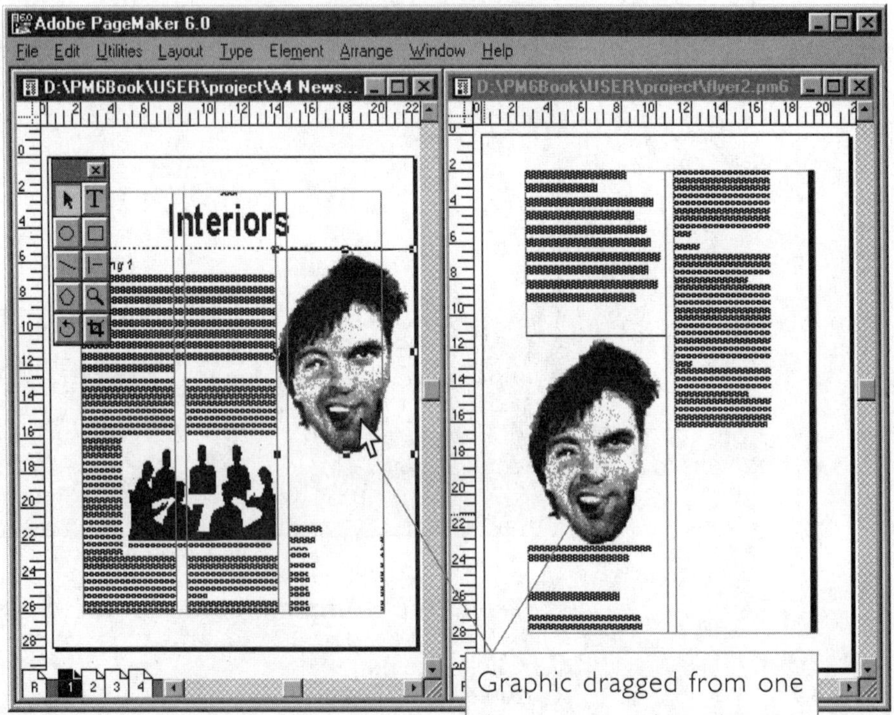

Graphic dragged from one document to the other

You will be able to view both publications side by side.

3. Locate the item to be copied in one document, then move to the proposed destination in the second.
4. Simply drag the element from one document to the other (the original will not be removed from the first document).

Special Keyboard Characters

Use these combinations of keys to enter special characters into your documents (^ represents the Control key).

Description	Symbol	Keyboard
Bullet	•	^ Shift 8
Copyright symbol	©	^ Shift O (letter "O", not zero)
Paragraph marker	¶	^ Shift 7
Open quote	‘	^ [
Close quote	’	^]
Open double quote	“	^ Shift [
Close double quote	”	^ Shift]
Registered trademark	®	^ Shift G
Section marker	§	^ Shift 6
En space		^ Shift N
Em space		^ Shift M
Thin space		^ Shift T
Non-breaking (hard) space		^ Shift H
Discretionary soft hyphen		^ -
Non-breaking hyphen	-	^ Shift -
Non-breaking slash	/	^ Shift /
En dash	–	^ =
Em dash	—	^ Shift =
Page no. marker		^ Shift 3
New line (soft return)		Shift Enter

Using PageMaker on the Mac

Although this book was written specifically for the Windows environment, Macintosh users should have little trouble in following the text, since PageMaker is virtually identical on either platform.

If you are a Macintosh user, bear in mind the following:

1. If a Windows keyboard command makes use of the **Control** key, use **Command** on the Macintosh.

2. Similarly, replace references to the Windows **Alt** key with **Option**.

3. Macintosh menus, windows and dialog boxes, whilst containing essentially the same information, have a different cosmetic look on each platform:

   Pop-up menus, indicated by a small downward-pointing arrow in Windows, appear as an option within a drop-shadow box on the Macintosh.

   Macintosh windows have a square Close box (in the top right corner) which is used to shut down the window.

   Unlike Windows, the type of a file is not necessarily indicated using a three-letter suffix in its name.

   The Macintosh operating system has its own WIMP filing system which does the job of both the Windows 3.1 File Manager and Program Manager, or Windows 95 Desktop and Explorer.

Index

A

Additions. *See* Plug-ins
Aligning Elements
  Align Dialog 39
  Control Palette 37-38
Alignment (paragraph) 67
Arrange menu 54
Attributes
  Character-level 66
  Paragraph-level 67
Autoflow 88

B

Backspace key 28
Baseline shift 74
Bitmapped graphics 58-59
Bold 66
Book 126
Boxes 27
Bring Forward 54
Bring to Front 54

C

Change 116-117
Character-level attributes 66
Clipboard 43
Closing 24
Colour palette 11, 137
Column breaks 101
Column guides 93-94
Compose to printer 19
Compressing TIFF files 144
Constrained lines, drawing 26
Contents. *See* Table of Contents
Control palette 11, 33-38, 76-79
  Repositioning mode 35
  Resizing mode 36
Copy 43
Copy Master Guides 91
Cropping 61
  Using Control palette 77
Custom line 41
Cut 43

D

Defaults 50-52
  Global 51
  Graphics 50
  Restoring 52
  Text 68
Define Styles 120
Deleting elements 28
Desktop Publishing 8
Dictionaries 97, 115
  Adding to 107
Document window 10
Double-sided document 19
Draw-type graphics 60
Drawing tools 25-54

E

Edit menu 30, 43, 45
Edit Story 114
Element menu 40-41
Ellipses 27
Encapsulated PostScript 60

F

Facing pages 19
File menu 56
Fill/Line 40-42
Find 116-117

Fit in Window 14
Floating palettes 11
Fonts 66
Force justification 67

G

Go to Page 21
Graphics
- Contrast 62
- File formats 57-60
- Importing 55-62
- Lightness 62

Grouping elements 32
Guidelines 47-49
- Column 93-94
- Guide Manager 112
- Horizontal 48
- Locking 49
- Using 49
- Vertical 47

H

Handles 29
HTML Author 143
Hyphenation 107

I

Image control 62
Import filters 57
Include in TOC 127
Indents 67, 104-106
Indexing
- Create index 134-135
- Cross-references 132-133
- Example index 135
- Making an entry 130-131
- Page ranges 133
- Subtopics 132

Inline graphics 108-109
Insert Object 140-141
Insertion point 64
Inverted image 62
Invisible characters 118
Irregular columns 94

J

Justification 67

K

Keep with next 100
Kerning 71-72
Keyboard shortcuts 15

L

Layout menu 15, 21, 49
Layout view 14-15, 118
Leaders 105
Library palette 142
Line/Fill 40-42
Lines, drawing 26
Links 138
Loaded graphic icon 56-57
Locking elements 80
Long Document Features 125-138
LZW compression 144

M

Mac, using PageMaker with 152
Margins 19
Master pages 21, 89-94
- Multiple 92

Metacharacters 117
Mini-save 21
Moving elements 29, 35, 59
Multiple Paste 45-46

N

New (publication) 10, 18-20
Numbers 20

O

Objects
  Editing 141
  Inserting 140
Older PageMaker Files 20
Opening a publication 9, 20-21
Orientation 18
Orphans 98-99
Ovals 27

P

Page 10
  Breaks 101
  Dimensions 18
  Icons 21, 90
  Inserting 22
  Numbering 18, 20, 126
  Orientation 18
  Removing 22
  Setup 51
  Views 14-15
PageMaker screen/window 10
Paint files 58-59
Palettes 11
Paper fill 42
Paragraph rules 102-103
Paragraph specifications 97
Paragraph-level attributes 67
Paste 43-46
Pasteboard 10
  Show 15
PDF files 143
Place 56-57, 108-109
  Text 82-83
Plug-ins
  HTML Author 143
  Open template 144
  Sort pages 143
PMx.CNF 52
Point size 66
Polygons 27
Power Pasting 44
Preferences 12, 114
Printing 138
Program Manager 9

R

Rectangles 27
Reference point 35-38
Reflecting 76, 78
Remove Transformation 76
Resizing elements 29, 36, 59, 70
Resolution 58-59
Revert 39
Rotation 53
  Using Control palette 79
Rulers 12

S

Saving 23
Screen 10
Screening 62
Search and Replace 116-117
Select All 30, 65
Selecting
  Elements 28, 30
  Text 65
Selection box 31
Send Backward 54
Send to Back 54
Show Pasteboard 15
Skewing 76, 78
Small Caps 96
Snap to Guides 47, 49
Sort Pages 143
Spell-checking 115
Start button 9
Start page # 18
Starting PageMaker 9
Story Editor 113-118

Displaying style names 124
Stretch 29, 77
Styles 119-124
By example 123
Copying 124
In Story Editor 124
Palette 11
Subscript 96
Superscript 96

T

Table Editor 140-141
Table of Contents 127-129
Tabulation 104-105
Tall page orientation 18
Templates 144, 146-149
Creating 149
Replacing elements 147-148
Using 147-148
Text 63-74
Adding 64
Alignment 67
Attributes
Character-level 66
Paragraph-level 67
Blocks 69-70
Control palette 65
Editing 65
Importing 81-88
Paragraph styles 120
Reverse 66
Ruler 104-106
Selecting 65
Special keyboard characters 151
Style by example 123
Summary of terms 87
Threaded 84-86
Width, setting 74
Text wrap
Irregular 111
Regular 110
TIFF
Compressing 144
File format 58
Preview image 60
Toolbox 11
Tracking 73
Transformations 75-80
Type menu 67, 97
Type specifications 96

V

Views
Layout 14-15, 118
Story 113-118

W

Wide page orientation 18
Widows 98-99
Wildcards 117
Window menu 11, 21
Windows 95 shortcut 9
Windows Metafile 60
Windowshade handles 69-70
Wrap. *See* Text wrap

X

X-ref. *See* Indexing: Cross-references

Z

Zero Point, repositioning 13
Zoom tool 16